1987

THE PLANNING AND MANAGEMENT OF DISTANCE EDUCATION

The Planning and Management of Distance Education examines the problems faced by those who are setting up and managing distance education systems of various kinds. The book begins by considering definitions of distance education and various models which can be used to describe and understand distance education systems. The second chapter considers various general educational models and relates these to distance education. The concepts introduced in the first two chapters form a background to the rest of the book.

The next section looks at the aspirations of those setting up distance education systems, the economics and costs of such systems, and the process of planning a distance education system from scratch (chapters 3 to 5).

Chapters 6 to 11 consider aspects of planning and management — organisation, staffing, planning, and budgeting, the management of the academic processes related to materials development and the provision of local student services, production management (the management of materials production and distribution), operations management (the management of the delivery of student services) — and the impact of new technology on production and operations management, and finally, evaluation. The short concluding chapter draws together some of the themes running through the book.

Greville Rumble is Planning Officer at the British Open University

THE PLANNING AND MANAGEMENT OF DISTANCE EDUCATION

Greville Rumble

ST. MARTIN'S PRESS
New York

© 1986 Greville Rumble
All rights reserved. For information, write:
Scholarly & Reference Division,
St. Martin's Press, Inc., 175 Fifth Avenue, New York, NY 10010
First published in the United States of America in 1986
Printed in Great Britain

Library of Congress Cataloging-in-Publication Data

Rumble, Greville.
   The planning and management of distance education.

   Bibliography: p.
   Includes index.
   1. Distance education. I. Title.
LC5800.R86   1986   378′.17   86-13847
ISBN 0-312-61403-9

CONTENTS

1

PREFACE

This book had its origins in a request from David Croom that Tony Kaye and I should revise an earlier book - *Distance Teaching for Higher and Adult Education* - which we edited and which was published by Croom Helm in association with the Open University Press in 1981. While we were both flattered, neither of us were wholly enthusiastic about the suggestion, not least because in the intervening years a number of general works on distance education have appeared. For some months we struggled with alternative structures and contents lists in an attempt to produce a book which would be both a general introduction to distance education (and hence would be at least as comprehensive as our earlier book) and yet approach the subject from an original viewpoint.

The significant gap which we identified was for a book on the planning and management of distance education. Once we had reached that point, Tony decided to withdraw from any active writing and leave the book to me. Yet the history of our early labours is important because of the enormous debt I owe him. To start with, substantial parts of the first and second chapters were either written by him or had their origins in our early discussions and exploration of the implications of theories of adult education for distance education. Secondly, Tony read and commented on every aspect of the book. The shortcomings remain mine, but they would have been more blatant without his help. And finally, he encouraged me to continue with the project. This acknowledgement is little recompense for the time and trouble which he took in commenting on the manuscript.

My thanks too to my wife Anne and to Gavin and Stephen for

their support during the long hours the book took to write. In Anne's case this involved reading the book in its final stages, when her comments were invaluable. The second major book in three years, its completion marks a temporary end to the disruption to family life which is the other and all too often hidden cost of authorship.

I also owe a debt of thanks to my many colleagues at the British Open University and elsewhere - particularly at the Universidad Estatal a Distancia (Costa Rica) and the Universidad Nacional Abierta (Venezuela), but also in other institutions where I have worked. Many of them have contributed in some way to this book. They are, however, too many to name individually.

Finally, my grateful thanks to David Croom and the staff at Croom Helm who helped in the preparation of this book.

Greville Rumble
The Open University, United Kingdom

ACKNOWLEDGEMENTS

The author and publisher are grateful to the following individuals, publishers and organisations for permission to reproduce previously published material in this book:

A.W. Bates and Croom Helm Ltd for permission to republish as table 7.2 a table that appeared originally in 'The role of technology in distance education', edited by A.W. Bates.

The Commonwealth Secretariat for permission to incorporate into the section on 'Staffing for materials development and production' (chapter 7), and to use in table 8.3, material originally published in 'Costing distance education' by G. Rumble.

The Further Education Staff College for permission to adapt as figure 11.1, a figure originally published in Coombe Lodge Report 18 (3), 'Assessing educational effectiveness and efficiency'.

The International Extension College, Cambridge for permission to use in table 4.1, data originally published in 'The cost of distance education', by H. Perraton.

The OECD for permission to adapt as table 8.2, a table originally published in the International Journal of Institutional Management in Higher Education, 6 (1).

Unesco for permission to publish in redrawn form as figure 1.2, a figure originally published in Prospects, 11 (1).

Chapter One

CHARACTERISTICS OF DISTANCE EDUCATION

Definitions of distance education

There are a number of problems in attempting to 'define' distance education. Firstly, used in this sense the term 'distance' has different connotations. It is certainly not restricted to the notion of mere geographical distance from the source of teaching: a high proportion of students enrolled in distance education courses live in densely populated urban areas close to the physical location of the institution from which their course materials are mailed. Although, initially, distance methods may have arisen in some countries (e.g. Australia, France during World War II) because of students' difficulties in travelling to conventional institutions, it would be fair to say now that distance in the physical sense is not a major necessary defining feature of this form of educational provision.

Perhaps the most fruitful use of the term 'distance' is that proposed by Moore (1983:157) in the expression 'transactional distance', which defines the nature and degree of separation of teacher and learner in the educational process:

> Transactional distance is a function of two variables called 'dialogue' and 'structure'. Dialogue describes the extent to which, in any educational programme, learner and educator are able to respond to each other. This is determined by the content or subject-matter which is studied, by the educational philosophy of the educator, by the personalities of educator and learner, and by environmental factors, the most important of which is the medium of communication. For

7

example, an educational programme in which communication between educator and the independent learner is by radio or television permits no dialogue. A programme by correspondence is more dialogic, yet not to the same extent as one in which correspondence - or radio or television - is supplemented by telephone communication.

Structure is a measure of an educational programme's responsiveness to learners' individual needs. It expresses the extent to which educational objectives, teaching strategies, and evaluation methods are prepared for, or can be adapted to, the objectives, strategies, and evaluation methods of the learner. In a highly structured educational programme, the objectives and the methods to be used are determined for the learner, and are inflexible. In a linear, non-branching programmed text, for example, there is less opportunity for variation, according to the needs of a particular individual, than there is in those correspondence courses which permit a wide range of alternative responses by the tutor to individual students' questions and assignment submissions. .... In a programme in which there is little structure, and dialogue is easy, interaction between teacher and learner permits very personal and individual learning and teaching.

Using these dimensions, the most distant programme would be one in which there was neither dialogue nor structure - an example would be a wholly self-directed programme of individual reading. At the other end of the continuum, the least distant programme would be one in which there is a high level of dialogue, with little pre-determined structure - for example, an individually tailored tutorial programme. Most of what are commonly called distance education programmes fall somewhere between these two extremes - they have a measure of dialogue, as well as being more or less highly structured. This conceptualisation also helps explain how a student learning in a 'face-to-face' environment, whose sole educational activity is to go to lectures to take notes, can be at a greater transactional distance than a student on a distance education course who regularly meets, corresponds with, or telephones his tutor.

A second factor to consider in attempting any definition of distance education lies in the great diversity of practices, systems, and projects that are commonly covered by the term. Granted, they all have in common, as their defining element, and in opposition to traditional classroom-based practice, the separation in space and in time of teaching and learning activities, with teaching generally based on a combination of structured learning materials and the use of intermediaries (tutors, counsellors, 'animateurs') to assist learners in their use of these materials. But here the resemblance often ends.

Differences are attributable to a number of factors. Firstly, there has been a fairly rapid evolution of methods and structures, especially in the last few decades, which has contributed to considerable diversity in the field of distance education. This is all the more remarkable when contrasted with the conservatism and stability of conventional education: classrooms and lecture theatres, and what goes on inside them, look much the same anywhere in the world, and have done so for a remarkably long time. The similarities in the situations of members of a rural radio listening circle in West Africa, students enrolled in one of the many Indian University Correspondence Directorates, British Open University students working at home on multi-media courses, and 'On-Line College' students in New York State, are not so easy to spot.

The many forms of distance education as we now know them have evolved from a wide variety of different sources. In some countries, a strong tradition of commercial correspondence colleges has survived for a hundred years or more. Postal tuition, combined with weekly or monthly lessons of printed or cyclostyled course materials, is still a basic model which has often been adopted relatively unchanged by many publicly financed institutions. In other countries, most notably in Latin America, radio broadcasting organisations were among the pioneers of distance education, and this is reflected in the structure of many current systems where there is less emphasis on print and individual correspondence tuition, and more on locally organised listening groups with trained 'animateurs'.

The last decade has seen the creation of a number of distance teaching universities throughout the world, many inspired by the success of the British Open University. Many of them use print and broadcast media combined with face-to-face and postal tuition in an integrated manner. These institutions have contributed a great deal to creating a much more positive image for distance education, giving credibility, through the levels of achievement of their graduates, to methods which were previously often considered as second-best, if not third-rate.

For many years, at least in some countries (for example, Australia and the United States), institutions teaching conventional students have also accepted a role in the education of external students. Recently, as the competition for students has increased, more and more traditional institutions have developed new and often very flexible distant study programmes. In the last year or two, in the wealthier countries, the new communications possibilities opened up by data transmission networks and widespread home ownership of micro and personal computers are beginning to be exploited for educational purposes. It is too early to know yet what the longer term impact of projects such as the California-based 'Electronic University' will be, but there is no doubt that networking and electronic mail technologies have considerable potential for improving the quality and nature of tutorial and student contacts in distance education.

Thus the problem in trying to establish a definition of distance education lies in identifying the common features of enterprises as different from each other as correspondence colleges based on postal tuition, radiophonic schools, and university programmes using electronic mail to reach off-campus students.

Perhaps the most comprehensive general definition of distance education is that first proposed by Keegan in 1980 and subsequently modified in 1986. Keegan's definition is based inter alia on an analysis of the definitions proposed by Holmberg (1977), Peters (1973), and Moore (1973). Keegan (1986: 49-50) identifies seven principal characteristics which he regards as being essential for any comprehensive definition:

- the separation of teacher and student
- the influence of an educational organisation
- the use of technical media
- the provision of two-way communication
- the absence of group learning, with students taught largely as individuals (while retaining the possibility of occasional seminars)
- participation in the most industrialised form of education
- the privatisation of learning (in that learning occurs away from the group)

Characteristics of distance education

Separation of teacher and student

The separation in space and time of teaching and learning is a basic feature of distance education. It is worth stressing that this separation is not the exclusive prerogative of distance education systems. Some proportion of learning activities in conventional systems takes place apart from the presence of a teacher, increasingly so as one passes up the scale from school to university education, while many distance education systems include elements of face-to-face contact with teachers. What is particular to distance education practice in this respect is that the overall design of a system is premised on this separation, and that therefore the role of the teacher, and the nature of the transactions between teacher and learner, are completely changed.

The role of the institution

Distance education needs to be differentiated not only from conventional classroom based education but also from private study at home. People learn a great deal through their own efforts. What distinguishes distance teaching is that there is an institution that is consciously teaching its students.

Use of technical media

The use of 'technical' communications media in an integrated manner to provide the basic teaching elements is the factor which has perhaps most marked the recent growth of distance education. If the mass media can be used successfully as a principal vehicle for teaching, and as a substitute for a classroom teacher, then considerable economies of scale are theoretically possible. In addition, people who are unable to benefit from traditional education because of physical, economic, or social barriers to access, can be reached. Much of the rhetoric surrounding the use of the term 'open' in the distance education context stems from this notion of the relative accessibility to the public at large of print and broadcast media, compared with the relative difficulty of obtaining access to resources for face-to-face teaching. However, it is clear that mere physical access to print and broadcast media does not necessarily imply that they can be used effectively for educational purposes: potential learners need to be capable of studying independently and to know how best to use these media for learning. This can be problematic, especially for media which have become almost exclusively associated with the provision of entertainment or information.

Two-way communication (between individual students and mentors)

The technical means of communication most commonly used in distance education, with the exception of correspondence by post (which can be very slow), telephone (instantaneous, but also asynchronous in the case of answerphones), two-way radio (instantaneous), and electronic mail (both sychronous and asynchronous), are all one-way. One-way communication is a characterististic of educational technology, with which distance education is often confused (Keegan, 1986:44). The dominance of one-way communication in distance education explains why so many distance education systems are felt to be 'information processing' or 'systematic' models which basically treat learning as the processing, storage and retrieval of information, and in which the learner is a 'passive' recipient of educational messages devised by those who produce the materials. Keegan argues that 'it is important that the student in a distance education system can profit from dialogue with the institution that provides the learning materials', and that 'the student should be able to initiate this dialogue' (1986:44).

Two-way communication between the individual student and his or her mentor (eg. tutor or counsellor) is thus regarded as an essential component of a distance education system. Students may communicate with their tutors or counsellors in writing, by telephone and two-way radio, or in individual face-to-face meetings. In some instances, these contacts may be public - for example television or radio phone-in programmes which enable students to speak with the teachers reponsible for the design of a course (as opposed to local tutors who may not have been associated with its development). Generally, however, they are more private, involving discussion of assignment work that the student is submitting for evaluation or personal difficulties encountered in studying at a distance.

Group learning

Learning in groups is a feature of many distance education systems. In his 1980 definition Keegan argued that 'the possibility of occasional seminars' was a defining characteristic of distance education. At the very minimum, this would imply the organisation of regular face-to-face meetings of students in a particular area, with or without the presence of a tutor, counsellor, or 'animateur', or occasional longer seminars or workshops (such as the contact programmes run by many of the Indian universities' Correspondence Directorates, or the British Open University's residential summer schools). Subsequently Keegan modified his view. He argues that the presence of a learning group is fundamental to most conventional education whereas distance education does not compel students to join a group: 'most distance education systems treat the student basically as an individual' (Keegan, 1986:45). He holds (ibid.:46) that 'the separation of the learner from the learning group throughout the length of the learning process is a characteristic feature of this form of education which distinguishes it from conventional, oral, group-based education', although he accepts that many distance education systems do make use of group-based learning. This leads him to his summary conclusion that distance education is characterised by 'the quasi-permanent absence of the learning group throughout the length of the learning process so that people are usually taught as individuals and not in groups, with the possibility of occasional meetings for both didactic and socialisation purposes' (ibid.:49). However, new communications technologies are now being used to permit group interactions at a distance, either synchronously via audio and telephone conferencing, or asynchronously through computer conferencing (textual teleconferencing using terminals in students' and tutors' homes linked through the telephone networks to a host computer).

An industrialised form of education

We owe to Peters (1973) the introduction into the definition of distance education of a strong emphasis on the quasi-industrial nature of distance education systems. Peters is right to point out that the mass production and distribution of learning materials, as well as the logistical aspects of administering and coordinating the activities of dispersed populations of students and tutors, involves the application of principles drawn from the industrial sector. The division of labour that revolves around specialised tasks and technologies associated with the development and production of learning materials is a marked feature of some forms of distance education. The skills of production/operations management are needed to ensure that materials are developed and produced and services delivered on time to students. Explanations of these processes tend to be couched in the language of 'classical management' (based on the ideas of Max Weber, Henri Fayol and Frederick Taylor) which emphasise organisational structures embodying 'rational' working arrangements designed to operate in predictable fashions.

The introduction of such principles into an educational institution can be problematic. It is not always easy to match the relatively creative activities of course development to a rigidly scheduled production system, while many educators, used to a high degree of personal autonomy in their day-to-day work, resent the loss of autonomy that is implicit in such regularised and task differentiated systems. For some the environment proves stressful. This raises problems of interpersonal behaviour both within the productive group and between groups that require a more human-relations approach to management if understanding is to be achieved. Also the 'packaging' of knowledge which the quasi-industrial nature of many aspects of distance education practice implies also raises problems for many educators, most notably for those who believe that the educational process should focus on the personal needs of the student, and that this is something distinct from the training approach implicit in packaging.

Certainly there are those (Willén, 1981:244-5) and Bååth (1981:213) who challenge the belief that industrialisation is an essential feature of distance education (the latter arguing that some small systems are not industrialised even if larger ones are). Keegan himself argues that there are industrialised features, even in small-scale distance education systems (Keegan, 1986:47). However, he no longer insists that this is an essential defining feature of distance education (ibid.:48).

Privatisation

Keegan's last defining characteristic, which is really connected with the fifth, is the essential 'privatisation' of the learning process which he identifies as being present in distance education, by which he means that 'a distance system takes the student from the learning group and places him/her in a more private situation' (Keegan, 1986:49). Distance education, he says, is 'characterised by the privatisation of institutional learning' (ibid.:49).

Models of distance education

A number of attempts have been made to integrate the defining characteristics of distance education (such as those presented by Keegan and discussed above) into models or theories of distance education. The rest of this chapter introduces three of these - the first a systems model of distance education, the second a holistic model of distance education, and the third a transactional model of distance education.

A systems model of distance education

The systems model is one proposed by Kaye and Rumble (1981:19-22), based on the concepts developed by Miller and Rice (1967) for analysing organisations as open systems which exist by exchanging materials with their environment. The activities carried out by an organisation are divided by Miller and Rice into three categories:

  • operating activities: the specific import, conversion, and export processes which define the particular nature and role of the enterprise

  • logistical activities, which ensure the supply of necessary resources for the proper functioning of the enterprise (recruitment, training, purchasing etc)

  • regulatory activities, which ensure the overall coordination and control of all processes within the enterprise, as well as its links with the outside environment

The operating activities which are characteristic of distance education enterprises can be grouped into two major subsystems (see figure 1.1), which reflect the separation of teacher and student (or teaching and learning activities) to which reference has already been made.

The 'materials subsystem' covers the design, production, and distribution of mediated learning materials. Materials development embraces the activities of curriculum planners, teachers, contents experts, instructional designers, media producers and other 'transformers' (eg. editors, graphic designers) who help in the production of 'media products'. The output from their activities are prototype materials which, through the materials production process, are turned into finished products, in single or multiple copies, in print, audiovisual, and/or computer software form. These materials can then be 'packaged' together as a course and are then distributed to all the students and tutors involved in the course, through mailing, broadcasting, or data transmission facilities.

The student subsystem is separate in system terms from the materials subsystem, involving different activities, personnel and resources, all of which are basically concerned with facilitating the students' learning activities and managing their progress through the institution. It admits students to the institution, allocates them to courses, local centres and tutors and counsellors, collects fees, ensure that they receive course materials, assesses their progress, issues certificates, and maintains their records. The point of contact between the two subsystems occurs when the students receive the learning materials and start to use them.

The value of this simple systems model is that it clearly identifies the principal activities involved in running a distance education enterprise, as well as the inter-relationships that exist between them. It underlines the importance of the quasi-industrial processes that characterise the production and distribution of materials, and lays stress on the specialisation of tasks and division of labour. It defines the difference between an educational publishing organisation (which would only require a materials subsystem) and a distance education institution (which must also provide an appropriate student subsystem). It also helps pinpoint the activities which are independent of student numbers (eg course development) and which are therefore susceptible to

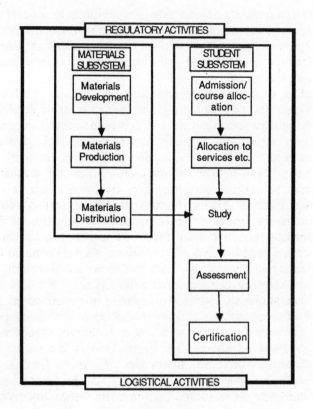

Figure 1.1
A systems model of distance education showing
the materials and student subsytems

economies of scale, and is hence a useful starting point for financial modelling. Finally, it underlines the fact that, theoretically and in practice, different groups and organisations can collaborate in providing a distance education system, each perhaps taking on responsibility for different activities, or clusters of activities, within each subsystem.

A holistic model of distance education

In contrast to the rather technocratic model presented above,

17

which is adequate in its way for helping to understand the activities which define a distance education system, a more global theoretical structure has been developed by Perraton (1981:22-4) which effectively displays the argument in favour of distance education. It is summarised below and in figure 1.2 as a linked sequence of fourteen elements, most of which have already been mentioned in this chapter; the summary is of great value in that it takes these various elements and brings them together in a logical manner, thus providing a useful synthesis of the cost, access and educational arguments favouring distance education. The summary below is to be read in conjunction with figure 1.2.

> Educational media are similar in their effectiveness, but differ in the ways they can readily be distributed (box A). This makes it possible to move away from the fixed staffing ratios necessary to face-to-face study (box B), thereby changing the role of the teacher (box C) and making possible a reduction in costs (box D). It is then possible to reach audiences different from the traditional ones, through distance teaching, and to do so at a reasonable cost (box E). The equivalence of the media however, presents us with problems of choice (box F), best resolved by a multi-media approach (boxes G and H) which allows for feedback (box I) and encourages active learning (box J). In working out the approach to be used, the organisation of any face-to-face element is of key importance (box K) and leads us to consider how to use distance teaching to ensure dialogue (box N) - something which is facilitated if a concern with new audiences and a new relation between education and the community (box L) lead to the use of groups as a basis for adult learning (box M).

Perraton's argument starts with the hypothesis that different media are similar in their effectiveness for teaching; this is based on the results of comparative studies of the use of print, radio, film, television, and live teachers, as reported, for example, by Schramm (1977). Many such comparative studies have been carried out. The general conclusions from them are that it is factors such as the pedagogical quality and clarity of presentation, the relevance of the content, and the motivation and interest of the learners, which are the significant variables, rather than the

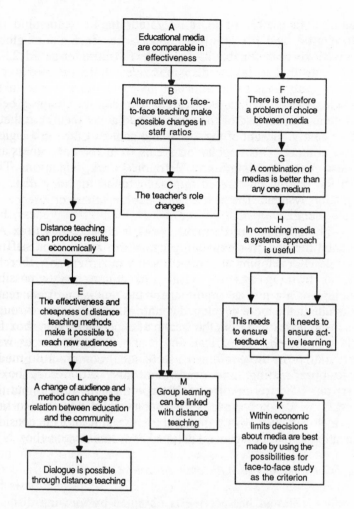

Figure 1.2
A holistic model of distance education

From H. Perraton (1981) 'A theory for distance education',
Prospects, 11 (1), p.23, reproduced by permission of Unesco

particular medium of instruction. The next elements in the argument presented in figure 1.2 follow on logically from this initial premise: the face-to-face teacher's or tutor's role becomes that of a facilitator of learning rather than a transmitter of information, and the group becomes a key forum for debate, discussion, and feedback. In fact, Perraton concludes by suggesting that in taking decisions over choice of media, the specific functions to be allocated to group activity should be considered first, within the overall cost constraints applying in particular cases. Use of the various media can then be decided subsequently, in light of the extent and nature of face-to-face and group contact. This conclusion stems from the community- or society-centred orientation of Perraton's work, which contrasts with the institution-centred approach found in many distance education systems. The next chapter explores these differences in greater detail.

Although much of Perraton's work is concerned with use of distance methods for expanding education as economically as possible in developing countries, notably in Africa, and often for teacher training and for rural and community work, his conclusions are just as important for the provision of education for adults in the more developed countries. In fact, there are many lessons to be learned from the wealth of experiences gained in this field by a number of African and Latin American countries, particularly in the combined use of local community groups, radio broadcasting, and print materials (see, for example, Perraton, 1980, on the use of distance methods for community education). The importance of Perraton's holistic model is that it provides a convincing argument for the adoption of distance education as part of a general national educational policy.

A transactional model of distance education

A rather different perspective is obtained by viewing distance education from the sometimes competing perspectives of the principal 'actors' involved in the process, and the relationships or transactions between them (see figure 1.3).

In traditional education, the vast majority of the learner's transactions are with individual teachers who, in addition to actual teaching and assessing, may give personal advice on course choice, help with administrative problems, and generally monitor the learner's progress. These 'transactions' - whether with teachers or with others - usually take place within the physical boundaries of the institution.

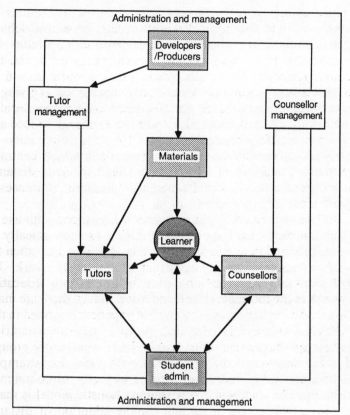

Figure 1.3
A transactional model of distance education

Note: this model assumes a certain kind of distance education
system similar to that of the British Open University. Other models
will have different transactional patterns

In distance education, however, the situation is quite different. Learners have three principal types of transaction to
maintain, and each of these has a different site within the system:

• 'transactions' with the learning materials - reading,
viewing, listening, manipulating, selecting, interpreting,
assimilating, synthesising, and so on; the locus of these
interactions is generally the student's home, but may be a

local centre.

• transactions with 'intermediaries' such as tutors, counsellors and 'animateurs', who are there to help in interpreting and using the course materials, and to promote group discussion and interactions with other learners; the locus of these transactions varies: local study centres or occasional residential sessions for group work, the home or place of work for exchanges by post, telephone, or other communications channels.

• transactions with the institution - or at least that part of it set up to provide student services and to deal with administrative and general queries and problems. These are of necessity often impersonal, having to be carried out a distance, and may be perceived by learners as problematic (the 'unfeeling bureaucracy of the faceless institution' etc). However, the institution may at times deal with students on an individual basis through personal counselling services and the 'faceless' bureaucracy may be humanised to the extent that such services are available (Henri and Kaye, 1985:124-5).

Beyond this circle of transactions in which the learner participates is a complex set of invisible (to the student) activities and interactions which are necessary for providing, coordinating, and maintaining learning resources, the network of intermediaries, and student services. These activities were outlined above in our presentation of the course and student subsystems (see figure 1.1). The principal agents responsible for these activities include:

• educators and subject-matter experts responsible for selecting, organising, and developing the content and curriculum of a particular course.

• 'transformers' of various kinds, who work with the subject-matter experts in developing and producing the specific media products which make up the learning resources. These include editors, graphic designers, media producers, educational technologists, and computer software programmers.

• managers responsible for planning, the formulation of policy, organisation and staffing, coordination and control.

• evaluators concerned with monitoring the functioning of

the system, providing and analysing information for decision-making, and recommending necessary corrective actions. In some cases these will be specific individuals based in an evaluation or management information unit; in others evaluation may be done by managers and educators as a normal part of their work.

Viewing distance education systems in transactional terms emphasises the human relations aspects of management, in contrast to the systems approach of Kaye and Rumble which tends to stress the 'rational' aspects of management.

Conclusion

This chapter started by indicating the diversity of form and practice in distance education, and then went on to discuss the characteristics of distance education presented by Keegan's (1986) definition of distance education. The next chapter develops this theme by examining three models of education and then considering Keegan's seven determining characteristics of distance education against these general educational models.

The latter part of the present chapter looked at three models of distance education, all of which are useful in that they provide a perspective against which the planning and management of distance education can be viewed. At different times one of these perspectives will prove more useful than the others, and they therefore form a backcloth to the arguments developed in this book.

Chapter Two

EDUCATIONAL MODELS AND DISTANCE EDUCATION

Educational Models

Before considering the planning and management of distance education, it is worth reviewing the variety of different general models of education that have been proposed at one time or another, and the implications of these for the nature of distance education. In particular, it is worth considering the extent to which the seven basic characteristics of distance education identified in the last chapter are affected by the general model of education underpinning a particular distance education system. (By 'a general model of education' in this context is meant a coherent and organised body of concepts and ideas, based on a particular world view or philosophy, from which prescriptions for principles and methods of teaching and learning can be derived.)

A number of different classifications of models of education exist. The most comprehensive are probably those proposed by Joyce and Weil (1972) and by Bertrand (1979).

The framework developed by Bertrand divides educational models into three broad categories: institution-centred models, person-centred models, and society-centred models.

The main feature of institution-centred models lies in maximising the effectiveness and the efficiency of educational practice. Bertrand groups here, under the heading of systematic models, those models which basically treat learning as the processing, storage, and retrieval of new information (what might be called information-processing models). Bertrand also includes Skinner's (1968) behavioural approach in this group.

24

Person-centred models, on the other hand, analyse education from a humanistic perspective, putting the main emphases on individual growth, on the 'meaningfulness' and the personal significance of learning experiences, and on the motivation of the learner. Carl Rogers' (1969) model for non-directive teaching represents the best known application in this area. Finally, Bertrand's third category covers models which are based on social action and social interaction approaches, where the main role of educational activity is to bring about change in society, and in social structures and institutions.

Institutions and projects do exist which are exclusively designed around a particular educational model: neighbourhood or community education projects aimed at bringing about social and political change, or schools purporting to teach according to a particular behavioural or humanistic philosophy, would be examples. Generally, however, the educational models which underlie the design of a specific project or institution are not made explicit in the terms used above. Decisions about teaching styles and educational methods are usually left to the initiative of individual teachers and departments and, in the best of cases, choices will be made from among the whole range of different models in such a way as to suit the particular curriculum, learners, and situation. The potential and actual variety in possible teaching approaches and educational models is one of the major advantages of many conventional educational institutions, allowing teachers to flexibly adjust their methods to the particular context in which they are working, and to the changing characteristics of students and their needs.

Many distance education institutions and projects emphasise in their publicity the flexibility as to time and place of study which they offer to their students, as well as the open-ness of access which they provide. Some emphasise the freedom for individual learners to choose the course or curriculum that suits them best. There is no doubt that some of these claims are justified, and that there are obvious practical advantages to independent study at a distance, as compared to attending face-to-face classes, lectures, and seminars. However, it would be foolish to equate this sort of flexibility with a real potential for variety and flexibility in the application of different educational models in the distance teaching situation.

25

Educational models and distance education

Perhaps the majority of distance education projects in the formal education sector (ie. concerned with secondary and tertiary level academic education) are what Bertrand would call institution-centred, inspired predominantly by systematic models of education. An over-riding concern often appears to be that of making the system as efficient and cost-effective as possible: educational planners, operational staff, media producers, instructional designers and evaluators are often assigned key roles in institutional structures. Actual teachers may seem relatively peripheral, recruited as consultants to write learning materials to order, or as part-time tutors and correctors, assigned to the roles of intermediaries between the teaching system and its clientele. The very reliance of distance teaching on the use of media and communications technologies can be said only to have served to strengthen the temptation to apply educational models of the information-processing variety to the design of specific institutions. Although this process has undoubtedly led to a high degree of professionalism in the production of learning materials, as well as to overall levels of efficiency that are the envy of many traditional institutions, it could be argued that this has been achieved at the expense of diversity and flexibility in the range of educational models made available to the adult learners and teachers involved. At times, the emphasis on systematisation and efficiency has led to teaching methods which rigidly pace and assess students' work, leaving little scope for personal initiative or for variations in the teaching/learning situation.

However, not all distance education systems are of the institution-centred type. It is possible to design person- and society-centred models. What is important is that the underlying purpose or philosophy of education should be made explicit. Considerable misunderstandings can arise if the underlying premises and assumptions are not clearly defined at the start. This happened when the Venezuelan Universidad Nacional Abierta (UNA) sought to model itself on the distance teaching systems developed by the British Open University and the Spanish Universidad Nacional de Educación a Distancia.

UNA's planning document (COUNA, 1979:42) made it clear that its curricular model should be based among other things on the concept of the student as 'an individual who is capable of identifying, asking for, selecting, choosing, and using the resources necessary for his personal and professional formation'. The model derived from ideas about open education which are predicated on a person-centred model of education. Confusion arose because distance education came to be seen as not only integral to the concept of open education, but also as equivalent to it. Thus, for example, the US National Association of Educational Broadcasting in its report on *Open Learning* identified one of the essential characteristics of open learning as the ability 'to accommodate distance between the instructional staff resources and the learners, employing the distance as a positive element in the development of independence of learning' (cited in Mackenzie et al, 1975:16-17). Mackenzie and his colleagues were under no such illusions. They made it clear in their introduction to the influential UNESCO book *Open Learning* that the concept of open learning 'is far removed from that which seems to have been in the minds of the British [Open University] Planning Committee' (ibid:17), but Escotet, a member of UNA's Organising Commission, says that UNA's planners along with many Latin Americans mistakenly came to believe that, in adopting distance education as it is exemplified in the British Open University system, they were also establishing an open education system (Escotet, 1978, 69-70).

In fact the British Open University is largely predicated upon an institution-centred model of distance education. Personal experience has demonstrated the confusion and incomprehension of visitors whose outlook has been informed by person-centred or society-centred models and who have visited the Open University believing it to be an open educational system. It is crucial that such misunderstandings should be clarified at the outset.

Institution-centred educational models

Many distance education projects in the formal educational sector conform to institution-centred models in which the primary focus is on increasing the efficiency of the institution as a purveyor of mass education. They define the educational aims and specify the objectives, content, and learning tasks required of those taking their courses, the conditions under which learning occurs, and the means of evaluating the learner's achievement, in ways that are fundamentally incompatible with a humanistic, person-centred approach to education.

In such models learners are 'incorporated' into the institution to receive, store, process and retrieve the information that is provided. In a sense they cease to be free-agents once they have decided they wish to enrol in the system. This is not to say that they do not have some freedoms - for example to choose particular courses from a range on offer or to skip certain sections of a course. Nevertheless, there is a real sense in which they are passive recipients of the educational message devised by the materials producers. The lack of personal choice given students in the development and shaping of their own courses is reflected in standard course models. In many institutions there is a tendency to assume that their work should be paced. As a direct result considerable emphasis is placed on scheduling (fixed examination times, assignment cut-off dates, planned study timetables, course start dates, etc.). Administrative processes are developed to deal with students *en masse*. The channels of communication between institution and learner focus on the interaction between the latter and those responsible for administering their progress through the institution (often admissions and student records clerks and administrators), for delivering the learning materials to them (warehouse operatives), and for tuition, counselling and assessment (academic intermediaries). The latter typically work within detailed guidelines governing student progress that are laid down by the centre. Direct communication links between learners and materials producers are often weak or non-existent. The materials are prepared by academics who are separated from the students and whose concerns focus on the scheduled delivery of prototype materials to those who produce and deliver it. Those describing the system frequently use language reflecting the industrialisation of the process - materials production, distribution, project control - while analogies are drawn with publishing and mail order businesses. The system is geared to what in Latin America is referred to as the *massification* of education. Figure 2.1 deliberately shows the student incorporated within the institutional framework and attempts to reflect an institution-centred approach to education..

Escotet has argued that such a system is primarily a means of *instruction* and not one of *education* (1980a:11-12, 15-17). He maintains that distance education (by which he means institution-

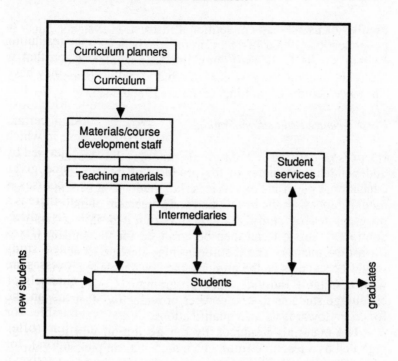

Figure 2.1
Institution-centred distance education model

centred distance education) fails to establish the real and permanent contact between student and lecturer and student and student which must be based on mutual respect and dialogue and which distinguishes education (with its implicit social and cultural context) from instruction (the transfer of information without the necessity for dialogue). While he is deeply critical of much conventional education which he characterises as 'face-to-face instruction', he appears to believe that distance education can never be a truly educational experience - although its shortcomings can be mitigated by various strategies such as study circles, tutorial groups, seminars, and socio-cultural activities (Escotet, 1981:110-11). He admits that what he calls 'distance instruction systems' can fulfil the informative role that the university actually has, with better quality, less cost, and a greater number of users' than conventional instruction systems, but it is not education (1980a:15-16). Certainly he believes that neither the British Open University nor the Venezuelan Universidad Nacional Abierta are providers of what he calls 'open education'. They are 'centres of training' (Escotet, 1980b:247).

Person-centred educational models

In person-centred educational models the learner is an 'independent' consumer of the products of the system, be they educational materials or services. For students, a person-centred model emphasises the negotiation and agreement of individualized programmes of study that are incorporated into a learning contract. Support can then be arranged for the student in the form of a mentor. The institution may decline to accept some would-be students on the grounds that it is unable to provide them with a suitable individualized programme. Conversely it may encourage students to take courses provided by other institutions for credit towards its own qualifications.

The materials produced by the institution will tend to be regarded as a resource from which students can pick and choose, rather than as something which they must study. More reliance may be to placed on existing resources such as text books and less on the development of purpose built materials. Because programmes are personalised there is likely to be more emphasis on personal tuition and tutors are likely to have greater responsibility for negotiating study programmes with students. Tutors will be unable to deal with large numbers of students so that the potential for 'massification' is much reduced - and with it the tendency to 'industrialisation'. Administrative procedures are more likely to deal with students on an individual basis and study programmes are likely to place less emphasis on 'fixed schedule' pacing. Where students are 'paced' in the sense that they are encouraged to achieve learning goals by a given date (and all responsible systems will monitor students and seek to encourage their progress), the pacing mechanisms are likely to be flexible and subject to renegotiation between tutor and student. In such circumstances distance teaching methods based on the use of materials are likely to be regarded as one among a number of means of enabling students to study. These may include independent study.

Cirigliano has pointed out that 'open education transcends face-to-face and at a distance methods and implies that the student endowed with his own set of instruments, through the possession of a method or design, organises his own learning situation having recourse to many sources of knowledge, and that the institutions utilise the educational potential of the social environment that offer many routes to knowledge' (Cirigliano, 1983:21). In open education the method of acquiring knowledge is not of prime importance (ibid:9); open education implies a responsibility and a discipline in the scheduling of one's own learning and does not require individuals to separate themselves from their social milieu and, above all, from their work (ibid.:10); indeed, in 'open education the student interacts much more with reality than with the teacher' (ibid.:15). While distance education enables people to learn at home and while working, what they learn is structured (ibid.:19, 20-1). In contrast, open education 'presupposes the possibility that the subject can define his own objectives ... [and] implies the liberty to organise his own curriculum including the possibility of designing it' (ibid.:21).

Figure 2.2 attempts to reflect the underlying approach to person-centred models. Three variants are shown: (1) learners as independent users of educational materials (which they may have bought), in the study of which they receive no help. As independent users they are depicted (in figure 2.2) as being outside the institution's boundaries; (2) learners as users of an educational service, receiving both materials and teaching from the institution within the context of a defined course, but able to vary their pace of study and, to some extent, the content of what they are studying. Certain guided-study and project-based courses at the British Open University, while still paced, have a degree of choice as to precisely what is studied, and fall into this category; and (3), learners in a contractual relationship with the teaching institution, having access to its materials where this is felt to be necessary, but essentially determining what they learn.

Examples of the third variant include contract learning programmes in which the individual agrees a programme of study with the institution and the latter agrees to help him or her achieve it (as at Empire State College - see Hall and Palola, 1979) and distance-based research degree programmes (as offered by the British Open University). The individualised 'question answering'

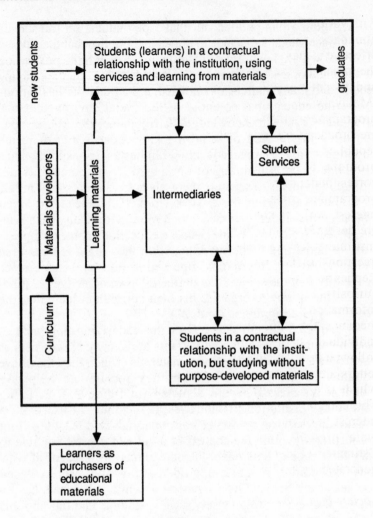

Figure 2.2
Person-centred distance education models

service offered by the Instituto Centroaméricano de Extensión de la Cultura (ICECU) is an example of an individualised educational service model. Established in 1963 'to diffuse general culture to adults and adolescents of all classes, but especially to those who have had little or no possibility to benefit from formal systems of education' (Malavassi, 1978: vol. 1, 253) ICECU operates throughout the Central American region. Having experimented with various media, it came to base its system on radio, a yearly almanack, and correspondence by letter. Radio is its most effective means of mass communication but is regarded as merely the initiator of the system, used 'to seek out those forgotten people and to put oneself at their service' and 'invite participation' (Malavassi, 1978: 1, 302, 304). The main object of the radio programmes, which have an estimated audience of 3 millions and are broadcast on local transmitters in all six Central American republics in both Spanish and some indigenous languages, is to promote a response from the listeners in the form of correspondence with the Institute. Two of the weekly radio programmes constitute talks and discussions on items of general interest, while the other four are based on listeners' letters and are designed to answer the queries raised by them. In 1982 the Institute received some 6,000 letters containing about 12,000 questions, each of which was individually answered by the staff. Replies are short and accurate and aim to increase the *campesinos* curiosity to find out more rather than saturate them with information. Files are kept by subject area (beekeeping, herbal medicine, the moon, the internal combustion engine, etc.) and by individual. It is not uncommon for the Institute's replies to be followed up by a further letter months or even years later. The letters are also a source of inspiration for the yearly Almanack which is a 200 page reader distributed throughout the region. This contains short one to three page articles on matters of general interest or of relevance to *campesinos*. In 1982 566,500 copies were printed. The selling price is deliberately kept low. Estimated readership tops three million. The Almanack also generates considerable correspondence.

Society-based educational models

Distance education materials can usefully be utilised in society-based educational projects provided that an appropriate group organisation is set up to help learners use the materials as a resource *within* the context of a community education project rather than as something that is isolated from the community.

In community-based education projects the educator aims to help whole communities meet their needs. Learners meet in groups but have an interest in institutions and individuals outside the group. The purpose of the educator is to help the whole community to identify what is to be learnt, to find the resources for learning, and to evaluate what has been learnt.

The term 'community education' is imprecise and is used in a variety of contexts. Particularly important is the size of the community since this determines whether or not the educator can meet with the whole community to negotiate the nature of the programme. Sometimes this is possible but generally the educator has to meet with representative groups with which he can plan programmes for the benefit of the whole community. Various approaches may be adopted: the aim may be to involve a wide spectrum of the population in tackling a particular problem - for example, cleaning up a neighbourhood. This approach is process-centered. Alternatively the aim may be to achieve particular social or economic goals by solving specific problems. Here the approach is one of social planning and is task-orientated. Yet another aim may be to achieve fundamental change in society - by for example helping deprived or disadvantaged groups to improve their position. This social-action approach may lead to conflict with the authorities.

The social-action approach stresses the role of the adult educator as a change agent who organises people to learn and, through learning, to alter society by individual or group action. Various approaches can be taken within the context of social-action programmes, although there is widespread support for ones which emphasise the role of the group, within which the adult educator acts as a facilitator or 'animateur' to help with the mutual clarification of situations and the identification of action to effect change. The Canadian Antigonish Movement which developed in Nova Scotia the 1920s and 1930s established 'study clubs' and 'kitchen meetings' (and used mass meetings, conferences, short courses, and radio discussion groups) to engage large numbers of adults in an extensive educational programme linked to social action and in particular a redistribution of economic power through cooperatives and credit unions. The movement was later influential in both developed and Third World countries. In Tennessee the Highlander Folk School which was established in the 1930s played an important role in the development of trade unions and later in the civil rights movement. It sought to emphasise cooperation and linked action to intensive short-term workshops. In Northern Ireland Tom Lovett has drawn on these and other ideas in developing an approach to education in working class districts in the Province (see Lovett, Clarke and Kilmurray, 1983). In Latin America adult education projects have developed based on what Diaz Bordenare (1980:165) has called a 'humanising communication model' in which agricultural extension workers join with farmers to solve problems rooted 'in reality', and where the role of the educator or extension worker is more akin to that of an *animateur* or 'guide', working as an equal partner with the learner, to achieve change through consensus, so that, in Friere's words, 'through dialogue, the teacher-of-the-students and the students-of-the-teacher cease to exist and a new term emerges: "teacher-student with students-teachers"' (Friere, 1972:67).

This kind of approach is very different to institution-centred models where the emphasis is on instruction. It stresses the work of the group in identifying problems and relating these to the personal experience of its members before there is any resort to texts and secondary facts. This radically changes the role of the distance educator and of the centrally produced materials. The latter become aids to the group learning process which can be drawn upon where this is felt to be useful (see figure 2.3). Local groups also may produce materials for their own use and for inter-group exchange.

Some social problems may be so widespread and pervasive that they lend themselves to massive intervention by field workers (adult educators, agricultural extension officers, local health officials) who may make use of centrally produced teaching materials to help educate the target populations. This kind of campaign approach was pioneered successfully by the Canadian Farm Forums in the 1940s with their slogan - 'Read Listen Discuss Act'. However, whereas in campaigns there is an element of 'indoctrination' which derives from the fact that the materials producers are necessarily remote from those using their materials, in more generalised social action programmes it is quite common and, one may suggest, very important that the learners should be able to feed their ideas back to those creating the materials, thus influencing the content. Indeed the successful use of distance education materials within community education projects requires both a local group setting and a feedback loop. In the absence of either it is likely that the materials will fail to have the desired effect firstly because there will be no mechanisms

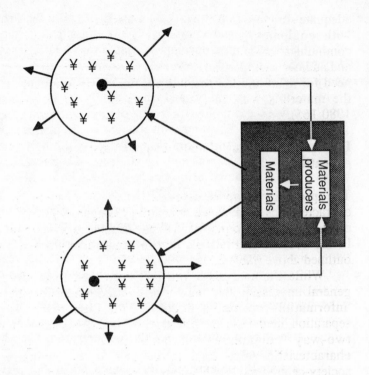

Key

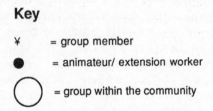

¥ = group member

● = animateur/ extension worker

◯ = group within the community

Figure 2.3
Society-based model of distance education system

to transform reading and listening into action, and secondly because the materials may seem (and indeed may well be) alien to the needs of the community. This argues against (1) the tendency to communicate with mass audiences without first establishing an adequate structure to facilitate group learning, (2) the fascination with equipment at the expense of human (interpersonal) communication; and (3) the compulsion to produce printed, visual and audio-visual materials without previously considering the real need for them and the possibilities for distributing and utilising the materials with the intended audience (Diaz Bordenare, 1980:165).

Implications of educational models for distance education

The previous chapter discussed Keegan's seven defining characteristics of distance education (Keegan, 1986:49). These can very crudely be plotted in terms of their relative importance in the various institution-, person- and society-based models outlined above (table 2.1).

While the analysis is crude it does tend to reinforce the general impression that institution-centred models are basically 'information-processing' models with high teacher-student separation, media use and privatisation, and low to medium use of two-way communication and group learning. These characteristics also tend to be shared by campaign-type society-centred models. Conversely, society-centred social-action models tend to have lower reliance on media and higher reliance on two-way and group communication, and these features are also shared by contract learning programmes and project-type courses. [Private individualised study (in the sense of study outside of the educational institution's influence - of the 'teach yourself' kind) is not referred to in the table. Characterised by a high use of one-way media and no communication with mentors, it should not be confused with independent learning (of the contract and project type), and it falls outside of Keegan's definition of what can constitute a distance education system.]

Conclusion

Unless the underlying philosophy of the system is explicit there is a grave danger that it will fail to meet its objectives. Failure will generally manifest itself not in the materials subsystem but in the student subsystem (for an explanation of these see chapter 1). For example, a system designed to achieve change within the commun-

Table 2.1
Correlation between educational models and distance education

	Institution-centred	Person-centred		Society-centred	
		Project-type course	Contract learning	Campaign	Extended social-action programme
Influence of an education organisation	HIGH	HIGH	MEDIUM	HIGH	LOW TO MEDIUM
Separation of teacher/student	HIGH	MEDIUM TO HIGH	LOW	MEDIUM	LOW TO HIGH
Use of technical media	HIGH	MEDIUM	LOW	HIGH	LOW TO MEDIUM
Two-way communication	LOW TO MEDIUM	MEDIUM TO HIGH	HIGH	LOW	MEDIUM TO HIGH
Group learning	LOW	MEDIUM TO HIGH	LOW	MEDIUM TO HIGH	HIGH
Industrialised form of education	HIGH	MEDIUM	LOW	HIGH	LOW
Privatisation	HIGH	HIGH	MEDIUM TO LOW	HIGH	MEDIUM TO LOW

ity will fail unless careful attention is paid to the role of the local groups and the *animateur* who is central to its success. Conversely, where the emphasis is on instruction (defined here as the transference of knowledge from one who knows to one who does not) the provision of tutorial services are more likely to be based on traditional correspondence structures and the emphasis on distance is likely to be much stronger.

As indicated, the underlying educational philosophy will influence the extent to which particular defining characteristics of distance education are emphasised or not. It also affects the choice of political goals.

A few distance education programmes (and it is very few) are person-centred in the sense that they set out to meet the personalised needs of individuals. However important educators may feel this to be, politicians on the whole have little interest in establishing systems to meet the personal needs of individuals. They seek instead to solve national educational problems or to effect social change through education. The vast majority of distance education systems are established primarily to provide equality of opportunity of access, to support modernisation programmes, to provide continuing education and opportunities for training, or to control what is learnt and where. Distance education systems with these objectives are likely to be institution-centred. Some distance education systems, however, are specifically designed to help rural development and community education programmes. Where this is the aim, the system needs to be society-centred.

The kind of system that is set up thus reflects the political goals underpinning the establishment of the system. The next chapter therefore looks at the political goals which distance education systems may seek to satisfy.

Chapter Three

THE POLITICAL PERSPECTIVE

In the nineteenth century distance education was developed primarily for commercial or altruistic reasons to provide alternative access to formal education and training. The early models were institution-centred and predicated on information-processing approaches to education. The use of distance education to meet needs within the context of community- or society-based models came later.

As the century drew towards its close a number of universities, particularly in the US, began to establish departments designed to cater for 'external' students. By the end of the century it was clear that correspondence education was a valid and effective means of meeting educational and training needs, and the twentieth century, while continuing to see the growth of private correspondence schools, has witnessed the development of distance education as a recognised component in *national* education systems. Many of the national institutions have as their objective the solution of major national educational problems.

Commercial correspondence schools have usually begun as small businesses, although some of them have developed into sizeable enterprises. In addition many conventional educational institutions have established departments to teach students at a distance. While there are exceptions - the Universidad Pedagógica Nacional in Mexico is one such example, with 3,000 conventional students and 60,000 distance ones in 1980 - most of the latter are small with relatively few distance students. A survey of 304 institutions with distance teaching programmes showed that 'the average number of distance-learning students dealt with by conventional institutions [undertaking some distance teaching] is small, never rising to 3,000, whereas the number of students dealt with by 'pure' distance-learning institutions is much larger. Even in Australia, with its very scattered population, it is over 7,500 and in Asia it rises to 55,000' (Perry, 1984:9).

Distance-teaching units set up in conventional educational institutions are often seen as marginal to their main purpose. They also compete for resources with departments teaching conventional courses. While their establishment may be accepted when resources are plentiful, it is likely to be strongly resisted in situations where resources are at a premium and particularly where they are reducing. Even where resources are readily available there may be little interest in developing distance education programmes. Thus in both Britain and the Netherlands, where distance teaching universities have been successfully established and are meeting a demand for the part-time education of adults at a distance, the existing conventional universities had earlier shown little interest in the needs of adults (Perry, 1976:5; de Moor, 1983:59). Generally the solution of major national educational problems by distance means has required the establishment of a purpose-built distance education system.

Examining the planning processes which led to the establishment of new distance teaching universities in the 1970s and early 1980s, Dodd and Rumble (1984:232) identified 'the strong personal support of an influential Government Minister' as a crucial factor in those planning processes that came to a successful conclusion. In the United Kingdom 'by far the most important factor [in the successful foundation of the Open University] was the personal interest and commitment of the Prime Minister [Harold Wilson]' (Hall et al, 1975:265). In Israel the foundation of the distance teaching Everyman's University (EU) owed much to the role played by the Labour Party leader Yigal Allon who, as Deputy Prime Minister and Minister of Education and Culture, 'was the driving force that made EU a reality in near-record time' (Halperin, 1984:28). In contrast, the absence of support from political leaders has led to proposals foundering. In Colombia a proposal in the mid-1970s to establish a national distance teaching university, put forward by the Instituto Colombiano para el Fomento de la Educación Superior and subsequently elaborated in a project plan, came to nothing because ICFES lacked essential support from the Colombian Ministry of Education (Dodd and Rumble, 1984:234-5).

The presence of political support alone may not be enough to save a project. In Nigeria the support of the President was insufficient to obtain the passage of the Open University of Nigeria Bill through the Nigerian Senate in 1981 (Dodd and Rumble, 1984:245). In the Netherlands all-party political support for the Open Universiteit might not have saved the project in the face of financial cutbacks had it not been for the fact that the Cabinet had decided to locate the University in the south eastern part of the country which had suffered heavily from the closure of its coal mines in the 1960s and was consequently regarded as a priority area for development (de Moor,1982:168; 1983:62).

Sometimes governments have encouraged the examination of distance education as an option without giving a lead on the question of whether or not it should be adopted. In both Sweden and Australia the terms of reference of the government commissions convened to consider the need for and desirability of establishing a distance teaching university were left open-ended. The Commissions were free to recommend against the establishment of a national distance teaching university, and both did so (Dodd and Rumble, 1984:236-8). In Australia vested interests in the continuation of the existing arrangements under which a number of Australian universities had a major commitment to external study argued against a single national institution, and the Karmel Committee (1975:80) agreed: 'the creation of a single major institution like the British Open University, ... might actually reduce the likelihood of existing institutions adopting innovatory policies'. In Sweden too a decentralised distance education system based on existing universities was adopted.

While open-ended enquiries may seem rational they are far less likely to lead to change and innovation than is the vision and determination of political leaders. Yet - setting aside the degree to which distance education projects may be established as 'memorials' to a particular government or ministry - political action must to some extent depend on a belief that distance education can play an important role in the national provision of education.

The Early Development of Correspondence Education

Correspondence education had its origins in the mid-nineteenth century. It was made possible by the development of cheap and reliable postal services, improved printing, and the general advances in learning reflected in book publishing and newspapers, the foundation of libraries, and the development of charity schools, debating societies, the Sunday School movement, scientific clubs, workingmen's colleges and institutes, lyceums and chautauquas, all of which made the emergence of home study practicable as well as desirable.

The first correspondence programme was started in the United Kingdom in 1840 by Isaac Pitman to teach shorthand. Pitman reduced the principles of his shorthand system to fit on small cards which he sent to his students. They transcribed passages of the Bible into shorthand and returned these using the 'penny post' service that had been established in the same year. The passages were corrected by Pitman and returned to the students.

In the years that followed further correspondence schools and colleges were established by private individuals who were motivated by a mixture of altruism and commercial acumen. The fact that some of those who set them up were motivated more by a desire to make money than by a desire to teach led, from the early twentieth century, to the establishment of bodies designed to accredit and regularise the activities of correspondence schools and colleges. Among these were the US National University Extension Association (established in 1915), the US National Home Study Council (1926), and the Association of British Correspondence Colleges (1955).

Early examples of correspondence schools and colleges include Charles Toussaint and Gustar Langenscheidt's correspondence school for teaching modern languages, founded in Berlin in 1856; Skerry's College, a business school based in Edinburgh which began postal instruction in 1880 and which was followed within a decade by the establishment of several correspondence schools in England; the Berlin-based Rustinsches Fernlehrinstitut, founded in 1894 to prepare students by correspondence for university entrance examinations; and the Swedish Hermods School (now Hermods-NKI Skolan) which has been offering correspondence courses since 1898, and which was based on the earlier experience of Hans Hermod in offering postal tuition to a number of his students who had moved away from Malmo where he taught.

In the United States, private correspondence schools generally followed on from the work of Thomas J. Foster of Pennsylvania who began in 1870 by using his newspaper as a vehicle to improve mine safety in the state, expanded his campaign into a question and answer service aimed at helping mine inspectors and superintendents qualify for the certificate of competency which became a legal requirement in 1886, and moved on to providing printed pamphlet lessons on mining and other subjects and a staff of teachers to grade assignments. In 1890 this work was taken over by the International Correspondence School.

At the primary school level, too, there were efforts to meet the needs of children who might otherwise be deprived of an education. One of the first ventures in this area, the provision for 'the education of children at home by correspondence', was aimed at children of primary school age who for reasons of remoteness, illness or itineracy could not attend a normal school, and was advertised in 1905 by the private Baltimore, Maryland-based Calvert School, the first students being enrolled in 1906.

By the end of the nineteenth century correspondence education was also influencing the universities. In the United Kingdom the University of London under its first charter was limited to conducting examinations and conferring degrees. Teaching was a responsibility of its constituent colleges and students who wished to sit an examination had to follow a course of study at one of these. In 1858, however, this restriction was removed and anyone could be admitted to read for a degree provided matriculation requirements were met and fees paid. This paved the way for the matriculation of external students. The University, however, took no responsibility for teaching them and it was left to private correspondence colleges to prepare those 'external' students who wanted this form of help for the University of London examinations. Many people considered the University 'to be no better than an examining board, rigid and remote, scarcely a thing to foster a university education' (Marriott, 1981:15) The provision for external students fell far short of the ideal of a university education as it was generally conceived by those interested in extending the role of the universities to meet the needs of the mass of the people. Subsequently pressure grew for the establishment of a teaching university in London - a demand eventually satisfied by the reconstitution of the University of London in 1898, as a result of which it began to teach 'internal' students through its recognised 'schools' and 'colleges' while retaining a continuing responsibility for the examination of 'external' students, the majority of whom were self-taught or prepared by one of a number of commercial correspondence colleges.

In the United Kingdom the idea that universities should have a responsibility for lecturing to the working classes ('university extension') had first emerged in the early 1870s at the University of Cambridge but had subsequently been lost sight of as efforts were put in to the affiliation of provincial colleges (at Lampeter, Nottingham and Sheffield) to one or both of the universities of Oxford and Cambridge. Those interested in extension criticised the affiliated colleges for failing to meet the needs of a wider section of the population, particularly as they rapidly began to press for university status in their own right. For a few years the extension movement was threatened with total collapse then, in about 1882/3, there was a revival of interest in the idea. Conceived in part as the provision of lectures to the working classes, it was recognised that this fell far short of what might be done, and by 1884 the leaders of the British university extension movement were pressing for 'a part-time, non-residential teaching university operating a system of academic credits' (Marriott, 1981:15). Not everyone, even within the movement, agreed with all of this and the idea was ahead of its time. However, Richard G. Moulton, one of the movement's leaders and the author of 'the fullest and most vivacious account of the theory of the open university' (Marriott, 1981:20), was later to go to the US where his ideas were well received during a lecture tour in 1890/1, and where he spent 1892/3 helping William Rainey Harper set up the Extension Department at the newly constituted University of Chicago.

In the United States a number of developments had paved the way for the adoption of correspondence methods by the extension departments of American universities. As early as 1874 the Illinois Wesleyan University began to offer a series of undergraduate and graduate courses that could be pursued in absentia. Forty courses were required for a bachelor's degree and course examinations were invigilated in distant communities by distinguished citizens. Final examinations were conducted at the University's campus. The programme was discontinued in 1910.

Another venture was the foundation of a Correspondence University at Ithaca, New York (1883). Staffed by teachers from various institutions, it was designed to provide correspondence courses to students unable to attend their regular institution. Although acclaimed at the time, the venture failed.

In 1879 William Rainey Harper, then a young professor at Chautauqua (an organisation originally established in 1874 to offer short residential summer school courses for Sunday School teachers and church workers), agreed to help his students continue their studies in Hebrew at home by providing them with an outline course of study and further advice through the mail. This became the forerunner of the Chautauqua home study programme. In 1883 Chautauqua received a Charter from the New York State Legislature and for a number of years a limited number of degrees of bachelor of divinity and bachelor of arts were conferred on graduates of its correspondence study programme, but as the major universities in the United States instituted correspondence work, the programme was run down and eventually closed. Meanwhile Harper had taken his ideas with him when he moved to become President of the University of Chicago (1891), where he established a correspondence course division offering credit courses by mail. The idea was rapidly taken up by other universities, notably the University of Wisconsin.

By the end of the century correspondence education was widely practiced and accepted to a greater or lesser degree as a valid means of studying. This acceptance paved the way for developments in the twentieth century.

The role of distance education systems in national education systems

The twentieth century has seen further growth in the commercial correspondence sector as well as the adoption of correspondence and distance teaching systems by professional associations (for example, the American Hotel and Motel Association, the American Association of Medical Record Librarians, etc.) and, latterly, for in-service training purposes within large companies (for example, British Telecom). It has also been marked by diversification away from the traditional media used in correspondence courses (notably printed lessons and question papers, and written assignments from students which are marked by tutors) to other media including broadcasting, audio-visual materials, and computers used in computer-assisted learning and for communications purposes. At the same time the emergence of 'fleximode' or open learning systems combining distance learning with more conventional approaches, coupled with the tendency of many distance systems to make use of some face-to-face contact between student and tutor, has led to a blurring of distinctions between conventional and distance learning.

The successful early development of correspondence tuition made it certain that sooner or later distance education would be adopted as an instrument of state education policy. Australia was the first country to do this on a large scale to meet the needs of a dispersed population of school-aged children. It was followed by the massive expansion of correspondence education in the Soviet Union and elsewhere.

This is not the place to provide a detailed history of the development of distance education. What is interesting are the underlying factors that have led to the adoption of distance education as an instrument of national educational policy - egalitarianism, modernisation theories, rural development and community education, continuing education and the need for training, and totalitarianism. In discussing these various factors a distinction is drawn between the developed and less developed countries since their needs are to some extent different. Brief reference is also made to the economic arguments favouring distance education, although this aspect is considered more fully in the next chapter.

Egalitarianism

The twentieth century has seen increased interest in distance education as a means of equalising the provision of education and reaching deprived sectors of the population. These include children and young adults who for geographical, economic or social reasons are unable to attend a class-room based system and those for whom the state has been unable for financial or other reasons to provide sufficient places to meet demand for access.

In Australia and subsequently in Canada and New Zealand correspondence education was adopted by national or state (provincial) governments as a means of extending the school system to those who would otherwise be deprived. The Australian correspondence school system originated in 1914 when a group of trainee teachers in Victoria agreed to send lessons by post to the children of a parent who had written to the Education Department asking for some kind of provision to be made. Similar developments occurred in New South Wales (1916), Western Australia (1918), Tasmania and British Columbia (1919), South Australia (1920), Queensland and New Zealand (1922), Alberta (1923), Saskatchewan (1925), Ontario (1926) and Manitoba (1927). Most of these schools began by offering primary level courses and later expanded to include secondary courses. All were specifically aimed at the remote student. Originally based on the provision of printed lessons which were supervised largely by the childrens' parents and the use of correspondence-based assignments, the development of two-way radios which allowed for an element of interaction with the teacher and other pupils led to the formation of Schools of the Air in Australia (from 1951) and, most recently, in the Falkland Islands (Penberthy, 1982; Leonard, 1985). At the higher education level the Act creating the University of Queensland (1909) required it to provide correspondence courses and was an early example of government interest in the potential of this form of education. The Act reflected the egalitarian philosophy of the legislators who wanted a university that would serve the interests of the whole state and not just those of the capital city.

During the 1920s the Soviet Union began to exploit correspondence education as a means of widening educational opportunities. Literature aimed at helping the home learner began to be produced, such as the *School at Home* series under the general editorship of N.K. Krupskaia, and publications such as *The People's Home University, The Workers' School at Home,* etc. Between 1923 and 1929 correspondence courses began to be offered and in 1926-7 certain Moscow-based higher education institutions opened correspondence divisions (the Second Moscow State University, the M.V. Lomonosov Mechanics Institute, etc.). A Central Institute for Correspondence Education was established in 1927 while the end of the 1920s saw the opening of more than 30 correspondence divisions at agricultural higher education institutes and the development of correspondence branch institutes in the higher technical education sector. During the period 1929-32 the large correspondence institutes were established, including the All-Union Industrial (now Polytechnic) Institute in

Moscow, the Leningrad Industrial (now Northwestern Polytechnical) Institute, and the All-Union Institute of Finance and Economics, Moscow. Further developments occurred during the 1930s, and 'correspondence education became an organic part of the general system of public education in the USSR' (Great Soviet Encyclopedia, 1975).

In the early part of the century correspondence education most interested those governments faced by the problems of educating a scattered population over vast distances. In Europe it remained in the hands of commercial and private interests until after the Second World War. Only in France was there an early recognition (in 1939) that correspondence education might be a means of alleviating the disruption to childrens' education resulting from the Second World War. As a result the Ministry of Education created a national centre for correspondence teaching which survives to this day.

Distance education continues to be recognised as a means of overcoming the problem of providing educational opportunities to those who are socially, economically and geographically disadvantaged. For example, the objectives of the Universidad Nacional de Educación a Distancia in Spain include specific provision for those living in remote areas of the country while those of the Costa Rican Universidad Estatal a Distancia suggest that the University will 'provide a solution to the problems facing the agricultural and working population who have the ability to enter a university but who, for economic, social or geographical reasons could not enrol in the existing universities'. In the United Kingdom the Open University was seen by its Planning Committee (1969:5) as having 'an unrivalled opportunity to rectify [the] long-continuing imbalance' between the educational opportunities available to men and those available to women. Distance education can also serve the needs of those who are kept at home - for example, women in purdah in Islamic coutries - and those confined in institutions - as in the United Kingdom where the Open University caters for the needs of the institutionalised and home-bound sick or handicapped persons and long-term prisoners.

Egalitarianism has also extended in some cases to the provision of educational opportunities to adults who for one reason or another had been unable to enter school or college at the normal age or had to finish before they had obtained a leaving certificate.

The provision of 'second chance' educational opportunities has occurred at all levels of the education service. Thus, for example, Radio Santa Maria in the Dominican Republic provides courses covering the whole primary-school curriculum adapted to the needs of the rural adult population. At the higher education level a number of the distance teaching universities established in the 1970s had as one of their objectives the provision of higher education opportunities to adults who had been unable to go to a conventional university. Coincidentally the provision of second chance opportunities was at times extended to those who lacked the normal minimum educational qualifications to participate at a particular level (so that for example the British Open University and Everyman's University in Israel allow open admission to their first degree programmes).

The ability of distance education to reach deprived groups is such that Pagney (1982:109) has commented that 'the project of democratic education could not be fully realized without including a provision for distance education'. From the many examples cited it will be clear that egalitarianism is a matter of concern in both developed and less developed countries.

Modernisation theories

In the 1950s and 1960s decolonisation focused interest on the development of the newly emerging countries of Africa, Asia and elsewhere. Modernisation theorists maintain that low-income countries are at an earlier stage of development than high income countries but that their development will follow a similar path. The general aim is to accelerate development by, for example, transfering capital and technology from high-income countries to low-income countries. Educational policies focus on the need to expand post-primary level education to the levels found in high-income countries (Harbinson and Myers, 1964:176-8) or to improve teacher training (Beeby, 1966:111-31).

A number of distance education projects were established to provide for the in-service training of teachers who were untrained or under-educated. In 1963 the United Nations Relief and Works Agency and UNESCO established a joint Institute of Education which used correspondence methods to train teachers serving the needs of Palestinian refugees. Similar projects were established in Botswana, Nigeria, Kenya, Tanzania and elsewhere to train the thousands of teachers needed to support the goal of universal primary education. More recently Tanzania has used distance teaching methods to provide initial training for teachers prior to their deployment in the schools. Elsewhere the Allama Iqbal Open University in Pakistan has as one of its specific objectives the training of teachers, while the first professional degree programme developed by the Universidad Estatal a Distancia in Costa Rica was a bachelor's degree in education for teachers in primary and secondary schools.

Media-based distance education techniques also came to be used to provide schools where none had previously existed. In Niger Télé-Niger began in 1964 with the aim of increasing access to primary education, the class-room teacher being replaced by a televised lesson and a coordinator able to help the children to a limited extent. In Mexico the Telesecundaria was established in 1966 to provide alternative secondary schools, particularly in rural areas, to students who had no chance of attending regular schools. The children are taught by televised lectures supported by workbooks, with each class having a coordinator to help them. Similar systems include the Malawi Correspondence College which was established in 1964 to provide secondary education to primary-school graduates unable to get into secondary school, and the Brazilian Fundação Maranhense de Televisão Educativa which provides television classes to children who cannot find places at school. Those Third World countries that have struggled to attain universal primary education are now looking for less costly ways of providing secondary education. Distance education may well offer the only hope of significant expansion of educational facilities at this level.

At the higher education level similar arguments prevail. For example, the distance teaching Universidad Nacional Abierta in Venezuela was established in part to help meet a demand for university education which could not otherwise be met; the Indira Gandhi National Open University, India, has been set up 'to provide opportunities for higher education to a larger segment of the population'; and the Allama Iqbal Open University, Pakistan has as one of its objectives the provision of facilities 'to the masses for their educational uplift'.

Central to the modernisation theorists' position is the belief that it is the modern sector of the economy of Third World countries that will lead to their development and that in consequence a major role of the education system is to meet the manpower needs of this sector. This led educational planners to estimate future national manpower needs primarily on the basis of the projected needs of the modern sector. Expenditure on education was seen as an investment in human capital which would yield benefits to the individual and society in the form of increased earning power and productivity. This encouraged the expansion of secondary and tertiary education, notwithstanding the fact that there was evidence available, certainly by the early 1970s, of increasing un- and under-employment of secondary and tertiary education graduates (Carnoy, 1975). It also affected the choice of curriculum, particularly at the higher education level, by placing emphasis on the development of specialised job-related courses. The theory influenced educational planners concerned in the establishment of distance teaching universities in, for example, China, Costa Rica and Venezuela (Rumble and Harry, 1982:208). In Venezuela it was hoped that UNA's graduates would help to meet the shortages of skilled manpower that had been identified in the fifth national development plan (1976-1980), while in China it was hoped that the Central Radio and Television University would help promote the modernisation of the country by providing trained graduates.

Modernisation theories are likely not only to affect the curricular objectives of distance education programmes, leading to an emphasis in job-related skills and the development of vocationally and professionally orientated programmes of study, but may also affect the choice of target audience, leading to a concentration on younger adults who may be expected to have a productive life of 30 or 40 years within the modern sector of the economy. Furthermore, since the purpose of education is seen in terms of the training of individuals to fulfil particular roles within the economy, distance education institutions serving this purpose are likely to be based on information-processing or institution-centred educational models (see chapter 2).

Rural Development and Community Education

More recently underdevelopment theorists have come to question the connection between modernisation and the attainment of high-income status. Foreign economic penetration has come to be associated with social and political underdevelopment, and has been seen as a positive hinderance to development as investment is channelled into mineral extraction and cash crops which do not contribute to the growth of the indigenous economy. Underdevelopment theorists argue that existing educational systems support foreign economic exploitation by giving priority to secondary and higher education, the purpose of which is to produce an indigenous elite trained to act as intermediaries for the process of capital exploitation and inculcated with the political and social values of the ex-colonial countries (Fanon, 1967:36, 120). In these circumstances the education of the mass of the people is ignored, thus supporting their exploitation (Freire, 1970:20-5, 46-53).

To counter these tendencies underdevelopment theorists argue that there should be a more equitable distribution of educational opportunities with emphasis placed on basic education for the mass of the people, locally controlled, related to the needs of the rural population and aimed at raising their collective consciousness so that they become agents for social and economic change (see for example, Freire, 1969:97-113; Malassis, 1975:69-88). Lowe (1983:302) has noted that while the chief justification for the shift away from educational strategies based on modernisation theories towards those concentrating on rural education and development is 'to alleviate the effects of under-nourishment and disease by raising rural incomes, it is noticeable that many countries which strove to achieve rapid industrialisation are now persuaded that national prosperity depends first and foremost upon the maximum utilisation of land resources and on the generation of capital surpluses for investment'.

Such developments may be regarded with deep suspicion, being seen as an inherent threat to existing agro-commercial interests. It is not surprising that community-based education systems using distance means have been the subject of right-wing threats and action in countries such as Guatemala, Honduras and El Salvador. On the other hand, where the political climate is favourable, there is little doubt that distance education can play a part in providing basic educational materials which can be used by the adult population to enhance understanding of their situation and to enable them to acquire further skills which can help improve their standard of living.

The implications of these theories for distance education are profound for they suggest that, rather than focus upon the production of more graduates with secondary and tertiary level educational qualifications, distance educators should use their systems for society- or community-based education. This will affect not only what is taught, but how it is taught and to whom. The effective implementation of community education schemes is heavily dependent on the participation of those adults who occupy positions of power and influence within the community, and on meeting the participants' perceptions of their educational needs. Those creating centrally produced materials must therefore be sensitive to these needs. Furthermore since effective community education leading to rural development demands action as its end product, participation needs to be group- rather than individual-based, with the group organisers providing the feedback to the materials producers which enables the latter to keep participants' needs in mind (Perraton, 1980:59-60).

Continuing Education and the Education of Adults

While less developed countries have been greatly influenced by modernisation theories and more recently by a concern with community education, the development of distance education in the developed countries has been particularly influenced by three factors, egalitarianism (discussed above), a concern for the education of adults, and a concern for continuing education.

The OECD (1976:4) defined adult education as 'any learning activity or programme deliberately designed to satisfy any learning need or interest that may be experienced at any stage in his or her life by a person who is over the statutory school leaving age and whose principal activity is no longer in education'. This definition, which encompasses vocational and non-vocational, formal and non-formal learning, undertaken for both individual and community development, rightly stresses the fact that the process of adult education is deliberate, planned and organised, undertaken with the conscious intention of bringing about change in the knowledge, attitudes and skills of the learner, and that the learner is aware of this intent and actively involved in the process.

The concept of adult education overlaps with others - for example, that of continuing education which the British Department of Education and Science (1980) defined only by reference to initial education: 'Initial education can be defined as the continuous preparatory period of formal study, to whatever level, completed before entering main employment. Continuing education covers anything which follows'. Generally speaking a distinction is drawn between continuing education of a vocational and professional nature and non-vocational adult education. This is not just a matter of content; it frequently subsumes issues related to the funding of provision and hence of access.

It is often argued in advanced industrial countries that the costs of adult education should not be a charge against public funds. A number of reasons are given for this including for example, adherence to a 'front-loaded' model of education which undervalues the education of adults; the belief particularly in respect of non-vocational adult education that since it is the only the individual that benefits, it is a private affair which should be paid for by the individual; and the feeling that there are no votes to be lost or gained in espousing adult education. So far as continuing education of a vocational or professional nature is concerned, it is often argued that the costs should be met either by the individual or the employer.

There is, however, another perspective which argues that the education of adults is not a luxury. During the 1970s increased awareness of the rate of technological and social change was coupled with a recognition that the knowledge acquired during initial education has a limited life and that individuals would need to update themselves if they were to keep abreast of their field. The pace of change is so rapid that those working in industries at the forefront of the technological revolution point out that technologists and scientists now have to be wholly retrained every five to ten years if their skills and knowledge are not to become obsolete. Significantly, professional updating now needs to be a continuous process rather than an occasional activity.

Some governments have legislated to provide workers with an entitlement to paid educational leave (for example, various state laws in the Federal German Republic). Elsewhere specific provision has been made to help with the continuing education and training of adults in remote areas. The government of British Columbia, acknowledging demands from the rural communities and professional associations for the provision of in-service training facilities for professionals working in isolated communities, established the Open Learning Institute in June 1978 to provide distance courses to isolated areas of British Columbia. Satellite campuses were established in a number of larger communities and mobile learning centres equipped so that tutors could visit outlying areas not served by a permanent centre. Subsequently in May 1980 the Knowledge Network of the West Communications Authority was established to provide post-secondary institutions with a telecommunications system for delivering educational courses and materials by cable television and satellite transmission. The programme appears to have been very successful in increasing the range of courses on offer to people in rural areas, and it has attracted increasing numbers of students.   In the United Kingdom the government-funded Manpower Services Commission's Open Tech Programme is providing the initial investment capital for the development of learning packages and delivery systems for distance and open learning projects in key areas of adult training, particularly at the technician level. Finally, large corporations such as Hewlett-Packard in the United States and British Telecom in the United Kingdom are using distance learning methods to continue the education and training of their staff.

Governments are increasingly aware of the need to train large numbers of people in the new technologies, a generic term encompassing developments in the fields of automation, robotics, micro-electronics, telecommunications and so on, but face the enormous problems of scale and cost. Attitudes towards work have also changed as unemployment has increased in many of the advanced industrial countries of the west. Surveys have shown that those who are unemployed want, among other things, the chance to gain skills and knowledge that will increase their chances of emloyment. In response governments have tended to support programmes related to the training of skilled labour in areas where there are acknowledged shortages.

The emphasis on professional and vocational continuing education has often appeared to be at the expense of liberal adult education. Nevertheless there are those who argue that one of the tasks of adult education is to cater for the pursuit of leisure, for new forms of work (self-employed, household and community work) as a valid alternative to employment, and for an extension of education into the 'Third Age' (that stage in the individual's life-cycle that follows the end of formal working life). Given the demographic structure of a number of advanced industrial countries, the latter is an area of increasing importance which has received recognition in such developments as the University (in the sense of 'universal' rather than an institution of higher education) of the Third Age movement in France and the United Kingdom.

Distance education, because of its flexible and modular approach, because it is not confined to metropolitan and urban areas, because it is convenient for those who have jobs and are unable to commit themselves to attend class-room based instruction, and because it is home-based and hence meets the needs of people with mobility problems (including the aged) can help to satisfy needs for continuing education in the vocational and professional fields and provide increased opportunities for non-vocational liberal adult education.

Politicians have to decide whether or not they will support the development of adult and continuing education within the public domain for the benefit of all those who want access, whatever the subject; whether their support will be limited to meeting the demand for professional, vocational or job-related education and training; or whether it will be left to private enterprise to exploit the potential of the new technologies for the benefit of those who can afford to subscribe to their services and in fields where demand is such that a commercial profit can be assured.

Where government help is given, it can be direct in the form of free access as of right (which given the present position in respect of the financing of education seems unlikely) or help with the costs through mandatory or discretionary and perhaps means-tested grants; or it can be indirect in the form of tax allowances to offset the costs of studying (or at least some of them) for some people. McIntosh (1981:28-9) suggests that most education of adults falls into three categories - refreshment and personal development which is of greatest interest to individuals who should therefore meet more of the costs; updating knowledge and skills, which is of greatest interest to employers who should therefore pay more towards the cost (recognising that many small employers may find the cost too great or be reluctant to accept it where there is a likelihood that staff will move on to other jobs); and recycling or retraining people to help them with unemployment and re-entry into the labour market, a matter of importance to the state which should therefore pay more towards this kind of training.

Politicians are rightly concerned with questions of demand and the costs implicit in satisfying it. In spite of the general support given to the concepts of lifelong, continuing and permanent education, governments have simply not had enough money to meet every demand. Their position is not made easier by the fact that demand is difficult to quantify, thus increasing uncertainty as to the financial implications of policy initiatives. Thus McIntosh (1981:29-30) reports that there was little clear evidence of demand for distance-taught university-level studies before the British Open University was established, yet since its foundation it has consistently had to turn away applicants. The Dutch Open Universiteit was founded without any research into needs or demand (van Enckevort, 1984:73). In fact initial demand far exceeded the initial planning estimates and at least in the case of the British Open University - now in its fifteenth year of operation (1986) - there is no evidence that it is diminishing. In Japan, where comprehensive studies of demand for a University of the Air were conducted in 1970 and again in 1975, the results showed that a huge number of people wished to study with the university (Neil, 1981:51-2).

The 'neo-Keynsian' view of education that was common in the 1960s and early 1970s and which regarded education as an end in itself has been challenged by those seeking to reduce public expenditure. At the higher education level this has involved limits on student numbers in certain fields and increased emphasis on vocational studies, and at the secondary level a reduction in the range of choice available to students coupled with efforts to make the secondary curriculum more employment related. In countries where such views are commonplace, education is regarded as an 'ancillary vehicle' acting in support of the economy. In spite of the rhetorical value placed on general, liberal education, many governments now feel that they cannot support both liberal and specialised education and there is a tendency to argue that the former is a luxury which must to some extent be curtailed in pursuit of the production of those trained professionals who will, it is asserted, subsequently generate the wealth that will enable more money to be spent on education. Opponents hold that this is a narrow view of the purpose of education and that liberal education has positive virtues beyond the intrinsic merit of the subject areas it covers - for example, in the training of minds.

Whatever the virtue of the arguments on either side of this

divide - and it is not the place of this book to discuss them - there is no doubt that they affect distance educators as much as their counterparts in conventional education. Yet, rather than reduce provision across the board, it is possible that distance education could provide an alternative and cheaper means of access to certain general courses, even for those attending traditional institutions who might take distance courses as a part of the requirements for the more specialised degrees offered by the conventional institutions.

Totalitarianism, Social Control and the Control of the Curriculum

So far we have been considering the benefits which may derive from the use of distance education. There is unfortunately a darker side to distance education which should be mentioned.

It is a feature of distance education systems that the students are isolated from one another and kept at home. While many distance educators see this as a problem which needs to be overcome through the establishment of local centres or use of the new communications technologies, politicians may see positive advantages in it. Houle (1974:41) commented that many non-South Africans believe that the distance teaching University of South Africa 'is an instrument of apartheid because correspondence interaction is a method ideally suited to such a purpose', a view supported by Dieuzeide (1985:45) who sees it as a vehicle for providing education at a distance to black South African students who, since 1952, have been barred from attending campus-based universities. Critics of the Free University of Iran alleged that it was established by the Shah as a means of increasing the output of graduates without having a further concentration of students in Tehran and other Iranian cities. In Latin America the 1960s saw the politicisation of the campuses. Distance education was an obvious means of preventing this and was recognised as such. In Colombia conventional students at the University of Antioquia opposed the expansion of its experimental distance teaching department on the grounds that distance education implied fewer on-campus students and a dispersion of student power leading to the depoliticisation of the student body (James and Arboleda, 1979:272). Similarly the development of university-level distance teaching in China after the cultural revolution was a response to the discontent of the young students sent out to work in the rural communes and a means of allowing them to study part-time while maintaining the contol of the commune over them (Dieuzeide,1985:42)

Distance educators and their critics have also drawn attention to the 'packaging' of materials in distance education systems, including the definition of objectives and content and the control over what is learnt implicit in this; the isolation of the distant student from libraries and hence from books and ideas other than those provided by the institution; the implications for the tutor's role where he or she is seen as supportive of the printed, audio-visual and electronic media produced by the institution rather than as a source of knowledge and opinion in his or her own right; the control of assessment; and the danger that the student will become a passive consumer of what is provided (Harris, 1976:44; Kaye, 1981:238, 241-5). Reviewing the impact of new information technologies on education, Gueulette and Hortin (1981:54) warn that 'the best-intentioned educational programmes could be reduced to highly controlled behavioural management strategies that would enslave the user and also would be very vulnerable to mismanagement or political or economic interests'. This constitutes a possible misuse of distance education which it would be foolish to ignore.

Lowering the cost of education

In a number of cases those founding distance education systems have regarded them as means of meeting demand at a lower average cost per student than would be the case if additional provision were made available in conventional institutions. In its planning report the Organising Commission of the Universidad Nacional Abierta (Venezuela) expressed the hope that the establishment of a distance teaching university would 'contribute to a significant diminution of unit costs in higher education' (COUNA, 1977:32); Schramm, Hawkridge and Howe (1972:65) in their report to the Hanadiv on the proposed Everyman's University envisaged that 'Everyman's University, if it develops as anticipated, may provide some welcome relief from the present unit cost of higher education in Israel'; and the Andhra Pradesh Committee on the Establishment of an Open University (1982:55-56) cited evidence drawn from early cost studies of the

British Open University to the effect that the average recurrent and capital cost per student in the latter was less than that in conventional British universities, and implied that in their view the foundation of an Open University in Andhra Pradesh would be cheaper than any alternative course of action. Whether or not these expectations were realistic is the subject of the next chapter.

Conclusions

There can be little doubt that distance education has a valid and important role to play in national education systems and can serve a variety of ends; that it can be a profitable field of activity for private enterprise; and that it can be used by large companies as a means of training their employees. Because of its flexibility, distance education is one of the most important means of providing for the education of adults both for ongoing vocational and professional training and in non-vocational fields.

Generally speaking, it is less likely that large-scale distance education systems will be developed where the existing educational system has already diversified into distance teaching. This is because at the national level, there will be a temptation to believe that the job is already being done, while at the institutional level it is often difficult to achieve a significant diversion of resource to distance education programmes. Distance teaching departments in conventional educational institutions frequently give the impression that they are marginal to the main concern of the institution. They remain dependent on the 'good will' of the institution for their continued survival and this gives them a fragility not necessarily shared by larger 'independent' distance teaching systems. On the other hand, such systems have an important role to play, not least because their absolute costs can be lower, hence making them attractive options where finance is constrained or potential student numbers small.

Experience shows the critical importance of political leadership in establishing large scale distance education institutions. The real issue at the present time is whether politicians wish to invest in distance education. The cost of establishing a large-scale distance education system is likely to be considerable and can act as a disincentive to politicians trying to balance expenditure across a wide diversity of educational and non-educational programmes. These tendencies may favour the growth of commercial correspondence interests or a laissez faire attitude that encourages the emergence of a series of innovative projects run by enthusiastic staff on minimum budgets.

To take one example, much of the present development of open and distance learning systems in the United Kingdom, with the notable exception of the Open University, fits the latter pattern. While such efforts should not be decried, they cannot be regarded as a serious attempt by the state to develop a national strategy which makes use of distance education to tackle educational problems. Indeed, such a strategy may lead to overprovision by conventional institutions vying with each other to increase their student numbers (as happened in Australia [White, 1982:272-4]), or an over-concentration on those areas of provision likely to be immediately profitable in commercial terms (with a consequential failure to invest in areas of low profitablity but high national need). Moreover, where the task of developing programmes is left to ill-funded public institutions or commercial ventures more interested in profit than in the success of the students, the requisite investment in materials development, infrastructure and student support systems may not occur, with the result that drop-out rates may be high and distance education in general be discredited.

Yet distance education can provide politicians with a way of meeting the educational needs of large numbers of those leaving conventional schools who are unable to enter the next level of education because there are insufficient places available; it is peculiarly appropriate as a means of teaching and training adults; and it can, as the next chapter shows, do this at a lower unit cost per student than is achievable in conventional systems.

Chapter Four

THE ECONOMIC PERSPECTIVE

As the previous chapter made clear, one of the attractions of distance education, at least for politicians, is that the unit costs of teaching are said to be lower than those in conventional class-based education, thus holding out the expectation that more students can be educated for a given level of investment than is the case in conventional systems. This chapter considers the comparative costs of distance and conventional education systems, the internal cost-efficiency and the cost-effectiveness of distance teaching, and the policy implications of the economics of distance education.

Distance education: the basic cost function

Traditionally most costs in conventional educational institutions are treated as variable costs directly related to student numbers. Distance education changes the production function of education by substituting a range of media for teachers. In essence capital replaces labour, offering to educationalists what Wagner (1982: ix) described as 'a mass production alternative to the traditional craft approach'.

In distance education very significant costs can be incurred in the preparation of teaching materials (printed texts, television and radio broadcasts, video and audio materials, computer-based instructional programs, and so on) before students enter the system and irrespective of the number likely to be enrolled. Their development and production costs can only be justified in economic terms if, at a later stage, there are sufficient numbers of students enrolled in the system to make the investment worthwhile. At the same time, the direct cost of teaching students can be significantly lower than is the case in conventional systems.

At its simplest, the cost function of any educational system can be expressed in the form:

$$TC = F + VN$$

where TC is the total cost, F is the fixed cost of the system, V is the variable cost per student, and N is the number of students. In distance education systems the value of F is likely to be much higher than that found in conventional systems, while the value of V may be significantly lower. The very high level of investment involved can be justified if the number of students is sufficient to bring the average cost per student down to a reasonable level. The average cost (AC) is simply the fixed cost divided by the number of students N plus the variable cost per student (V):

$$AC = F/N + V$$

Laidlaw and Layard's study of the comparative costs of courses at the British Open University and conventional universities provides an idea of the difference in cost structure between the two systems. They showed, for example, that the fixed costs of the first Open University Arts Foundation Course, which they defined as covering the cost of the central academic staff who developed the course, certain other central academic faculty costs, consultants, design, the fixed costs of the printed correspondence materials and of television, radio and audio-visual supplies not given to students, and certain central administrative costs, was £162,558 (at 1971 price levels). The variable cost per student, which covered the annual recurrent costs of printing supplementary materials with a one year life (such as for example assignment question papers), the variable costs of the printed correspondence materials, and the costs of tuition, postage, packing, residential schools, audio-visual aids given to students on a non-returnable basis, and examinations, was £56 at 1971 price levels. In comparison the fixed costs in a typical conventional university for an arts course were £401, while the variable cost per arts student was £117 (Laidlaw and Layard, 1974:454). Other courses had different cost structures.

Wagner (1977:360) pointed out that generally the ratio of

fixed to variable costs in conventional British universities was 1:8 whereas in the Open University it was 1:2000. Laidlaw and Layard (1974:454) showed that the variable to fixed cost ratio of one early mathematics course at the Open University was 1:1936 (course M201), that of an education course 1:3035 (E282), and that of a biology course (SDT286) 1:1562. In contrast the average variable to fixed cost ratio in conventional British universities was 1:7.6 for mathematics courses, 1:7.7 for social science (and education) courses, and 1:3.1 for physics and biology courses.

Figure 4.1 shows the comparative unit cost per student in a distance and conventional system where the fixed costs of the distance system are three times those of the campus-based system and the variable cost of the distance student is one third that of a conventional student. It is clear from this that when student numbers are low it is cheaper to teach by conventional means (depicted in the A 'zone' of the figure), but that there is a crossover point 'X' beyond which it becomes progressively cheaper to teach students by distance means (the B 'zone' in the figure). However, eventually the curve flattens out and further significant economies of scale cease to be realisable (the C 'zone' in the figure).

It is arguable that the most important measure of cost-efficiency is the cost per graduate since it is the output of graduates that measures the efficiency of an educational system. Since drop-out rates are usually higher in distance systems it is quite possible for a distance system with a lower annual unit cost per student to produce graduates at a higher unit cost than is the case in conventional systems.

Those planning a distance education system in the hope that they will reap economies of scale must ensure that the variable cost per student V in the distance system is less than that found in conventional systems operating at a similar educational level; that the number of students N is large enough to bring the average fixed cost per student F/N down; and that the drop-out rate is kept at a reasonable level (and preferably as low as possible). The first condition has very significant implications for the choice of media. While in theory distance educators have a wide choice available to them, in practice this is often constrained not only by the absolute costs of a particular medium but by the effect its adoption may have on the average cost per student. The second has important implications for market research. The third has

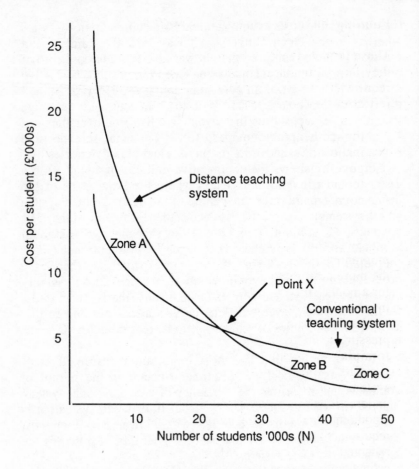

Figure 4.1
Student numbers and unit costs in conventional and distance learning systems

implications for the resources put into student support services. Since these are a direct cost per student (that is, variable with student numbers) the degree of investment in student support services has to be weighed against the effect of this on the variable cost per student and hence on the ability of the system to reap economies of scale. Unless these conditions are met it is impossible for a distance system to be cheaper than conventional systems.

Funding distance education projects

Those involved in distance education have long recognised that they face particular difficulties in justifying the level of funding required to set up a project. Snowden and Daniel (1980:76), reflecting their experience at Athabasca University, wrote of:

> the considerable difficulty we have in describing the institution's operations and its economics to officials in government and funding agencies, to members of other (conventional) institutions and, to some extent, to our own counterparts in other SDEs [small distance education systems].

Swinerton and Hogan (1981:1) point out that nontraditional programmes 'cannot be driven by the same financial flywheels as the more customary academic programs'. Generally 'the budget for a nontraditional degree program is a nightmare for everyone involved'. In those cases where it is funded 'by the same mechanisms as traditional programs, ... there is an inevitable pressure to mold the program itself to fit traditional funding formula'.

One result is that the level of funds required to establish a system - in effect to meet the fixed costs - can be seriously underestimated. Perry (1976:20) recounts how in 1966 Lord Goodman, then preparing a report on the costs and broadcasting requirements of the proposed British 'University of the Air' (later renamed the Open University) for Harold Wilson's government, estimated that the whole project would cost £3.5 million annually with an initial capital expenditure of over £1 million. He seriously underestimated the cost of the project. As he told the House of Lords on 23 May 1974, 'When I see the figure I mentioned and the figure it is now costing [£14.6 millions in 1974] I ought to blush with shame.' He did not, however, because it 'might not have been established except for my foolish miscalculation.'

It was the Open University's good fortune to be set up at a time and in a country where the government was able and willing to continue to fund its expansion. In Venezuela the fledgling Universidad Nacional Abierta was not so lucky. It found itself committed for political reasons to a plan (COUNA, 1977) to develop seventeen specialist (professionally orientated) degree programmes even though the National Congress had abruptly reduced the level of funds required for 1977 by more than 80 percent (Casas, 1981:418). There was both a general failure to recognise the effects which a massive cut in the University's fixed costs was likely to have on its long term plans, and a sharp appreciation of the likely effects on its political credibility of a decision to cut back its declared programme. Its failure to retrench caused considerable problems over the next few years. Ultimately the number of degree programmes was cut to five.

There have been a number of attempts to develop cost equations which are simple to understand and describe the fundamental cost-inducing variables in distance education systems. One of the first of these was developed by the British Open University in the mid-1970s. It was based on two fundamental variables, the number of students and the number of courses under development and on offer to students:

$$C = a + bx + cy$$

where:

a = the fixed costs.

x = the number of courses, itself a function of the number being developed (and weighted as 1.0) and the number in presentation (each weighted as 0.1 of a course under development)

y = the number of students

b = the average cost per course

c = the average cost per student.

For several years from the mid-1970s this equation was used as the basis for determining the level of funds provided to the Open University by the Department of Education and Science. The approach was taken up and developed in a number of other distance teaching universities. At Athabasca University Snowden and Daniel (1980:76-82) developed a rather more sophisticated costing model which they hoped could be used as a tool to project costs and evaluate policy options; Guiton (1982:178) has developed a cost function for distance education systems within Australian 'two-mode' (ie. mixed distance and conventional) universities; and Rumble developed cost models which could be used to analyse the future costs of the Universidad Estatal a Distancia in Costa Rica and the Universidad Nacional Abierta in Venezuela (Rumble, 1981a, 1982).

While models such as these had the virtue of simplicity, Rumble, Neil and Tout (1981:235) remarked that they 'do not specify the fundamental variables, which affect costs, in sufficient detail to be of practical value to people who are trying to prepare an operating budget for an institution'. This can lead to a number of problems. Firstly, the resources available may be insufficient to achieve the defined objectives of the institution. If the model used to plan its growth and development is unable to define the fundamental variables affecting costs and the relation between these with sufficient precision, the institution may overstretch itself. Secondly, the resources provided may exceed the absolute requirements of the institution in respect of its defined objectives. While the excess resources may be used to fund new developments, they may also be used to 'gold plate' the system unnecessarily with the result that costs escalate. Finally, the resources may be sufficient to achieve the objectives but they may be deployed in the wrong way, resulting in internal inefficiencies and poor performance.

Rumble, Neil and Tout (1981:248-70) identified a whole series of cost functions that would make explicit the fundamental variables affecting costs in large scale distance teaching universities similar to the British Open University. They acknowledged that the equations they developed did not 'strictly speaking represent a mathematical modelling approach' and that they had distinct limitations, not least in that 'models cannot recreate the complexity of the organisation they seek to reflect' (p. 236). Nevertheless they perceived 'a pressing need for suitable cost functions to be developed to enable planners, decision-makers and accountants to forecast budgetary requirements with a reasonable degree of accuracy' (p. 269) and enable 'the cost implications of a variety of alternative policy decisions' to be understood (p. 235-6).

Cost-efficiency and cost-effectiveness

An organisation is effective if it achieves its objectives: it is efficient if it does this with the optimum use of resources. It follows that it is possible to be effective without being efficient but it is not possible to be efficient without also being effective. Effectiveness will depend upon the quality and quantity of the output. Efficiency will depend not only on these factors but also on the consumption of resources as an input to the system.

Comparisons of the average costs per student and per graduate in distance and conventional teaching systems usually make the assumption that the quality of the teaching and of the outputs (graduates) is the same. Clearly this is by no means always the case. Academic standards can vary enormously not just between conventional and distance systems but also between institutions of the same type.

The evidence shows that distance teaching can be cheaper per capita (i.e. more cost-efficient) than conventional education. Wagner's study of the comparative costs of distance and conventional university students and graduates in the United Kingdom showed that in 1973 the average annual recurrent cost for an Open University student was about a quarter that of conventional university costs, although allowing for the fact that the Open University spent less on research than conventional universities reduced this cost advantage to a third (1977:365). The average cost per graduate was about one half that of a conventional university graduate in comparable subject areas (p. 377-8). In a similar study of costs at the Costa Rican Universidad Estatal a Distancia, Rumble (1981a:398) showed that the average cost per year per student of US$795 (at 1980 price and exchange levels) compared very favourably with those found in two of the conventional campus based universities where they were $1,301 (Universidad de Costa Rica) and $2,033 (Universidad Nacional). Moreover, there was every possibility that the Universidad Estatal a Distancia would reap further economies of scale with expansion in student numbers (p. 399).

Muta (1985:286) reports that the 'direct current expenditure [per student] of the [University of the Air of Japan] is 1/4, 1/3 and 2/3 of that of national universities, public universities and day programs of private universities respectively, and is equal to that of evening programs of private universities.' The cost per graduate at the University of the Air of Japan (UAJ) is dependent on the graduation rate. Muta calculates that 'the direct current expenditure per UAJ graduate is calculated to be equal to that of the evening programs of private universities, day programs of private universities, public universities and national universities when the graduation rate is about 60%, 50%, 25% and 20% respectively' (p. 290). However, 'with a lower graduation rate UAJ is not necessarily economical compared with conventional universities' (p. 290). Otsuka (1984) reports that the direct current expenditure at the Radio and Television Universities in the People's Republic of China is two thirds that of full-time students and one-third that of part-time students.

Perraton (1982:24-7, 30-1) has summarised costs and success rates for distance teaching systems at primary and basic levels, secondary level and tertiary level and compared the comparative costs of distance teaching and orthodox education where this is known. Table 4.1 summarises some of his findings. It is important to note that distance teaching systems are not always more cost efficient than conventional ones.

The question remains whether claims that distance teaching is cost-effective in comparison with conventional educational systems can be sustained when questions about the quality of the teaching and graduates are taken into consideration. Wagner (1977:360-1) discussed this issue and argued that, whatever the intention of those working in a nontraditional programme are, 'any judgement on this matter is likely to be a subjective one'. He went on to suggest that at least in the case of the British Open University there was no evidence to suggest that the final academic standard of its degree was any different to that of other conventional universities in the United Kingdom.

A study comparing the results of Open University economics course students and economics students at conventional UK universities showed that the former scored at the same level as first year conventional students in microeconomics, and significantly higher than third year conventional university students in macroeconomics (Lumsden and Scott, 1982:573). More generally Eicher et al (1982:75-81) discussed evidence on the cognitive effects of media based teaching in a variety of projects. They concluded that research on the effects of technology in education upon scholastic achievement indicates that 'there is no reason to doubt that Schramm's (1977) summary still holds good: motivated students learn from any medium if it is competently used and adapted to their needs' (p.79).

However, those who accept that the quality of the *learning* of distance and conventional students is equivalent may still be reluctant to acknowledge that the quality of the *education* is the

Table 4.1
Costs and success rates in distance teaching systems

Institution & country	Educational level	Measure of success	Rate	Distance teaching costs relative to conventional
ACPO Colombia	Primary equivalent	Number taking end of course examination	53-56% (1962-6)	D/t is cheaper
Radio Santa Maria, Dominican Republic	Primary equivalent	Number taking promotion examination	56-69%	D/t is cheaper
IRDEB Brazil	Secondary	Examination passes	37%	D/t probably more expensive
Radio ECCA Canary Islands	Upper primary/ lower secondary	Number promoted	72-75%	D/t is cheaper
Correspondence Course Unit, Kenya	Teacher training	Teachers promoted following course	90%	D/t is more expensive
Air Correspondence High School, South Korea	Secondary	Examination passes as % of enrolments	13%	D/t more expensive than day schools, cheaper than boarding schools
Open University UK	University	Graduates	54%	D/t is cheaper
Everyman's University, Israel	University	Graduates as a proportion of enrolment	37% (forecast)	D/t is cheaper

Table 4.1 continued

Athabasca University, Canada	University	n/a	n/a	Costs are within the range of comparable Albertan universities
Doncaster Institute of Higher Education, UK	Professional qualifications	Final examination passes	52%	D/t is cheaper
South West London College UK	Professional qualifications	Final examination passes	35%	D/t is cheaper than evening classes, more expensive than day-release classes

Source: Perraton, H. (1982) *The cost of distance education,* Cambridge, International Extension College, pp.24-7, 30-1, reproduced by permission of the International Extension College, Cambridge.

same. Carter, responding to an earlier (1972) paper by Wagner on the economics of the Open University, commented that:

> the comparison ... is between two quite different kinds of educational experience: one full-time, involving close relations with other students in a wide variety of activities, free from the pressures of earning a living and from most other responsibilities; the other requiring the dedicated use of spare time, in a life subject to the discipline of other responsibilities. I am not saying which educational experience is better - ... But they are *not* the same, and Mr. Wagner's remark that "the output of the Open University is planned to be similar to that of conventional universities"

might give currency to the belief that those who can pass the same examination have had the same education (Carter, 1973:69).

The assumption that the academic quality of distance and conventional university education is the same was also questioned by Carnoy and Levin (1975:396). They suggested that the cost savings of the Open University system might be 'obliterated by a smaller educational product.' They argued that the average university student 'receives not only instruction and instructional materials, but he receives substantially more tutorial services, contact with fellow students, access to libraries, computers and campus lectures than does his Open University counterpart.' Elsewhere Escotet (1980a:11-12, 15-17), drawing on his experience at the Universidad Nacional Abierta in Venezuela, has found distance teaching universities deficient in the provision of social and cultural learning. He does not deny that what he calls distance instruction systems 'can fulfil the informative role that the university actually has, with better quality, less cost, and a greater number of users', but it is not *education* (1980a:15-16).

Cost benefit analysis

A further criticism concentrates on the earnings potential of distance taught graduates. The benefits of education are often measured by economists in terms of the effect which it has on the individual's earning power. This cost-benefit approach usually concentrates on the age-earnings profile of workers with different levels of education, and tries to assess the financial benefits of the education against which is offset the private costs of studying (cost of books, fees, etc.), and the social costs of education (including expenditure on educational institutions and the opportunity cost of students' time measured in terms of income foregone during the period of study).

The value of education may depend on the reputation of the institution offering it as well as on the level attained. Carnoy and Levin (1975:390) pointed to the credentialing effects of higher education institutions and argued that 'to assume that the value of an Open University degree will be similar to one from Oxbridge or the "Red Bricks" ... simply ignores the credentialing effect of higher education institutions.' They suggested that 'the Open

University seems to be a solution to pressures for university training for working class youths, but only for a university training which increases some competencies without necessarily providing credentials for higher paying jobs which are reserved for graduates from the "real" universities' (p. 402). They concluded that:

> a more realistic premise is that the limited nature of the Open University education as well as the credential effect of particular institutions on earnings and occupational attainments would suggest that the Open University graduate is not likely to receive either consumption or income benefits from his education that are as high as those of the person from the more conventional university setting (p. 396).

Generally distance education systems appeal to individuals who have not had the opportunity to study earlier in their lives as well as those who wish to continue and 'renew' their education. Mace (1978:299-300), noting that the average age of an Open University graduate is 37 against 22 for conventional university graduates, and assuming a retirement age of 65, points out that conventional university graduates enjoy the earning benefits derived from their education for a longer period of their lives: indeed 'the period of higher earnings of OU students is one-third shorter' (p. 299). He also points out that 'labour market studies suggest that by age 37 most people are established in their jobs, and in addition there are powerful institutional forces, such as internal labour markets, that will inhibit mobility' (p.300). These two factors 'indicate that the economic benefits of an OU degree will be below those of a CU [conventional university] degree' (p. 300).

Mace has subsequently acknowledged that 'economists are more aware of the difficulties of establishing the link between education and income' (1984:44) while Eicher et al (1982:103) have drawn attention to the fact that there is great variance of income between persons with the same level of education, that education does not explain a large part of the variance of labour earnings, and that (crucial for any assessment of the relative worth of distance education in cost-benefit terms) earnings are affected by the perceived quality of the credentialing offered by a particular institution.

Certainly in countries such as the United Kingdom where the norm is for students to study full-time, any assessment of the relative benefits of studying part-time at a distance must take account of the earnings foregone by those who study full-time. Swift (1980) found that the majority of Open University graduates (83 percent) were in full-time employment when they commenced their studies with the University. Similarly, in countries where students commonly work their way through conventional higher education, the value of their part-time earnings needs to be compared with what they might have earned had they gone straight into employment while at the same time studying part-time at a distance.

There is no doubt that many Open University graduates do benefit financially as a result of their studies. Swift (1980) found that while less than half of a sample of 3002 graduates (45 percent) were specifically interested in promotion, better pay, or a new occupation when they began studying, the experience encouraged two in three of them to try to better their jobs. Thirty eight percent reported that they benefitted solely because of their Open University degree, 16 percent indicated that the degree had helped them, 15 percent said that they had progressed independently of their qualification, and 31 percent said that the degree had made no material difference to their circumstances. Unfortunately no information is yet available on the effect progress had on individual earnings.

While in principle it should be possible to measure the cost-benefit of a distance taught qualification and compare it with that of a conventional one, there are a number of practical problems to be faced. The measurement of 'value added' is simplified if all the institutions being compared have similar entry standards, but a number of distance teaching institutions (including some at the higher education level where selection is normally practised) have open entry schemes or accept applicants with less than the normal university entry qualifications, while the quality of mature entrants will differ depending on their 'life-experience' as well as their past educational qualifications. In these circumstances it could be that the 'value added' to the distance student is proportionately greater or less.

A further factor which needs to be taken into account is the value of recurrent education in maintaining the earnings potential of graduates over their lifetime and in facilitating career changes. It is widely accepted that initial education will not in itself be sufficient to last a lifetime. It is now clear that graduate engineers, scientists and technologists need to be wholly retrained every five to ten years. Significantly, 71 percent of a survey of Open University graduates said that their studies had helped them improve their job skills and their ability to perform their work (Swift, 1980). Whether their studies also helped maintain their employability is unclear. Until such time as detailed studies have been undertaken, much of the above remains supposition. What is clear is that there is a demand for distance-based higher education, that a significant proportion of students do benefit financially from their studies, and that increasing numbers of employers recognise the worth of distance education.

Internal cost-efficiency and financial management

In considering the cost-effectiveness of the Open University, Mace (1978:305) argued that 'it is necessary to consider whether the costs of individual items in [its] budget are inflated because of inefficient practices'. He went on:

> It is a singularly pointless exercise to compare the relative efficiencies of two systems for producing graduates (external efficiency) and not consider the internal economies or diseconomies operating within the system (internal efficiency).

Mace's point is obviously important. Since the early 1980s education has been under considerable pressure in many countries as governments have reduced public expenditure. Governments have argued that it is not the comparative cost-effectiveness of distance and conventional systems that is important but whether or not they are as internally efficient as they might be. As a direct result individual institutions in both sectors have had to achieve significant efficiency savings on their operating expenses.

Forced to cut their costs, institutions have returned to more basic principles of financial management in which individual projects are costed and evaluated within a context of financial stringency. In this situation last year's budget is not relevant for this year, let alone for the next. To achieve savings and free resources for new developments, a form of zero-based budgeting needs to be adopted in which all activities are reviewed. From an institutional point of view the aim should be to 'destruct test' the budget to the point at which it is too tight for individual managers to achieve their objectives. Only then should some resources be made available to allow managers some flexibility.

There are clearly limits to the volume of efficiency savings that can be achieved. Distance teaching systems face particular difficulties in times of financial stringency because the ratio of fixed to variable costs is so high. Within the context of the total budget, enforced savings of, say, 20 percent can have a disproportionate effect on the operation of the institution and require far more drastic cancellation of courses and cuts in student numbers than would be the case in conventional institutions facing a similar proportion of cuts. Moreover, just as expansion can help achieve economies of scale, so cuts in student numbers can rapidly lead to marked diseconomies that are reflected in rising average costs. Because the underlying cost structure is different to that of conventional institutions, great difficulty may be found in explaining the effects of cuts both on the operation as a whole and on average costs. A rise in average costs may itself become a liability if a government or funding agency uses simplistic measures such as comparative costs per student between distance and conventional systems as a measure of efficiency. The danger is that in the 'post-cuts' phase the increasing inefficiency of the operation may become the excuse to close it down.

A further problem arises from the nature of courses in distance teaching institutions. In conventional institutions course costs are dominated by the costs of staff. With some exceptions, for example, where courses make use of central media resource centres and computing facilities, the costs incurred by the course are contained within the departmental budget. Cost reductions can be managed by the department and can be achieved by a reduction in student numbers which then leads to cuts in staff. In distance courses a high proportion of the costs of development and production and some of the costs of presentation are fixed irrespective of student numbers. Many of the development costs and all the costs incurred in buying in stocks of materials are sunk costs which cannot be recovered, and which can only be justified if the course is allowed to run its complete life.

Achieving cuts may be more difficult in distance education systems because the individual cost elements involved in the development and presentation of a course are usually controlled by a number of budget holders in both academic and administrative areas. If cuts are imposed on a departmental basis, with each budget holder responsible for proposing savings on his or her own budget, then the integrity of individual courses may be jeopardised. It is therefore essential that the costs of developing and presenting courses should be analysed on a course by course basis, taking into account those cost elements that are 'fixed' once the course is presented (an example might be the transmission costs of television or radio broadcasts associated with the course) and those that are variable with student numbers (for example, postage costs and tuition). Given assumptions about student numbers, an idea of the total costs of individual courses and of the overall programme of activities in a term or year can be obtained. Savings can be achieved by cutting elements from individual courses where this will not damage the essential educational experience irrevocably (eg. by reducing the number of tutor marked assignments) and by constraining student numbers on particularly expensive courses. Such savings are essentially marginal. Significant savings will only result if the fixed costs of the institution are also cut. This means reducing the number of development and production staff (academics, designers, editors, etc) and staff involved in supporting presentation. If this is done then the number of courses on offer may need to be reduced, the lives of existing courses may need to be extended so that they are replaced less frequently, and the number of students enrolled with the institution cut. More significantly, the institution may have to review the media available and choose to use only those that are cost-efficient given its circumstances. Thus, for example, the British Open University takes account of the relative costs of video-cassettes and over-the-air transmission for different numbers of students in deciding how to deliver its audio-visual programmes on particular courses.

There are a number of studies on the relative costs of media (eg. Perraton, 1982:8-17; van der Drift,1980) but the results need to be treated with care, since they either provide broad generalisations or are institution-specific. With media costs affected by so many local factors and by changes in the relative cost of different technologies, institutional managers will need to cost their operation before they can come to any conclusions about the relative costs of media to their institution. Institutions having to retrench significantly may reach the point at which they have to stop using a particular medium, either because of the need to make absolute savings or because it no longer makes economic sense to continue to use it given the student numbers remaining in the system.

If, as the research shows, students learn equally well from any media, then it makes sense to use those which are most cost-efficient. This is not to deny that different media have particular educational advantages but, other things being equal, the choice should be governed by criteria which take account of the relative cost of the media for given student numbers, the ease with which students can access the media, the cost implications of particular media for students, and the ability of the institution to provide the necessary infrastructure to support the media.

Student costs and market penetration

The vast majority of cost studies of distance education concentrate on the institutional costs of the system as reflected in the operating budget. Relatively few studies look at the costs of the system as these affect students. Student costs include such items as fees, the costs of course materials, books and consumables which students have to buy, and the incidental costs of studying at a distance including postage, telephone and travel costs.

Students may also incur capital costs in equipping their homes for learning at a distance. Some of this equipment may already be widely available in people's homes. Other equipment may be less common, so that many of those wishing to enter a particular system may first have to buy items themselves before they can take advantage of particular courses. Such costs can be considerable. Among the equipment which it might be necessary for students to have access to are radios, televisions, video-cassette players/recorders for viewing video-cassettes and off-air recording, audio-cassette players, record players, personal computers with word processing and other application packages, together with a printer and perhaps a modem, microscopes, and assorted scientific and other equipment. In some cases students will be provided with the equipment by the distance teaching institution on a loan basis; in others arrangements may be made to make it available at local study centres although this has the disadvantage that the student is obliged to attend the centre; in yet others the institution may require the students to provide their own equipment.

Whatever the case, institutions need to take account of the costs falling on students and try to assess the likely affects of increasing student costs on access.

Distance education systems may find themselves facing increasing competition as the number of educational institutions seeking new markets through the use of distance education methods proliferates. This could lead to a price war in which institutions seek to cut the costs falling on students. Lower average costs and hence fees can only be realised if the number of students are increased (if possible - and even then there is a point beyond which further significant economies of scale are not achievable) or the costs of the system reduced. Unfortunately the cost structure of distance education (with high fixed and low variable costs) makes it difficult to cut the costs of the system. The danger is that in a price war students might be offered cheap and shoddy programmes with few support services. This will be contrary to the best interests of students not just because drop-out will be encouraged but also because the quality and hence the wider reputation of distance teaching and of the qualifications offered by distance education institutions will suffer.

Policy implications

At very low levels of student numbers it will almost certainly be cheaper to teach by conventional rather than distance means, although the level at which this is true will depend on the extent to which use is made of available materials rather than specially developed ones, media choice, and the level of support services offered to students.

An option is to graft distance education systems onto conventional campus-based systems. There is evidence that the add-on costs of developing distance teaching materials out of conventional class-room based courses by, for example, video-taping lectures or writing up lecture notes which can then be 'wrapped around' commercially available textbooks, are relatively small (Leslie, 1979; Wagner, 1975). Although there are arguments in favour of the development of purpose-built distance education systems in cases where student numbers, whether on individual courses or in the distance system as a whole, are likely to be small, the practice of grafting a distance teaching system onto a conventional education system makes considerable sense.

In Canada where this approach has been adopted by a number of universities the cost of the distance education programme is treated as a marginal additional cost. By failing to attribute some of the costs of developing the original course to the distance programme, the costs of the latter are effectively understated, and direct comparison between the additional costs of 'add-on' distance education programmes and 'purpose built' distance programmes made more difficult. Determining the add-on costs of a project is clearly important for internal decision making, but to assume that distance education projects working out of conventional universities will be more cost-efficient than purpose-built programmes in all circumstances is clearly wrong. In each case the full costs have to be assessed and assigned to particular programmes on an equitable basis so that fair comparisons can be made. Rumble (1986:23-31) discusses various approaches to the costing of 'two mode' systems teaching both by conventional and distance means.

Finally, there is the commercial option. As chapter 3 pointed out, the history of distance education owes much to the development of commercial correspondence schools and colleges run on a profit-making basis. While there is no suggestion that some distance education provision should not be funded by the state, there is in many countries a reluctance to extend such provision into the field of adult education. With the education service coming under increasing financial pressure there are those who argue that at least in respect of continuing education each department or course needs to be financially self-sufficient, covering its direct costs and making a positive contribution to general institutional overheads, and in the case of distance education, creating working capital for new developments. This approach, which may also be applied to whole institutions, is commercial in orientation and is found not only in commercial correspondence colleges but also in some publicly funded institutions where particular programmes are not supported from public funds. An examples is the British Open University's Continuing Education programme which has to be financially self-sufficient. In this respect it is interesting to note that the Italian Universita' a Distanza has been funded by a consortium of private and public bodies and is expected ultimately to run at a profit, making a return on investment while at the same time generating further funds for its future development.

The successful privatisation of distance education depends on the size of the market and hence the possibility of bringing the unit cost per student-course down to a point which matches the ability and willingness of sufficient potential customers to pay for the educational services received. This raises particular problems for institutions where specialist courses may attract very few students. Very early on in the development of the British Open University, Laidlaw and Layard (1974:458) argued that the case for developing higher-level courses with relatively small numbers of students had to be justified 'on the grounds that they are an integral part of a system providing wider access to complete degree courses rather than that they are a cheap way of doing this.' Given this, pressures to privatise distance teaching institutions may threaten the existence of programmes and courses central to their overall goals simply because they are beyond the ability of students to pay the fees needed to recover costs. Ultimately this must raise questions about the commercial viability of higher-level distance education in the private sector.

Conclusions

There is little doubt that distance education can be a cost-efficient and cost-effective way of teaching provided that the cost structure of the various media and the likely number of students is taken into account. The high fixed, low variable cost structure of distance teaching which makes it such an attractive option when seeking to expand the educational service, makes it equally vulnerable when the education service is being cut. It also limits the scope for privatisation of higher-level and 'specialist subject area' distance education.

It is clear that the introduction of new technologies will affect the cost structure of distance education. The extent to which particular technologies will be adopted will depend in part on their absolute cost and in part on their market penetration into the homes of those wishing to learn at a distance. In this sense distance education may well become increasingly 'parasitic' upon the facilities which students have available in their own homes as an aid to home-based learning. However, as private individuals acquire technology so the potential for its use in home-based learning will be realised, leading to changes in the nature of distance education. The ownership of personal computers, printers and modems and the ability to access mainframe computers to obtain information and to communicate with tutors and other students using electronic mail systems is technically possible but inhibited by cost factors. For an institution to equip its students would be immensely expensive. On the other hand, the assumption that students will be able to equip themselves raises questions about the ability of all but the more well off to benefit from the technological changes now taking place. It would be ironic if distance education, once seen as a means of bringing education at a lower cost to the educationally deprived and economically disadvantaged, were as a result of the pressures of reduced government funding, changes in cost structures resulting from its further 'technologisation', and a shift in the financing of the learning environment from the educational institution to the student, to become too expensive for all but the relatively well off.The trend towards increased reliance on technology in distance education is also likely to increase the 'resource and facilities gap' between distance teaching systems in developed countries and those in the Third World.

Meanwhile, the most significant advantage of distance education remains its ability to reach large numbers of individuals who for a variety of reasons would not be able to attend classroom based activities, to provide flexible learning materials which students find easy to use, and to do so relatively cheaply given sufficient students in the system to enable economies of scale to be reaped.

Cost-effectiveness is not, however, always an end in itself. Distance teaching may be the only practical way of reaching some target groups and the cost of doing so may be a secondary consideration. It may well be that the political objective of reaching a particular group of students (for example, doctors, teachers and other professional people living in rural areas) outweighs simple cost considerations. Perraton (1982:33) draws attention to the Tanzanian radio campaigns and the Botswana Tribal Grazing land radio campaign, both of which used radio, print and group meetings to meet the needs of adults, and neither of which could have been offered by conventional means.

Whether or not governments will seek to reach groups which can not be reached by conventional means will depend in part on the needs that have been identified and in part on the political perspective of the government or agency mounting the campaigns. So far as the costs of such programmes are concerned, Perraton (1982:35) concludes that in respect of non-formal education, 'comparisons between distance-teaching methods and alternatives are so difficult that we can only say that some, large-scale, non-formal programmes look cheap in comparison with other kinds of expenditure on education or social welfare'. Similar cost advantages do not apply in all cases. The per capita cost of providing updating courses to rural doctors, for example, may be considerable, but the cost of doing so may be a relatively unimportant consideration provided that the system itself is internally cost-efficient.

Still, the potential for savings is often an important factor in the minds of those establishing distance teaching systems. Whether or not a given distance education system is likely to be more efficient than a comparable conventional one will then depend on a number of factors including decisions taken by those planning the system in respect of choice of media, student support services and the administrative infrastructure supporting the system.

Chapter Five

ESTABLISHING A DISTANCE EDUCATION SYSTEM

The pre-planning phase

Some of the factors favouring the establishment of a distance education system were discussed in chapter 3. Important indicators that the existing educational system is failing to meet needs include (1) a large pool of frustrated demand from school leavers; (2) a similar demand from adults; (3) significant numbers of disadvantaged persons unable to enter conventional educational establishments for geographical, social or economic reasons; (4) large-scale needs for training or retraining in professional, technical and vocational fields; and (5) a recognition that the absolute cost of a conventional solution is beyond the capability of the State, and the search for more cost-efficient solutions to the problem.

The existence of educational needs that can be satisfied by distance methods does not automatically mean that distance education is the best way of satisfying them. Distance education is not, for example, the most efficient way of meeting a demand from relatively small numbers of people for courses where the target population needs considerable guidance and support in their studies (in the form of distance teaching materials), although it may meet the needs of small numbers of students who are able to study independently, working from pre-existing textbooks with the minimum of materials specially prepared to support them. It is not the most efficient way of meeting the needs of a fairly concentrated but small population of learners able and willing to attend class-based instruction, but it may be the only way of meeting the needs of such a population in cases where they have difficulty in attending classes regularly. It is likely to be an appropriate means of meeting large scale demand for standard courses, and this will be true whether or not the population is geographically dispersed or concentrated, and irrespective of that population's ability or otherwise to make use of class-based facilities (assuming they exist or could be provided).

All too often, however, those charged with setting up a distance education system are not given the choice to recommend against it. Tiffin (1978:195), discussing the initial planning of eight Instructional Television systems in Latin America, noted that in at least three cases the planners were not asked to conduct a needs analysis or to consider the use of alternatives to television, but instead were told to plan to put into operation decisions already made, begining with the implantation of studio technology. The Advisory Committee on the proposed British 'University of the Air' (subsequently the Open University) was 'invited ... to consider the educational functions and content of a University of the Air, as outlined in the speech made by Mr. Harold Wilson in Glasgow on 8th September, 1963' (Advisory Committee, 1966:4). The subsequent Planning Committee on the Open University was charged with the task of 'work[ing] out a comprehensive plan for an Open University, as outlined in the White Paper of February 1966, "A University of the Air", ...' (Planning Committee, 1969:1). Wilson's commitment to the project was not based on any fundamental analysis of needs, but rather on an instinctive appreciation of the possibilities inherent in correspondence education and educational broadcasting. Similarly, in Andhra Pradesh, India, the State Government had already taken the decision to establish an Open University before it set up the Committee charged with preparing a project proposal (Committee on the Establishment of an Open University, 1982:2). In other words, in these cases, and often against a background of extreme scepticism on the part of the traditional educational establishment, the political agenda had already been set and those charged with planning the system had only to get on with the job.

On the other hand, the Enquiry Commission on Everyman's University in Israel was not only charged with looking into the need for such a project in Israel (Schramm, Hawkridge and Howe, 1972:70), but considered and reported at length on the educational problems and needs of the country (ibid.:21-35) and on some alternative solutions to these (ibid.:36-48), before finally recommending the foundation of a distance teaching university. Similar 'open-ended' reviews occurred in Australia and Sweden where both the Karmel Committee (1975) in Australia and the TRU Commission (1975) in Sweden decided that there was no need to establish a distance teaching university (Dodd and Rumble, 1984:236-8).

The planning phase

Planning is the systematic development of activities aimed at reaching agreed objectives, by a process of analysing and selecting from among the various strategies and opportunities that have been identified as being available. It is regarded as a rational process that is comprehensive in its scope and leads to results, but it is bedevilled by the irrational - unthought out policy statements, flashes of inspiration, or sudden decisions to change well established ground rules; it is often far from comprehensive; and it may lead to nothing.

Figure 5.1 illustrates the basic planning process and sets it within the context of the need for information derived from market research and evaluation. The process illustrated in figure 5.1 is common to both the planning required in the period leading up to the establishment of a distance education system and the on-going planning that is a normal part of the managerial function. In this chapter we are concerned only with the former. The latter is the subject of chapter 8.

Fundamental role ('Mission') and markets

The political decision to establish a distance education system will usually be justified in terms of a broad statement of the fundamental role or 'mission' which the proposed institution will have. An institution's 'mission' therefore expresses the expect-ations which society has of it. It is also a broad statement of the conditions on which its continued existence is predicated.

Mission statements usually have their origins in the political aspirations of those setting up the institution or system. Politicians will normally make it clear whether they are thinking in terms of a formal or non-formal educational system, its educational level (primary, secondary or tertiary), the nature of the target audience (school-leavers unable to enter conventional secondary or tertiary

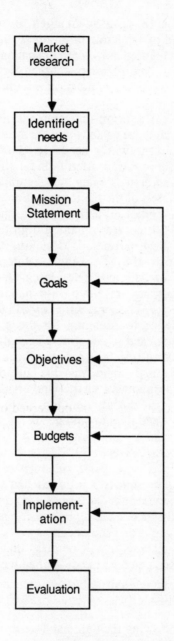

Figure 5.1
The planning process

education, adults, those disadvantaged for a variety of reasons, etc) and the kind of academic programmes (academic liberal arts and sciences, technological, vocational and professional, etc.) that are to be offered. The planners charged with implementing the project are then expected to develop it within the guidelines that have been laid down.

In theory an institution's mission and goals should relate to the needs to which those establishing the system are responding. In practice, the extent to which needs are clarified and the level of demand properly assessed often falls far short of the ideal. The British Open University's Planning Committee commissioned a survey of the interest of the adult population in the proposed Open University. This indicated a firm 'commitment to register' from 34,000 to 150,000 individuals and a high level of interest from 170,000 to 450,000 individuals (Planning Committee, 1969:3), although McIntosh (1981:29-30) felt that in reality there was little clear evidence of demand. The Dutch Open Universiteit was founded without any research into needs and demand (van Enckevort, 1984:73). Schramm, Hawkridge and Howe (1972) discussed evidence for demand for the proposed Everyman's University in Israel and felt confident enough to suggest that there might be a pool of 250,000 people who might study with the University, but this demand was 'difficult to estimate' (ibid.:49). In Venezuela the planners of the Universidad Nacional Abierta pointed to the escalating demand from school leavers for university places and the national needs for professionally trained labour, and planned for an estimated student population of 50,000 within three year (COUNA, 1977:101), but the university failed to achieve this level. In Japan the planners of the University of the Air (Hoso Daigaku) undertook an exhaustive study (Ministry of Education, Science and Culture, 1975) indicating a massive demand for a distance teaching university as well as the demand across a number of broad subject areas.

From this analysis it will be clear that the extent to which needs are assessed and demand quantified has varied enormously.

Planning committees

The first step following the political decision to look into the need for (or even establish) a distance teaching system is, usually, to establish a planning committee. The planning committees set up to establish a number of distance teaching universities have been the subject of a study by Dodd and Rumble (1984) who drew attention to various of features including (1) the crucial importance of political backing (to which reference has already been made in chapter 3), (2) a tendency to isolate the committees from the normal bureaucratic processes of government, (3) the often highly specific terms of reference which they had, charging them with establishing a system and not with questioning the need for it (see above), and (4) the prestige of the committee members.

Recognising the opposition to the proposal to establish a distance education system, politicians have in a number of cases isolated those charged with planning the system from the normal and potentially hostile bureaucracy of government. In Costa Rica the idea for a distance teaching university had originally been proposed by the Office of Higher Education Planning within the National Council of Rectors (Consejo Nacional de Rectores). They proposed a five year experimental project (CONARE, 1975: VII-84 to VII-101). The proposal was taken up by the Minister of Public Education, Lic. Fernando Volio, who decided to establish a permanent distance teaching university rather than an experimental limited-period one. He set up a three-man advisory committee and then kept the planning process firmly under his personal control. In Britain the Minister of State with responsibility for higher education was not involved in the planning of the Open University, nor were the largely unenthusiastic civil servants in the higher education branch of the Department of Education and Science. The task was given to the junior Joint Parliamentary Undersecretary of State at the Department of Education and Science with special responsibility for the arts, Jennie Lee. A personal friend of the Prime Minister, she insisted on the unusual course of action of chairing the Advisory Committee on the University of the Air.

Planning committees are often prestigious. Jennie Lee was reported in *Sesame* (1979:7) as saying: 'I knew I had only one chance in dealing with all the snobberies of the [Department of Education and Science] and the establishment - I had to outsnob the snobs. Therefore I went for the Vice-Chancellors'. She had five vice-chancellors of traditional British universities and one principal of a Polytechnic, as well as other eminent people, on the 19 member Planning Committee. In the Netherlands, the Chairman of the Planning Committee for the Open Universiteit,

Professor dr. Ruud de Moor, was also Chairman of the prestigious and well-respected Netherlands Committee for the Development of Higher Education which, following ten years' work, had recommended the key objectives for Dutch higher education policy into the 1990s.

Goals and objectives

The goals of an institution are a reflection of the aspirations it has (or, perhaps more accurately, those held by the individuals and groups within it). Such goals may articulate aspirations in relation to a range of activities and policies - what should be taught, how it should be taught, to whom the institution should address itself, how the institution should be run, etc. Frequently many of the basic goals of an institution will be established by its planning committee and in a sense inherited by the institution. Woodley's study of the Open University shows the extent to which the Planning Committee report made a range of detailed proposals about teaching, degree structures, the structure of courses and the use of broadcasting, which subsequently became 'foundation stones' of Open University policy (Woodley, 1981:14-19). The subsequent transfer of such goals from the planning committee to the institution will be made easier if some of those who worked on the planning committee go on to take up posts with the university. As Dodd and Rumble (1984:248) make clear this is frequently the case, with members of the planning committee either taking up senior executive posts or sitting on the institution's governing council.

Goals may be overt or covert, formal or informal. It is well known that there can be conflicting goals within an institution. It is also quite common to identify goals that have the broad support of the institution (for example, the goal of integrating media within a teaching package) only to discover that they are at variance with practice (broadcasts produced by specialist production staff who have little contact with the staff preparing the written materials for the same course).

Goals should also be expressive of the general philosophy of the institution. It should be clear, for example, whether an institution is predominantly institution-centred, individual-centred or society-centred in its approach to education and training (see chapter 2 for definitions of these). This is not simply a matter of knowing clearly where one is going. It is fundamental to the choice of teaching strategy and media. Thus for example, an institution-centred system may well choose to concentrate on technical media (print, broadcasting, etc.) which will deliver a message to the student (and assess that student's understanding), and relegate to a secondary place any concern for 'two-way' communication between teacher and student and student and student. On the other hand, society-centred models concerned with the education of communities will focus on the group, on the interaction between its members, and on their interaction with the community beyond the group. This is why Perraton (1983:42), a 'society-centred distance educationalist', argues that planning should begin with the group, with the role of technical media being decided on subsequently.

Particular problems also arise where goals are in conflict, and particularly where multiple goals cannot be sustained within the resources available to the institution or system. In the latter case it is crucially important that planners should have an idea of the resource implications of individual goals and if necessary make a choice between them. On the other hand, as expressions of aspirations, there is no reason why goals should be immediately achievable.

Objectives are much more specific than goals and are commonly held to be commitments to action. Indeed, the aim should always be to be as specific as possible in the prevailing circumstances. Objectives should be capable of realisation within the financial constraints within which one has to operate, and their achievement should be measurable in terms of quantity, quality, time, etc. It is crucial that planners should consider whether or not a given set of objectives can be sustained before they embark on a programme of activities. The best way of ensuring this is to make clear the links between objectives and budget. This is as much a managerial issue as an issue for those planning a new institution, and it will therefore be considered further in chapter 8.

Planners (and evaluators) generally agree that goals and objectives need to be clearly defined. In practice this does not always happen. There is often widespread resistance to the more explicit definition of educational objectives (Cohen and March, 1974; Weathersby and Balderston, 1972), and many institutions go no further than the preparation of a statement of general goals, the measurement of which is virtually impossible. For example, it is suggested that if objectives are made too explicit, they can be over-restrictive and leave little room for initiatives and the emergence of new objectives. It is certainly the case that there should be some room for unplanned growth and development, but this ought to be accommodated within a general provision for institutional research and development. In general, the failure to specify objectives must be regarded as an abrogation of management.

Strategy: the problem of ways and means

Those planning a distance education system must not separate the conceptualisation and justification of the project from a fundamental and realistic assessment of the ways and means of achieving their aims. Any such separation is wrong in principle and fraught with dangers.

The general aims of an institution should extend down to a series of subordinate objectives that are clear, mutually consistent, and form a hierarchy such that the objectives (ends) at subordinate levels become the means by which higher level superordinate objectives are achieved. This should include, for example, the specification of academic programmes in terms of the numbers of courses involved, the likely use of media including the volume of output, the production rate of the various categories of staff developing and producing the media (see chapter 7), the number of students likely to be enrolled in the system by level and course, the range and quality of support services to be available to students, levels of admission of new students and assumptions about student rates of throughput (promotion, repetition and desertion), and costs. Throughout this process there is a constant iteration between the definition and redefinition of objectives and the specification of means.

The task is not particularly difficult in its essence, although experience shows that it is not necessarily easy to foresee every eventuality, to ask all the right questions, and to obtain answers which in the event turn out to be reasonable estimates of the volume and cost of the activities being undertaken. There are many instances where, for example, the resource needs of a distance education system have been severely underestimated or where the operational systems have proved inadequate to achieve the objectives or support the chosen strategy. It is the failure even to attempt to specify ways and means at the development stage that is wrong for, unless this is done, there can be no idea of how much it will cost to implement the plans nor whether they are achievable in administrative and operational terms.

At the same time one should not be too prescriptive in the early planning phase. Both the plans and the structures established should retain flexibility. The aim should be to avoid courses of action which restrict one's ability to evolve more suitable solutions in the light of practical experience and evaluation. For this reason it is desirable to avoid rigidity in the following areas: choice of media; organisational structures; staffing and the definition of staff roles; and administrative computer systems. Rigidity in any one of these areas can become a subsequent straight jacket.

The experience of the Venezuelan Universidad Nacional Abierta in respect of organisational structures appears to support this view. Bureaucratic pressures forced the university to adopt traditional university structures rather than follow the advice of its technical planning committee and adopt a 'brief general legal instrument ['Reglamento'] which would outline policies and principal directions, and be representative of the approved basic concepts of the project, while retaining great flexibility' (Casas, 1981:436). In the event the Reglamento was an 'excessively complex, casuistical, and contradictory' document which 'spelt out in detail an initial over-elaborate bureaucracy' (ibid.:436). This tendency was also seen in the basic planning document which specified in considerable detail the aims and objectives of the university as a whole and its organisational structure. A 'highly detailed document drawn up before the actual take-off ... [it] could not take into account situations that its authors with all their feasibility studies, knowledge of the educational system and good intentions had not been able to forecast' (Villarroel, 1980:6). As a consequence it 'became a veritable straight jacket that inhibited creativity when it was taken at face value' (ibid:6).

Development process

Once it has been decided that an institution should be set up, work needs to begin on the planning of the curriculum and media.

Firstly, in the light of the institution's agreed mission and goals, curriculum and institutional planners will need to determine the nature and size of the academic programmes which will be offered including (1) the nature of any awards offered, (2) the level of competence of the target population, (3) whether or not admission will be open to those without formal academic qualifications, (4) the number of courses, including policy on course levels, prerequisites, mandatory core courses and options, etc. In some cases use may be made of materials produced by another institution, although experience suggests that this raises problems of integration with home-produced materials as well as problems of the 'not-invented-here' kind.

The aim should be to produce a plan which will indicate for each academic programme (defined as any coherent group of courses leading to a particular academic qualification such as a degree, diploma or certificate, or within a defined area of study) a list of the number of courses (defined as any coherent grouping of materials and activities which can be studied either on its own or for credit towards an academic qualification) that will ultimately be presented in an academically creditable programme. Once this is done, the planner should specify the rate at which the courses will be brought 'on stream' - taking account of the needs of students to have a viable choice of courses available to them at any one time (eg. per term). This will determine the production load. As more and more options are brought on stream so the total number of courses in presentation will increase (the presentation load). Planners also have to take account of the need to replace ageing courses, and the implication of course lives for the overall production load. The importance of undertaking such studies should not be underestimated. Chapter 4 drew attention to the problems which the Universidad Nacional Abierta faced when it failed to reduce the number of planned specialist degrees established as an objective in its plan (Proyecto) following the massive budget cut it sustained in 1977.

Secondly, planners will need to consider the nature of the courses including the media which can reasonably be made available to those developing them, and the extent to which students will have access to local support facilities. Those planning society-centred models need to concentrate first on the provision of two-way interaction between animateur or tutor and student, and on group interactions, and then fit the technical media to the needs of the group. Planners of institution-centred models generally start with the technical media and consider face-to-face contact and group work second.

At the practical level the locus of learning in an institution-centred or individual-centred system may be in the home, with a consequential need to consider the facilities students have to hand there, whereas in a society-centred model the locus of learning will probably be the local 'community-based' learning centre, with a consequential need to provide facilities there. It is absolutely crucial that planners should seek to think their way into the situation of their students (in terms of their environment, the time they have available to study, the media they have access to, the ease with which students will be able to travel to local centres, etc.). The amount of time students will have to study should be related to the volume of material given to, and the range of activities expected of, students. A particularly useful way of checking on this is to specify a detailed calendar for each course which will show for each week the range of activities which a student on the course will need to undertake, and the time that is likely to be spent on each.

Planners will also need to consider the overall capacity of the system to provide access to media for all courses (for example, access to broadcasting networks may be limited to a very few hours a week, with implications for the number of broadcasts that can made and transmitted; and there may be physical limits or cost constraints on the extent to which certain media can be used). The total volume of media (in production and presentation terms) should also be related to the institution's future staffing requirements. Some of these questions are discussed in chapters 7, 8 and 10.

Finally, planners will need to consider the regulations which will govern student progress and assessment, including whether or not students will be required to study in a paced system (with defined schedules governing registration on courses, return of assignments, broadcasts, examinations, etc.) or in an unpaced system where they are allowed to begin studying a course at any time, progress at their own pace, and sit a (scheduled) examination when they feel ready to; the number of courses which students will be able to take at any one time (term or year); the number of times students can resit a course; the extent to which students are obliged to attend certain activities (eg. tutorials) or do certain things (eg. submit assignments).

It is not the purpose of this book to consider all the various factors which ought to be taken into account in the establishment of a distance education system. What concerns us is the process of planning. However, planners will obviously need to take account of those factors relevant to the issues under consideration. For example, when choosing media, planners will not only need to take account of questions of availablity, access, cost, etc, but also the pedagogic advantages and disadvantages of the options available. Many people believe that motivated students learn from any medium provided it is competently used and adapted to their needs (Eicher et al, 1982:79), but there are those who hold that because cognitive styles are culturally determined, some media are more appropriate than others in some cultures (Escotet, 1978:73; Sine, 1975:27). Whatever the truth of the latter view, it is worth noting that the various media have different pedagogic functions which tend to favour their use in given circumstances (see for example, Kaye and Rumble, 1981:51-4; Bates, 1984), and that it is important to choose those media that are familiar to the target audience and which they will find easy to use. In this connection it is interesting to note that Pacheco (1978:339) argued that one of the factors underlying the successful transfer of the concept of distance education to Costa Rica was the fact that the Universidad Estatal a Distancia utilised communication technologies - print, radio, television, etc. - that had already been successfully introduced and assimilated into Costa Rica. The major factors are nevertheless likely to be cost, accessibility, and results.

In implementing any distance education project a wide range of considerations need to be taken into account before the final choice of means is made. There can be no question of transferring a particular system from one country to another, no matter how successful it appears to be in its original setting. Each proposal must be considered within the context of the environment in which it will operate and having regard to its purpose. There are a number of guides to the planning of distance education systems which provide useful checklists and advice on the factors that should be taken into account by those establishing a new system (see for example, Erdos, 1975; Kaye and Rumble, 1981; Unesco, 1983:42-63; Dodd, 1985:136-50), while advice can also be sought from existing distance education systems and through aid agencies.

Implementation

The framework developed in chapter 1 for the specification of subsystems for the development, production and distribution of materials and for the administration, teaching and support of students provides a useful focus for the planning of distance education systems. The two subsystems can be analysed in terms of the resources required to support them and an overall idea of the costs involved can be obtained. More significantly, the crucial inter-relationships between the various component systems can be established and a proper balance between them achieved.

At each stage planners will need to check that the structure that is emerging is pedagogically, administratively and financially feasible, and can be achieved in the time available. A detailed project implementation schedule should be drawn up which will relate all the activities (development, production and distribution of materials, and design, testing and implementation of student administrative and teaching systems) to the first point in time when the materials or systems will be required. In paced systems this will normally be during the first term or year of operation for administrative and teaching systems, and for course materials production and delivery systems; and in the first term or year of presentation of a particular course for the specific materials. In unpaced systems the schedule will depend on the point in time when the system or a particular course 'goes live'. However, it will also be necessary to have specified some of the systems, strategies and policies (eg. media use, titles of courses, assessment and fees policy, admissions criteria, etc.) before the first publicity materials and prospectuses go to press.

One final issue deserves to be discussed here, and that is the rate of development of the project. Broadly speaking, there are three possible approaches: (1) to mount a small pilot project, evaluate the results, and then decide whether or not to expand the system to a major project; (2) to implement a full-scale project immediately; and (3) to adopt an incremental approach in which the basic infrastructure is fully implemented from the start but volumes rise year by year as the number of academic programmes, courses and students are increased.

The pilot project approach is most likely to be adopted in cases where the level of investment (in, for example, materials development and production and infrastructure) is small, where expectations are limited, or where there is a base from which a distance education system can be established on an experimental basis. A number of the distance teaching programmes set up in conventional educational institutions were originally conceived of as pilot projects. The application of distance teaching materials to community education may also be based initially on a pilot. The same is true of those systems where the intention is to apply media to boost the quality of the teaching in schools and colleges. Pilots also occur where there is a conscious commitment to formative evaluation as a strategy. The approach is not generally used where the intention is to establish a fully-fledged purpose-built distance teaching institution. However, in the case of Athabasca University in Alberta, Canada, the pilot approach was used as a means of ensuring the survival of the institution. Athabasca was originally established as an innovative campus-based university but it was threatened with closure as enrolments at the other three pre-existing Albertan universities began to fall in the early 1970s. It survived only when its President, Dr Tim Byrne, persuaded the Government of Alberta to accept his plan to allow the institution to proceed as a pilot project 'to test the various dimensions of its academic model' and become a 'research and development project in advanced education'. The government accepted the plan and appointed a new governing body empowered 'to undertake a pilot project for the production, testing and application of learning systems to provide study programs in the arts and sciences leading to an undergraduate degree, and for the application of technology and new procedures to improve educational opportunities for adults generally' (Hughes, 1980: 47-9).

The pilot approach is not generally satisfactory where the ultimate intention is to have a large-scale system because the scaling up which must occur in the move from a limited sized pilot to a large-scale system will usually involve fundamental changes in working patterns which will, inevitably, limit the value of any lessons learnt from the pilot stage. Also, because different media have different cost structures, the media which can be used by a small-scale pilot (for example, those with few economies of scale) are unlikely to be suitable for large-scale projects, while high fixed cost/low variable cost media suitable for large-scale projects will prove to be a very expensive mistake if the pilot in which they are used proves to be unsuitable for subsequent expansion.

Full scale implementation is most likely to occur where there is an intention to conduct a massive campaign which will result in fundamental change and where the objectives are relatively limited, as for example in literacy and basic education campaigns such as those in Tanzania, Botswana and Cuba.

The most common approach where a purpose-built distance education institution is being established is the incremental one, in which the institution or system is established with its infrastructure more or less fully formed in terms of administrative procedures and so on, and in which there is every intention that the volume of activities should increase rapidly in order to maximise impact and reap economies of scale. This has been the case with many of the purpose-built distance teaching universities, where student numbers have expanded rapidly, and where there has been an early commitment to large numbers. There are dangers in this course of action, which is why it has been suggested above that as much flexibility as possible should be built into the early plans of the institution. It is why Perry (1981:7) characterised the British Government's decision in 1967 to begin serious planning for an Open University as 'an act of faith that was quite remarkable and almost miraculous. ... the gigantic gamble of funding the Open University'.

Conclusion

This chapter makes clear the importance of specifying the underlying philosophy before starting to plan a distance education system, as well as the need to make explicit the mission, goals and objectives of the institution or system. Equally, it is vital to clarify the strategies which will be used and ensure that the ways and means adopted are sufficiently robust to enable agreed goals and objectives to be achieved.

Chapter Six

ORGANISATION

Experience indicates that systems with similar goals can be organised in many different ways, reflecting philosophical, cultural and technological differences (the latter involving issues related to the specialisation of the workforce), as well as differences in size and geographical coverage. There is therefore no 'right way of organising a distance education project. Nevertheless, all structures need to take account of the functions undertaken in a distance education system

Functions

Various attempts have been made to identify the functions undertaken by distance education systems. Typical lists mention curriculum planning; materials development, production, storage and delivery; student recruitment, admission and counselling; the organisation of study facilities and support services; the tutoring, assessment and examination of students; the monitoring of student progress; general and specialist administration and management (direction, personnel, finance, management services, purchasing, estates and maintenance, etc.); and research and evaluation. The range of media used in distance education systems provides an added dimension to the tasks which need to be undertaken. Notwithstanding this, there is much to be said in favour of Erdos' (1975:16) contention that any institution teaching by correspondence has three basic functions: '1. The preparation of the teaching material. 2. The distribution of the teaching material. 3. The correction of students' written and practical work.'

Organisational typologies

There are many ways in which organisations carrying out these three basic functions can be structured:

(1) The 'classic' organisational model is a purpose-built institution only involved in distance education, developing its own materials for this purpose, and teaching and examining its own students;

(2) Much commoner are 'mixed-mode' systems which teach both conventional classroom-based and distance students. Mixed-mode systems are structured in a number of ways, the main distinction being between:

(a) those *separated* distance teaching departments, sometimes invested with considerable autonomy and having the authority to decide what should be taught, to whom, and how, and

(b) those *integrated* distance education departments that have little or no autonomy, having to work closely with on-campus faculty, where the decision as to what should be taught at a distance and to whom is the product of a joint decision in which the influence of conventional teachers may predominate over that of teachers working in the distance education unit.

In integrated systems the distance education unit is frequently only an administrative unit. Indeed in some institutions the functions associated with the education of distance students are so integrated with those related to conventional students that to all intents and purposes no distinction is drawn between the two systems and there is no identifiable unit concerned solely with distance studies.

(3) Those distance systems that are based on consortia or federated structures incorporating a number of hier-archically distinct institutions. (A hierarchical institution is one in which the top management is not subject to the control of other managers.)

Some of the differences implicit in these models have been explored in the various taxonomies of distance education systems at the higher education level (El-Bushra, 1973:13-15; Neil, 1981:126, 140-41; Keegan and Rumble, 1982a:28-30; Keegan, 1986:136-63). None of the taxonomies are wholly satisfactory because individual systems tend to exhibit different features in a variety of permutations, making clear-cut classification difficult. Neil (1981:138-40) attempted to get round this problem by distinguishing 'the degrees of authority and control exerted in [four] key operational areas' (p.138): finance, examinations and accreditation, curriculum and materials, and delivery and student support systems. As he points out, 'the more a [distance learning] institution is embedded into communities of educational agencies in such a way as to increase specific mutual benefits ... the greater the extent to which that [distance learning] institution will have to share control (or, alternatively, share legitimate authority) in one or more of these key areas' (p.140).

Purpose-built distance systems

The 'classic' structural model for a distance education system is undoubtedly the purpose-built system which teaches only at a distance. The model originated in the nineteenth century with the development of commercial correspondence schools and colleges, while the twentieth century has seen the development of purpose-built distance teaching universities, initially in the Soviet Union and later in South Africa, but more recently elsewhere following the establishment of the British Open University.

The arguments in favour of purpose-built distance education institutions stem from the conviction that the administrative structures of conventional educational systems are not the most suitable ones for developing and managing distance systems (Peters, 1973:310; Perry, 1976:55; Daniel and Smith, 1979:64). Distance systems engage in a number of quasi-industrial processes. Their academic staff are a part of the production process, required to work in a disciplined manner and deliver the products of their labour to the production departments on time. The 'best' results are likely to be obtained where the 'corporate culture' encourages disciplined adherence to production schedules, with academics subjected to managerial controls and accountable for their work in ways that are at variance with the almost complete autonomy they enjoy in conventional universities.

It is also said that the requirements of distance students are likely to be better served if the institution is wholly dedicated to their needs. It is easier for purpose-built distance education institutions, or at the very least a self-contained and relatively autonomous distance unit operating within a mixed-mode institution, to develop new courses to meet the needs of distance students - particularly where they are adults studying part-time. Singh (1979:87) reports that Indian academics working in conventional universities dominate the various academic bodies which validate courses and that as a result 'they often turn down any innovations recommended by the correspondence course institutes with regard to new interdisciplinary courses, subjects of study, job-orientated courses etc'. Autonomous purpose-built distance education institutions or units are also thought to be more appropriate where the characteristics of the target audience are significantly different to those of the campus-based students, as is the case where the latter are largely young adults at the tertiary stage of their initial education while the former are adults with distinctive - adult - approaches towards learning. Also Peters (1973:310) believes that the pedagogy of distance teaching is different to that of conventional systems and that for this reason too it is better to have separate systems.

Finally, both Perry (1976:55) and de Moor (1983:59) suggest that significant innovation is more likely to occur outside the framework of traditional educational institutions. In both the United Kingdom and the Netherlands the traditional universities showed little interest in distance education or in the education of adults at the time when consideration was being given to the foundation of the British and Dutch distance teaching universities.

Mixed-mode institutions

Far more common than the purpose-built distance education institutions are those 'mixed-mode' institutions that teach by both conventional and distance means. These include institutions where a single department decides to offer courses at a distance on its own initiative, without involving the institution's central administration (as happened at the University of Waterloo where the Department of Physics was the first one to offer distance courses); institutions where a number of departments offer distance as well as conventional courses but there is a central unit to administer the distance programme (as at the University of New England and the University of Zambia where the academic staff in the departments are responsible for teaching both on-campus and external students); and institutions where a separate unit is established to teach external students across a range of subject areas and to administer the programme (as at the University of Queensland and in the Indian university Correspondence Directorates).

A major argument in favour of external students being taught by the same lecturers who teach internal students (with the distance education unit fulfilling a purely administrative role) is that this ensures parity of academic standards and hence legitimacy and credibility. Kevin Smith (1979:200) has argued that the full integration of external teaching into the mainstream teaching activities of academic departments at the University of New England did much to ensure parity of standards and an equal commitment to these dual responsibilities.

This integrated model is not without its critics. Siaciwena (1983:70), reporting on problems encountered at the University of Zambia where the University of New England structure was adopted, states that 'the system of assigning the same lecturers to both internal and external students has, in fact, been disadvantageous to the correspondence programme' because overworked lecturers tend to use the available time for internal teaching and ignore external teaching which they find exacting and difficult. Such negative attitudes 'undermine both the status of correspondence education and the very concept of parity of standards' (ibid.:71). Singh (1979:87) has also reported on the low status accorded lecturers in the Indian Correspondence Directorates by lecturers in the conventional 'wings' of Indian universities. Those who favour integration suggest that where distance or correspondence education is accorded low status and external students are taught by separate staff, the quality of the staff attracted to teach them is likely to be poor and this will further degrade the status of correspondence education. They regard integration as an answer to this problem. Finally, Ortmeier (1982) has criticised the integrated model on the grounds that it 'tends to transfer an internal teaching model to the external teaching situation'.

Organisation

Deakin University used to have a separate organisational unit to look after the needs of its external students. It included instructional designers and the off-campus operations, production and media departments. In 1982 this unit was disbanded and the various functions supporting the external programme were integrated into the main structure of the University. The change caused great controversy, opponents holding to the notion 'that off campus students need a special unit of their own because "out of sight, out of mind" can all too easily become true' (Jevons, 1984:27), but the new structure appears to be working well. Jevons suggests that the need for distance education programmes to be supported by separate organisational and administrative support structures can be exaggerated (ibid.:29), although the validity of this conclusion must to some extent be affected by the scale of the distance teaching operation.

Finally, distance education departments within mixed-mode institutions face a further problem - that of obtaining political support for their programmes within the decision-making organs of the institution. This point was made by Singh (1979:87) in respect of the ability of the Indian Correspondence Directorates to introduce innovative programmes. Distance education departments also experience difficulty in explaining and justifying their resource needs given the very different cost structures of distance and conventional departments. The pressure to force nontraditional departments to fit traditional funding formula can be considerable (Swinerton and Hogan, 1981:1). Integration may be an answer to such problems.

Consortia

The consortium approach to distance teaching is, for reasons which will be explained, not very common. The most usual form of consortium is that of a central materials development and production agency that provides materials to participating institutions which in turn deliver the materials to those of their students who are enrolled on distance courses. Examples of such systems include the Deutches Institut für Fernstudien an der Universität Tübingen (Federal Republic of Germany), the now defunct University of Mid-America (USA), the Universita' a Distanza (Italy), and the FlexiStudy system in the United Kingdom. Rather different form of consortia are exemplified by the Norsk fjernundervisning (Norway) and Massey University (New Zealand).

The Universita' a Distanza comprises an administrative centre which is responsible for organising the development and production of learning materials. The funds for this are provided by a consortium of public and private bodies including Olivetti and the universities of Rome and Calabria, each of which is covenanted to invest a fixed sum of money in the Universita' over a number of years. Local centres where tuition and other facilities are provided are funded in the main by local municipalities. Students are enrolled with conventional universities in the consortium (currently the universities of Rome and Calabria) and are examined and accredited by them.

FlexiStudy in the UK is an open learning system in which there is a national materials producer, the National Extension College (NEC), which develops materials that are then supported and taught by a number of local institutions. The teaching may be based on independent study, correspondence and telephone tuition, and some face-to-face tuition (an approach similar to that taken by many distance education institutions), but it may also involve rather more face-to-face study than is normally found in distance education systems. The NEC also teaches its own distance students.

The Norsk fjernundervisning (NFU) is rather different. It has an enabling, co-ordinating, initiating and approving role in the development of distance education but does not itself teach students, nor does it produce materials. It facilitates (1) the production of materials by the Norwegian State Broadcasting Corporation (NRK), Statens Filmsentral (the National Film Board), private film and video producers, and publishers, and (2) the delivery of courses by NRK, libraries, schools, educational organisations, voluntary associations, and correspondence schools. The only aspect over which NFU has complete control is the choice of project. The basic development costs are born by NFU. Students can obtain textbooks through booksellers and public libraries, and hire audio and video cassettes from Statens Filmsentral. They can register with correspondence schools. The majority of the courses are organised at the local level by correspondence schools and the various voluntary organisations which support adult education in Norway. NFU's main role is 'to act as a meeting point for all the partners invited to take part' in a project (Bakken, 1984:188). In 1983 NFU had only seven full-time staff. Bakken notes that in general collaborating partners have been reluctant to participate actively in the direct financing of NFU projects. Nevertheless, in the limited number of projects mounted between 1979 and 1983, the model 'has proved to work very well in practice' (ibid., p.190).

Massey University in New Zealand provides a rather different model of cooperation. Massey is a mixed-mode institution teaching its own campus-based and external students. It also has a responsibility for teaching the external students of other New Zealand universities. Any New Zealand university can exempt a 'country student' from attending lectures, but where Massey University offers an extramural course in the subject, the student is required to register for tuition on the Massey course, follow its teaching, and sit its examination. Passes gained on the course are credited to the student's home university as if the teaching had been provided there. This interchangeability of internal and external credits and use of Massey courses for credit at other universities has won confidence for Massey extramural courses from the other universities (Bewley, 1979: 250). There is also an agreement whereby students at the University of the South Pacific (Fiji) may register for tuition on Massey University courses for credit towards their USP degrees. The confidence of these universities in Massey, and the 'sharp respect for rationalizing and economizing efforts' which derives from the early federal structure of New Zealand universities and the centralised financing imposed by the Universities Grants Committee, gives the system a stability and acceptance and avoids unnecessary duplication (Bewley, 1979:250). This is not always the case. The Flexistudy system in the United Kingdom, for example, depends upon a range of fragile agreements between the NEC and the Colleges, with the teaching function often being undertaken by enthusiastic staff working on shoe-string budgets on small-scale projects that are marginal to the main concerns of the host institutions. As the experience at the now defunct University of Mid-America showed, distance education systems based on consortia are peculiarly fragile.

Reviewing the experiences of collaboration reflected in the papers prepared for the Open University's Conference on the Education of Adults at a Distance, Neil (1981:168) noted that 'practical schemes for collaboration are difficult to design and implement and are consequently rather rare. Further, even when a scheme is launched, there seems to be a rather high chance that it will atrophy or collapse after a depressingly short time'. Among the inhibiting factors identified by Neil (ibid.:172-6) are the 'not-invented-here' syndrome which inhibits the co-creation of courses and their shared use; the lack of any common ground with the result that institutions are poorly matched for collaboration; misconceptions about the absolute cost of collaborative schemes and their distribution between collaborating institutions; the failure of two or more well-entrenched bureaucracies to cooperate at a level adequate to initiate or sustain collaboration; technical incompetence on the part of one or more of the collaborating parties or the failure of one of the parties to sustain quality; failure to agree on technical questions - for example, on copyright; the feeling that one of the parties is over-dominant; philosophical differences about the nature of the educational process; and ideological differences in respect of the content of particular courses.

Bynner (1985) found that there was little active collaboration among the five Australian universities that teach at a distance. In only one instance - a Women's Studies degree offered jointly by Murdoch, Deakin and Macquarie, have any of these universities collaborated in the joint production of courses towards a given award, although Deakin University and the South Australian College of Advanced Education share some MBA courses (ibid.: 516). Bynner comments that 'the most that generally does happen is that common facilities, such as study centres, are used within a particular state. Thus Darling Downs Institute has the use of some of Queensland's impressive network of local study centres ... and Western Australia Institute of Technology (WAIT), Murdoch University and Nedlands College of Advanced Education, similarly use the same local centres and sometimes hold joint meetings with students' (p.516).

Bynner identifies the inhibiting factors as being, among others, (1) 'a simple distrust of other peoples' teaching" (p.516); (2) different philosophies which are reflected in the adoption of faculty-based (Murdoch, Deakin and Macquarie) and school-based (New England, Queensland) organisational structures (pp.520-1); (3) the failure of all departments to participate in distance teaching, even in those universities with the strongest commitment to external studies; (4) the different means of organising the distance education programme, including Deakin with no distance education department, Murdoch, New England and and Macquarie with administrative units supporting distance students and in the case of Murdoch supporting course design, and finally Queensland whose School of External Studies and Continuing Education undertakes the teaching of external students as well as administrative tasks connected with the programme. As he comments (1985:524), 'each of these different arrangements displays the distinctive distance teaching philosophy of each university...'; and (5) the use of different media and approaches to the design of the teaching package, Deakin for example placing the emphasis on high quality printed materials and audio and video materials backed by a first class library service, New England emphasing residential schools, and Macquarie taped lectures supported by notes and campus-centred non- residential courses (ibid., pp.525-7).

Nevertheless, while it is not easy to bring institutions together, consortia are valuable in providing a forum for diverse participation in decision making and an organisation for mutual support (Dolce, 1981), and can link different kinds of colleges, thus reducing territoriality and competition. Cooperative arrangements have provided opportunities for developing and influencing government policy on telecommunications. Successful consortia 'have not been imposed from outside but have been viewed by member institutions as the only way in which certain goals can be met' (Feasley,1983:45).

Model organisational structures

A number of writers have proposed model organisational structures for distance education systems (Erdos, 1975:14; Singh, 1975:32-38; Dodds, 1983:90-5). All these proposals assume a 'classic' structural model - that is, either a purpose-built distance education institution or a separated distance education unit - undertaking all the functions associated with distance education. As we have noted, there are other ways of structuring distance education systems which may result in very different organisational models - for example the wholly integrated approach taken by Deakin University, or consortia with coordinating committees or joint executive councils governing the activities of member institutions, each of which may undertake similar or discrete functions. Organisational models normally assume:

(1) An academic department (or a number of such departments based on faculties or schools) responsible for curriculum planning, the development of academic programmes and courses, and the development of academic teaching materials;

(2) Either incorporated within (1) or organisationally separate but linked to (1), a department responsible for the teaching of students, including tuition and counselling functions, and the organisation of local support services. Such departments commonly arise only in those institutions where there is a sharp distinction between those academic staff (or consultants) responsible for the development of materials and the staff responsible for the tutoring the students (eg. Open University, United Kingdom; Universidad Estatal a Distancia, Costa Rica; Universidad Nacional Abierta, Venezuela). Many systems require their academic staff both to develop the materials and to tutor distance students. (Interestingly, the fact that the department responsible for local teaching at the Universidad Nacional Abierta was located in the Operations Division, and had no direct responsibility to the Academic Directorate, was greatly criticised by UNA academics who felt that this separation was wrong in principle.)

(3) Production and distribution departments, the number of such departments reflecting the breadth of media used by the system (eg. print encompassing editorial, publishing, design and print production, warehousing and distribution; audio-visual; computer assisted learning, etc.). The precise number of departments also depends on factors such as the specialisation of function and labour. In some cases professional staff such as editors may be attached to academic units; in others they may be in a separate department.

(4) Administrative areas including finance, management services, buildings and estates, personnel, secretariat, student administration, etc.

The question arises whether any worthwhile generalisations can be made in respect of the organisation of distance education systems. Various attempts have been made to produce typologies of organisations. Glover (1985:72-3) suggests a practical typology that distinguishes between functional, product, area-based, project and matrix structures. Matrix structures are composite, mixed ones which are subdivided according to the diverse and varying demands of functional expertise, products, projects, geographical location and time and it is in this category that distance education systems tend to fall. To understand a matrix structure it is necessary to have an appreciation of the various elements that make it up.

Project structures are specialised by particular tasks which usually have a temporary nature. The course team approach to the development of materials, which brings together a range of specialists (academics, editors, designers, course manager, etc.) over a relatively short period of time to develop a course, is a prime example of this kind of structure. Generally, however, the various staff assigned to course teams on a temporary basis continue to have a functional responsibility to their specialist department. Thus editors, for example, while having day-to-day responsibility to the course team leader, may have a professional responsibility to a publishing department to maintain the 'house style' in respect of printed materials, and their deployment to work on a particular course may also be the result of a decision by the head of publishing rather than by anyone in the academic department.

Functional structures are based on specialised departments. Some distance education systems adopt a 'production line' approach to the development of materials which exhibits functional characteristics. The various specialists involved in the different stages of the development process work on the materials sequentially rather than as an interactive team: the process moves through a series of predetermined stages - content definition (by curriculum specialists), design of the overall teaching package (instructional designers), preparation of content (course writers, audio-visual producers), graphic and other design (designers), editing of materials (editors), etc. This functional approach, which is particularly common where materials are prepared by outside experts under contract (eg. Universidad Estatal a Distancia), is very different to the project structure commonly found in those institutions such as Deakin University and the British Open University which have adopted a course team approach. However, even those distance education systems that have adopted a project structure for the development phase may subsequently organise on functional lines for the production and distribution of materials (eg. printing, warehouse, postal despatch services), while the specialised staff assigned to work on a project usually retain functional links with their specialised management.

Functionalism also tends to determine the organisation of student administrative and support areas, particularly in large-scale institutions but also in smaller institutions. Specialised departments, offices or sections deal with admissions, fees, tutor-student allocation, assessment, examinations, student records, etc. The extent to which functions are differentiated depends, however, in part on the way work is organised and in part on the size of the operation. Öster (1965:80) recounts how the expansion of Hermods led to a need to reorganise the administrative systems with a separate system to handle student fees which was discrete from the basic student record. At the time this was regarded as a very radical change in the organisation.

In both the student administrative and support areas and the organisation of course development there may be a further structural distinction based on products: thus for example the British Open University draws a distinction between its degree and non-degree studies which, while by no means clear cut, adds another dimension to the organisational structure. While it integrates some of the production and distribution processes for its degree and non-degree studies, there is no intrinsic reason why these should not be divided into two areas serving the needs of product based degree- and non-degree-studies divisions. A similar product based distinction is drawn in those mixed mode conventional and distance education institutions that set up separate administrative and in some cases teaching arrangements for distance and conventional students.

Functional structures also dominate the general administrative and managerial areas of distance education systems (eg. finance, data processing, personnel, etc.) and are to be found in the organisation of teaching in a number of systems. At the British Open University there a sharp distinction between the full-time central academic staff who develop courses and the part-time academic staff that tutor them. Other systems (eg. the University of New England) require their academic staff to teach students as well as develop course materials.

The provision of local services to students adds an area-based dimension to the organisation of distance education. Various structures may emerge including two-tier structures consisting of the centre and a number of local centres where face-to-face tuition and counselling occurs, and where students can have access to a variety of resources (eg. Universidad Estatal a Distancia, Costa Rica), and three-tier structures consisting of the centre, a number of regional centres with various administrative functions (eg. tutor recruitment, hire of local centres, organisation of tuition and counselling, provision of information to students, etc), and the local centres (eg. British Open University). The services provided by such regional and local centres may be organised on functional and/or product lines.

From what has been said it will be clear that distance education systems can be organised in a variety of ways. Generally speaking, however, the structure of distance education systems is dominated by functional divisions which arise from the distinctions between development, production, distribution, and delivery systems, the use of a variety of media, and a much sharper division of labour than is the case in conventional systems. Again, and in general, the larger the system the more pronounced this is. The commonest form of consortia also appear to be based on a functional division between materials development and production on the one hand and teaching on the other (eg. Universita' a Distanza, Italy; Deutsches Institut für Fernstudien, West Germany; University of Mid-America), often with the central materials producer serving the needs of a number of area-based organisations that are responsible for teaching. This is also the pattern commonly found in systems where a materials production agency creates distance-type materials for use in community-based systems.

Hierarchic control of functions versus the contracting out of work

There are major differences of approach between those institutions that aim to control the vast majority of the functions integral to their system (and in this sense retain a hierachic control over them) and those which either devolve responsibility to another institution or contract functions out to external suppliers.

A prime example of a system of devolved responsibility is the University of London external studies system which has effectively 'devolved' responsibility for the teaching of its external students either to the students (in cases where they study by independent means) or to the various commercial correspondence colleges that have grown up to meet their needs. Consortia - particularly those which involve a central materials' production agency serving the needs of a number of institutions teaching distance students - also involve the loss of direct control over functions. As we have noted, the fragility of consortia derives from a variety of causes among which are concerns about loss of control over quality.

Generally speaking, however, the extent to which systems contract out functions is limited to the use of external suppliers for the production of particular teaching materials (print, audio-cassettes, television programmes, home experiment kit items, etc.). The reliability of these sources of supply is likely to be particularly crucial in cases where the materials are purpose-built items (eg. the Open University's MacArthur microscope, HEKTOR computer, and robot) rather than mass produced ones (eg. chemical glassware).

It is argued that systems need to exercise direct hierarchic control over the production process from development through to delivery, in order to ensure that the quality of the product is closely controlled at all its stages and disruptions to the production-delivery schedule minimised. There are certainly dangers in using external suppliers. The record company contracted to produce the small number of records needed by the British Open University's Health Education Programme twice put this work to one side - once to produce memorial records of Elvis Presley following his death, and then to do the same thing following the death of Bing Crosby. As a result the materials were not available in time for despatch to the students.

These problems may be lessened where the supplier sets up a separate organisational unit specifically to meet the needs of the distance education system. An example of such a system is the BBC's Open University Production Centre which is wholly managed by the BBC [British Broadcasting Corporation] but paid for (and ultimately owned by) the University. However, such arrangements can only be justified where there is a guaranteed minimum level of production each year. This effectively commits the institution to the expenditure necessary to support the facility, irrespective of actual need.

On the other hand there may be positive advantages in contracting out many of the jobs connected with the production of distance learning materials. Where hierarchic control is exercised, there is a geometric increase in the number of possible interactions between personnel and hence in complexity associated with an arithmetic increase in numbers of employees. Williamson (1975) has argued that the 'transactional cost' of communication, coordination and deciding have been greatly underestimated. He argues that if the transaction cost indicates that a function might be performed more efficiently by 'markets' (ie. outsiders) than by 'hierarchies' (ie. internally), then it should be contracted out.

One result of the use of outsiders is an apparent loss of 'tidyness'. For example, the editing and design of printed materials may be undertaken by commercial publishers rather than in-house editors. Under such circumstances a range of agreements may be possible from simple access to the services provided by a commercial publisher, which might thus produce a limited edition for the institution's own needs, to buy-back arrangements whereby sufficient copies of a commercially available finished product are sold back to the institution to meet its needs. Some of these agreements may result in a loss of control over the product - for example, in respect of house style. The identification of potential producers and negotiation of contracts, particularly given the non-standard nature of the product, may be time-consuming. In some cases it may not be possible to interest a commercial producer in the venture at all with the result that one requires not only adequate machinery for dealing with external suppliers but also an internal production unit.

On the other hand the benefits of contracting work out may be considerable. To begin with, once an agreement has been reached the only worry is to ensure delivery on time to the approved specification. The detailed planning, management and resourcing of that process is not a problem because it is not the distance education institution's responsibility. The use of outside contractors may also provide much greater flexibility. Where in-house facilities are available it is economically inefficient if they are idle. This imposes considerable constraints on production since there are cogent reasons for maintaining constant (and minimally viable) volumes of production. (Additional capacity can usually be bought in if necessary.) In fact there may be good reasons why the pace of development of materials cannot be kept constant, resulting in annual fluctuations in the volume of production of media. In addition the requirement to maintain volumes across a range of media may impose a broad standardisation on courses - at least in terms of their use of media - which is undesirable from an academic point of view. It may also inhibit experimentation and the use of 'new' media simply because it proves too difficult to reduce the level of dependence on the 'old' ones and there is not enough money available to accommodate both. Increased reliance on external suppliers may positively enhance flexibility.

It is not necessarily the case that a distance education institution will be in a position of weakness viz a viz an external supplier. It may in fact find itself in a position in which it is the major client of a particular supplier and thus in a strong bargaining position to obtain what it requires, particularly in cases where the market is saturated with alternative sources of supply. Much will depend on the skill of the institution's managers in exploiting the situation.

The arguments in favour of contraction out as against hierarchic control of functions are by no means clear cut, but they do warrant serious consideration by those managing distance education institutions.

Conclusions

It is clear that there is no absolutely right way to organise a distance education system.

Examination of the functional divisions common within such systems suggest that there are four main areas of activity: academic development, teaching, materials production and distribution, and administration. These functions are found in all distance education systems - purpose-built distance systems, mixed-mode distance systems, and consortia. The relative advantages and disadvantages of these models were discussed above.

The organisation of distance education systems is typically based on functional divisions, although there are other elements including project-based (notably in the course team approach), area-based (derived from local centre activity) and product-based (derived from the organisation of academic subject areas and differential between programmes of study) divisions.

The overall structure is extremely complex, and this may be a reason for trying to lessen the transactional costs of the structure by contracting a number of functions out to external suppliers. The advantages of doing this are, however, by no means clear-cut and the arguments for contracting work out will need to be examined in each case.

Chapter Seven

STAFFING

Categories of staff

The way in which jobs are defined in distance education systems depends on a number of factors including, for example:

- the size of the institution
- the range of media used
- the effect of technology on work roles
- the extent to which work roles are defined as specialised or generalised
- the organisation of staffing for materials development, materials production and teaching, and in particular the way in which academic staff roles are defined
- the effect of traditional work structures (eg. those found in broadcasting or the publishing industry) on the way work is structured in the distance education system
- the extent to which work is subcontracted to external suppliers
- institutional staffing policies.

In complex processes a number of work structures can normally be fitted to tasks (Emery and Trist, 1965). At one extreme a complex formal structure can emerge with 'simple' work roles - a pattern which Emery and Trist refer to as the 'conventional system'. At the other end of the scale the 'composite system' combines a simple structure with complex work roles. Where work roles are complex the way jobs are actually structured often depends on the aptitudes of individuals. In such circumstances the formal situation may break down, the actual role fulfilled by an individual depending not on some institutionally agreed and limiting definition of the job but on the way he or she develops the work.

Distance education systems typically involve a range of complex tasks which may be structured in simple (conventional) or complex (composite) ways. Composite work roles are typical of the areas responsible for developing courses. Academic staff frequently occupy a range of roles as their careers develop. Conversely, work roles in administrative areas dealing with the admission and registration of students are often simple. Thus, for example, Öster (1965: 75) favours the 'co-ordination of similar duties and tasks in homogeneous groups (specialisation)' as the basis for the organisation of staff in the administrative section of large correspondence schools.

In considering staffing requirements one also needs to distinguish between the staff required to support the activities of the system, and those required to support the activities actually carried out by the institution. For example, the Norsk fjernundervisning works with a handful of staff, the majority of the people involved in the Norwegian *system* of distance education being employed by other organisations. On the other hand, the British Open University, admittedly a much larger *system* in volume terms, is basically a hierarchic organisation in which the majority of functions are undertaken by staff employed by the *institution*. It employs over 2,000 permanent and 5,000 part-time staff.

Table 7.1 lists some of the staffing categories found in large scale distance education systems. It is by no means an exhaustive list. The table makes assumptions about the location of particular functions within administrative and other areas. Other arrangements are of course possible. It also makes assumptions about the way in which work roles are defined. For example, it is possible (1) to draw a distinction between the role of tutors (who are subject experts) and counsellors (who support students, help them with general learning problems, and act as intermediaries between the student and the institution), and (2) to distinguish between the roles of class-tutors who provide the face-to-face teaching and correspondence tutors who mark assignments. The British Open University in its first year of operation distinguished between class tutors, correspondence tutors and counsellors. In its

Table 7.1
Staffing categories in distance education systems

Function	Categories of staff
General management	Head of institution, departmental heads, and personal assistants and secretaries to these, planner with statisticians and other support staff, project control staff, institutional evaluators
Secretariat	Administrators (policy formulation and committee secretaries), secretaries/typists, filing clerks
Personnel	Personnel officers concerned with recruitment, training, industrial relations, terms and conditions of service, establishment control, secretaries and clerks
Management Services	systems analysts, programers, computer centre managers, in-put clerks, etc.
Finance	professional staff and supporting clerks concerned with accounts, staff payments, creditor payments, fees administration, financial planning, budgetary control, purchasing; some secretaries
Buildings & Estates	Buildings and estate planner, surveyor, services engineer, staff connected with utilities and services (plumbers, electricians, painters, carpenters), security guards, porters and internal mail staff, gardeners
Public Relations	Press and publicity officers, secretaries, house newspaper editor, etc.
Catering	Kitchen staff, serving staff, etc.
Materials development, production & presentation	Coordination by course or project leader, aided by project administrator, (and by scheduling and other professional staff as needed [eg. finance])
Library	Librarians

**Materials
Development**

All materials	Curriculum planners, subject experts, educational technologists
Print	Editors, typists, word processor operatives, designers, graphic artists and photographers, copyright editors.
Broadcasts & audio-visual	Producers, script-writers
Computer Assisted Learning	Programmers
Home experiments	Technicians (to design equipment)
Tuition and assessment	Senior tutors

Materials production

Print	Editors, typesetters, printers
Broadcasts/a-v	Designers, visual effects, model building & scenic construction staff, costume & make-up staff, floor managers, studio assistants, camera crews, sound recordists, film & sound editors, announcers. presenters, actors; copyright editor; transport staff, etc.
Home experiments	Production staff, assembly staff, technicians (to test equipment)
Computer Assisted Learning	Technicians

Materials storage and distribution	Generally: Storemen, packers, and despatch clerks
	For broadcasts on open and closed circuit transmission: appropriate staff concerned with their transmission
	For Computer Assisted Instruction: Operational and computer centre staff

**Student
administration
and teaching**

Admin.	Administrators, admissions and student records clerks, student enquiry service clerks
	Examinations administrators, examinations and assignment clerks
	Tutor records office administrators and clerks
	Regional and/or local centre administration, secretaries and clerks, security guards, cleaners, etc.
Teaching	Senior tutors and counsellors, tutors, demonstrators, counsellors, examination invigilators and script markers, etc.

second year of operation the two roles of class and correspondence tutor were amalgamated into a single role of course tutor. The separate counselling role was retained, although there were those who doubted its validity, the debate centring on whether it was more desirable for the counsellor to have a wholly educational role, untrammelled by the obligation to pass judgements on students' academic progress, or whether counselling could not be more effectively carried out by persons who had first hand knowledge of the individual student's academic work. In fact, while counsellors had from the second year of operation been encouraged to undertake a tutorial role wherever possible (subject to their having the necessary academic knowledge to tutor on a course), they were primarily employed as counsellors whose tutorial role was in practice more theoretical than actual. The debate was finally concluded in the mid-1970s with the introduction of a new role, that of tutor-counsellor, in which individuals were appointed to tutor and counsel about twelve new students on their first introductory course, and subsequently to retain a counselling role for these students as they progressed onto subsequent courses. The total counselling load carried by an individual tutor-counsellor varied but had a maximum of 56 (including the students for which they fulfilled a tutorial role). Specialist course tutors continued to provide face-to-face and correspondence tuition on higher level courses.

The example is interesting in that it shows how roles may be divided up in different ways and how educational debates can affect role definitions. However, sometimes even the role is unclear. The educational technologists at the British Open University are a case in point. Gale (1980:5) cites various Open University educational technologists in support of this contention. Among the roles identified are that of a consultant (Henderson, 1979; Macdonald-Ross, 1976); source of information (Henderson, 1979); an applied scientist implementing a technology of teaching (Macdonald-Ross, 1976); a systematic technician, starting with well-defined objectives and ending with multiple-choice questions (Macdonald-Ross, 1976); a problem solver (Macdonald-Ross, 1976); a students' advocate (Macdonald-Ross, 1976; Lawless and Kirkwood, 1976); an initiator who stimulates those developing the courses to consider issues of assessment and pedagogy when those of content are all pervasive (Lawless and Kirkwood, 1976); a transformer who mediates between the expert and the reader, putting the former's message into words which the latter will be able to understand (Macdonald-Ross, 1976); and a reactor to draft material (Lawless and Kirkwood, 1976a). Elsewhere Duchastel (1978:164-6) lists, with minimal comment and in caricature form, the diversity of perceptions which surround the role of Open University educational technologists. An explanation for this confusion and diversity of view is suggested by Hawkridge (1981:17) who stresses the multi-disciplinary origins of educational technology. More significant perhaps is the fact that a formal and limiting definition of the job is not seen to be appropriate, so that individuals have had great freedom to develop their own roles.

Riley (1986:7) has commented that when she joined the Open University in the early 1970s,

> it seemed fairly clear what my job was. There was a more or less agreed body of advice, such as to include objectives, advance organizers and self-assessment questions. There was a dominant philosophy, developed from programmed learning and ideas about the value of active learning. ... There were agreed procedures, such as organizing developmental testing or evaluation, ...

but that 'this initial consensus appears to [her] to be breaking down' (ibid.:8). She suggests (ibid.:8-10) five emerging roles for educational technologists - the 'traditional' role concerned with objectives, self-assessment questions, developmental testing and evaluation; the subject expert, concerned with the presentation of various knowledge structures, content analysis, and writing lessons; the 'executive manager' who seeks to gain agreement on procedures, organises and facilitates these, and sometimes chairs meetings and plans tasks; the social-analyst who seeks to diffuse anger and hostility between those working on a course; and the expert in a particular aspect of course design who advises those working on a course on this. Riley accepts that individual educational technologists may play a number of roles. She then goes on to discuss the focus, aims and 'reference group' of each kind of educational technologist: for example, the social analyst is interested in group dynamics, hopes to aid the creative use of group interactions, and 'refers to' psychoanalysts, counsellors and social psychologists, while the subject expert focuses on the course subject matter, aims to produce a model of the discipline's use of knowledge, and 'refers to' epistemologists. As Riley indicates (ibid.:13), each style may be welcomed or rejected by the particular group with which the educational technologist is interacting.

The educational model underlying a distance education system is also crucial to the definition of staff roles. In institution-centred systems the role of the tutor is likely to be severely circumscribed. In person-centred models the tutor's role is likely to be central to the system, fulfilling a similar role to that of the supervisor of a research student, and encompassing teaching, counselling and administrative functions, with consequential implications for the role of student administrative offices. In society-centred models the animateur is likely to be the central figure in the organisation of learning, the administration of the learning group, and the achievement of action within the community. Central records of students may not be maintained at all, the role of the centre being to develop and produce materials supportive of activities in the community based groups. Consortia in which there is a central materials development and production agency producing materials for use by a number of teaching institutions may exhibit similar characteristics, with no central student administrative system. To this extent the list in table 7.1 very much reflects the needs of institution-centred models, and particularly purpose-built distance systems.

The vast majority of distance education systems prepare some educational materials (the possible exception being those meeting the needs of contract learners and research students studying at a distance). How these materials are developed is one of the most significant decisions which any distance education system makes.

There are a number of possible kinds of appointments, but not all of these will be open to all institutions:

(1) One option is to appoint permanent course development staff whose major job is to develop distance materials and who as a result have no direct teaching commitments. They may, if they work in a university, have a commitment to carry out research, and this will keep them in touch with intellectual developments in their subject, but they lack day-to-day contact with students. They are also subjected to the discipline of continually developing new materials to (often) tight production schedules, and while they may be able to gain some respite through study leave arrangements, this can be a strain. While they may become good distance educators, unless they have the time to keep up with the development of their subjects through study leave and research, they may become out-of-date in their subject. Also, as the objectives of the institution change and it begins to respond to new markets, there is a danger that the staff will be unable to adapt and will become expensive liabilities. A bad appointment also tends to be a long-term liability, but at their best they will have a commitment to the institution, and as their mastery of the pedagogy of distance education increases they will come to rely less and less on help from educational technologists (a view supported by Riley, 1986:13).

(2) Course development staff may be appointed on short-term contracts, to work full-time on the development of distance courses. Such staff, where they are drawn from other (conventional) educational institutions, will have had recent experience of teaching students, but the skills they have as a class-based teacher may have little relevance to the needs of the distance education institution. They might, for example, be rather poor at writing. As a direct result they may rely more heavily on help from educational technologists. In

theory the distance education institution should be able to hire the best possible course developers but in practice it may prove very difficult indeed to arrange for the secondment of staff from another institution. Where contracted staff have no 'home base' to return to, and where the common practice of employment is one of permanency, the institution may be subjected to pressure to convert short-term appointees to permanent positions, thus negating the advantages of increased flexibility that come with such appointments. The temptation to extend contracts only exacerbates the problem as friendships and loyalty are built up, so that the central administration may then be seen as unreasonable when it insists that a contract is finally ended.

(3) Some institutions have their materials developed almost entirely by short-term consultants employed to produce a given piece of work. This gives great flexibility to the institution, but it also raises a number of significant problems. The best external writers are not always those who are the most renowned experts in the field. Contract writers and materials developers are rarely trained in the pedagogy of distance education. As a result there may be an urgent need to have a full-time staff of 'transformers' who will take the drafts prepared by the contract staff and turn them into 'proper' distance education materials. As we noted above, this is a role which may be undertaken by educational technologists. The consultants will also have to be fully briefed about curricula, content, principles of course design, and so on. Since courses at many distance education institutions cannot be written by a single person, it is crucial that the consultant's work should be co-ordinated with that of others developing the course. This places a further burden on the transformers. It is also crucial that the materials should be prepared in time for the transformers to work on them prior to production. Consultants may not deliver on time. To encourage them, some institutions insert penalty clauses into the contracts (eg. Universidad Estatal a Distancia, Costa Rica), but these are of little use where a consultant simply walks away from the job. (Having said that, it is also the case that permanent staff and staff on full-time contracts may fail to deliver materials.)

(4) Mixed-mode institutions may appoint separate staff to develop the distance materials (eg. University of Queensland) or they may require or request staff involved in the teaching of campus-based students to develop distance courses as well. The point was made in chapter 6 that such arrangements do not always work out to the best advantage of the distance education wing of the institution (the example cited being that of the University of Zambia). In mixed-mode institutions some departments may refuse to participate in the distance teaching programme at all (eg. Agricultural and Horticultural Sciences, and Science at Massey University; Architecture and Science at Deakin; Science and Rural Science at New England).

(5) In mixed-mode systems which have a limited geographical coverage, the materials developers may also tutor distance students. In large-scale systems which teach over an extensive area and have many students, it is more common for the materials developers not to have a responsibility for teaching, particularly where the tutorial role encompasses both class-based and correspondence tuition.

Generally speaking, those institutions which rely on permanent full-time academic staff are more costly, but they avoid some of the problems of coordination and commitment which are encountered in systems that rely on short-term appointments or make use of staff whose major commitment is to a conventional educational programme.

Determining academic staffing levels

It has been a common experience of many distance teaching institutions that they do not know how best to determine the number of academic staff which they should have in post. Indeed, in many mixed-mode systems the attempt is not even made. Bynner (1985:527) reports that academic staff who work in Australian mixed-mode university departments have a teaching load exceeding that of people working in conventional higher education or purpose-built distance teaching universities: 'The tradition of the typed lecture notes supplemented later, as in

Staffing

Macquarie [University], by the taped lecture, does not acknowledge the need for teaching time to design and develop external courses.' Neither Queensland nor New England universities recognise staff effort put into course development. At Murdoch University, however, lecturers are allocated sixteen teaching hours per week for the design of external course materials (ibid., p.528).

Staffing levels for face-to-face teaching

In conventional campus-based systems a very high proportion of total costs is spent on staff salaries and related costs, hence the importance in conventional institutions of staff:student ratios or instructional workload models. The student:staff ratio is quite simply the number of students (or full-time equivalent students) (S) divided by the number of staff (or full-time equivalent staff) (T), such that the average class size (ACS) equals $S \div T$.

$$ACS = S \div T \qquad \text{[Equation 1]}$$

The instructional workload model makes explicit the fundamental variables (class size, average number of taught-hours or contact hours which students receive, and average number of teaching-hours per lecturer), affecting the teaching load, and is for this reason held to be a powerful and flexible planning tool:

$$T = (S \times ASH) \div (ACS \times ALH) \qquad \text{[Equation 2]}$$

where:

T = the number of full-time equivalent lecturers determined by dividing the total class contact hours of staff by the average class contact hours of full-time staff

S = the number of full-time equivalent students, determined by dividing the total student taught hours by the average student taught hours (ASH) of full-time students in the same subject area.

ASH = the average taught hours of a FTE student which is obtained by dividing the total student hours by the number of FTE students.

130

ACS = the average class size determined by dividing the total student contact hours by the total lecturer hours.

ALH = the average lecturer hours taught by a FTE lecturer, determined by dividing the total lecturer hours by the number of FTE lecturers.

In institutions that teach both at a distance and by conventional means and in which staff are expected to undertake duties across both modes, a major problem faced by those planning the allocation of staff time is to establish some kind of equivalency between the workloads imposed by teaching on-campus students and tutoring distance students. However, the instructional workload model can be modified to do this, as Birch and Cuthbert (1981; 1982) have shown.

Their starting point was to note that lecturers in conventional Further Education colleges are required to spend a minimum number of hours per week in college, of which a proportion is to be spent in front of a class (in UK colleges 30 hours and 20 hours respectively). The balance of the time (10 hours) is spent on preparation, marking, administration, etc. However, where teaching patterns emerge which require the lecturer to spend more than the normal amount of time on preparation and marking and less on face-to-face contact, as happens in distance-learning situations, there has to be a way of negotiating an appropriate reduction of class-contact hours. They accordingly adapted the instructional workload model approach to provide an estimation of the number of staff required to support distance learners (Birch and Cuthbert, 1981, pp. 53-5; 1982, pp. 103-6). They concluded that 'any agreement which gave the teacher one hour's class remission for less than 6 students in his case load would lead to a unit cost for the open learning programme which was higher than for equivalent conventional work' (ibid.:105).

Another approach would be to assess the workload involved in tutoring an individual student by correspondence and a group of students by face-to-face means, work out the total workload given a particular case load of students, and then relate this to the full-time load of a conventional teacher. For example, it might be established that the correspondence and telephone tuition, and other contact with the individual distance student outside the *class* situation, is equivalent to 30 minutes per student, that the average distance student case load per academic is 25, and that each group of 25 distance students has one hour of face-to-face contact per week over a 15 week term. The total teaching commitment for a member of staff with a group of 25 distance students would be (0.5 hours x 25 students x 15 weeks) + (1 hour x 15 sessions) = 202.5 hours or 13.5 hours per week. If the normal load in the conventional programme was 15 hours, then the load imposed by a group of 25 distance students would be equivalent to 13.5 ÷ 15 = 0.9 of a conventional load.

This approach can also be used to determine the number of tutors required to support a given student population. The total teaching load (TTL) arising from tutoring a distance course might be established as follows:

$$TTL = (S \ w \ œ) + [(S \, /g) \ t] \qquad \text{[Equation 3]}$$

where:

TTL = the total teaching load on a course in hours
S = the number of student courses on the course
w = the number of weeks the course is taught
œ = the number of hours or the proportion of an hour which is allowed for contact with an individual distance student for purposes of correspondence tuition etc.
g = the average size of a tutorial group
t = the number of hours tutoring provided on the course

The average weekly teaching load (WTL) is:

$$WTL = \{(S \ w \ œ) + [(S \, /g) \ t]\} \div w \qquad \text{[Equation 4]}$$

If the full time load of a conventional class teacher (K) is defined as being 15 hours per week, the total staffing requirement (N) to tutor a distance course will be:

$$N = \{(S \ w \ œ) + [(S \, /g) \ t]\} \div (w \ K) \qquad \text{[Equation 5]}$$
$$= WTL \div K \qquad \text{[Equation 6]}$$

Example 7.1
Staff required to tutor a distance course [Equations 3-6]

There are 62 students (S) on a course taught over 10 weeks (w). Tutors are allowed 30 minutes per week per student for correspondence purposes (ie. œ = 0.5 hours), the average group size (g) is 20 and there are 5 hours of tutorials (t) during the term, then on the basis of Equation 3, the total teaching load is:

TTL = (62 x 10 x 0.5) + ([62 ÷ 20] x 5)
     = 310 + say (3 x 5)
     = 325 hours

The average teaching load per week is (Equation 4):

WTL = 325 ÷ 10 = 32.5 hours

The number of FTE staff required to support the programme (Equation 6) is:

N   = 32.5 ÷ 15 = 2.17 teachers

Staffing for materials development and production

The comment has already been made that, at least in certain mixed-mode institution, no allowance is given for the time that academic staff have to spend in developing and producing course materials. In purpose-built distance education systems where the staff are required to spend a large proportion of their time on this kind of work, there is an obvious need to determine staffing requirements by establishing some kind of relationship between the 'input' of staff time and the 'output' of materials and courses. This can be done by using a production-rate to determine the amount of staff time needed to prepare and produce a given measure of learning materials, and hence the number of staff likely to be required to achieve a given level of output. Where courses have a standard format it may be enough to establish the total amount of time of each class of employee required to develop and produce a course, and then multiply the result by the number of courses involved. Where courses differ widely in their use of media it is necessary to establish production rates for each media.

As Rumble (1986:35-8) shows, a production rate is derived by measuring the output of whole courses or of individual components and dividing this by the number of staff years of each category of staff involved, taking into account the proportion of time spent on other duties (such as research), and prolonged absences such as sick leave or maternity leave, etc. For example, assume that a particular institution has 37 full-time academic staff employed for 365 days each year. Weekends, public holidays, holiday entitlement and research leave account for a total of 164 days. In addition staff are expected to spend some time on administration (allowance 10 days). This leaves 191 'productive days' which can be spent on course development, teaching and research.

Assuming that the staff have no teaching and research duties and are employed full-time to develop distance courses, one can measure the output of standard courses or of particular components and derive a production rate for staff wholly employed in the development and production of distance materials and courses. For example, assume that the 37 staff developed 13 'standard courses', then the production rate per academic member of staff of 'standard courses' would be $13 \div 37 = 0.35$ per annum. Alternatively assuming that 120 hours of television or video programming is produced, then the production rate would be $120 \div 37 = 3.24$ programmes hours per annum.

The essential formula is:

$$p = X/N'$$ [Equation 7]

where:

p = the production rate
X = the product of output (be it a course of a standard type or a component of a course) which is being developed, produced or maintained.
N' = the number of staff of category N' involved in the activity of developing, producing or maintaining product X

and where by extension:

$$N' = X/p \qquad \text{[Equation 8]}$$

Production rates can be established for the various categories of staff (academic course writers, editors, broadcast producers, designers, course coordinators, educational technologists, secretaries, etc) in respect of whole courses or particular components (print, audio, video, etc). A judgment would need to be reached on whether or not the historical production rates (if they are derived from past data) or the assumed production rates (if they are based on estimates) are reasonable or not.

The next step is to use the agreed production rates against target output levels to establish staffing requirements for each category of staff. The total requirement for staff of category N'_1 would be:

$$N'_1 = [X_1/p_{X1N'1}] + [X_2/p_{X2N'1}] + ... + [X_n/p_{XnN'1}]$$
$$\text{[Equation 9]}$$

where $X_1, X_2, ... X_n$ are courses of a particular kind or length, or particular components, and $p_{X1N'1}, p_{X2N'1}, ...$ etc. are the production rates for that course or component. This would be repeated for other categories of staff. Example 7.2 shows how this might be done.

It should be borne in mind that while these equations indicate the number of academic staff required, this is related to the input of staff time over a given period and not necessarily to the number of staff in post. Thus the output in Example 7.2 could be achieved by 28.5 people over one year, or by 14.25 people working over two years.

The British Open University studied academic production rates in respect of the output of its courses. Broadly speaking the University's courses consist of multi-media materials loosely divided into 'packages' which equate with a week's work by a student. These are called 'units' and each one is approximately equal to 12 hours work by the average student. The University identified the number of units that had been developed by its academic staff, and then divided the total units produced by the

---

Example 7.2
*Use of production rates to determine staffing needs for materials
development [Equation 9].*

Source: Rumble, G. (1986) Costing distance education, London, The
Commonwealth Secretariat, p.38, reproduced by permission.

The example which follows shows how the academic staff
numbers required to support a particular programme of activity
can be derived using production rates for various media. If N'_1 is
the number of academic staff and the volume of printed materials
to be produced (X_1) is 120 course books of a standard length, the
volume of audio-cassettes of one hour duration (X_2) is 100, the
volume of video-cassettes (X_n) is 80 programmes of one hour
duration, the production rate $p_{X_1N'_1}, p_{X_2N'_1}, p_{X_nN'_1}$ for
print, audio-cassettes and video-cassettes of the kind described is
7, 40 and 9 per annum respectively, then:

$$N'_1 = (120 \div 7) + (100 \div 40) + (80 \div 9) = 28.52$$

---

number of years of academic staff time put into their
development. Although its courses were developed around a
standard multi-media model using print, broadcasting, residential
schools, home experiment kits, computing, etc., there were some
differences in the balance of media used in courses prepared by
different faculties. All courses had 28 to 32 correspondence texts
of a standard length, and about half the courses had residential
schools. All courses had assessments and examinations. However,
home experiment kits were particularly used by science and
technology courses and computing by mathematics courses; and
science-based courses (ie. those produced by the faculties of
science, technology and mathematics) had about twice the number
of television programmes but half the number of radio
programmes of courses produced by arts-based faculties (ie.

courses produced by the faculties of arts, education and social sciences). In addition it was argued that the planning and development of science, technology and maths based courses required a much more rigorous approach to the control of the curriculum and content since in these subjects it was necessary to define clearly the entry and exit skills and knowledge of the students, both at the course level and at the individual 'unit' level, if students were not to be hopelessly lost in the face of unfamiliar concepts. The staff involved in developing the courses had other duties, notably research (one third of their time) and as a result they had perhaps 120 'productive days' per annum to devote to course development. An analysis of the historical production rates showed that staff in the faculties of science, mathematics and technology were producing from 1.4 to 1.6 'units' of work per annum, while those in social science and arts had a production rate of about 2.3 and 2.6 'units' per annum respectively. Staff in education were in an apparently anomalous position in that their production rate was 1.6 'units' per annum (ie. equivalent to the production rate in science-based areas). The production rates were then used for many years as a basis for determining the number of academic staff in each faculty (Rumble, 1976:22-5).

Vázquez-Abad and Mitchell (1983:205) have suggested that production should be measured in terms of the number of person-hours needed to produce one hour of instruction through a particular medium. However, there is little information available on the amount of time it actually takes to prepare an hour's instruction. They point out that the quantification of production hours depends on the characteristics of the producer or production group. It also depends on the nature of the material, as the experience at the Open University seems to bear out. A further factor is the way in which the material is produced. It is generally thought that the course team method of working is more labour intensive than solo (individual) production. Nevertheless Vázquez-Abad and Mitchell suggest that an assessment can be obtained from people experienced in materials development as to the likely time in may take to develop one hour's worth of student learning material. Indeed, Sparkes (1984:219) provides some indication of production rates for various media worked out on this basis (see Table 7.2).

Table 7.2
Production rates of various media (number of academic staff hours to produce one hour's worth of student learning)

Media	Academic work (in hours)
Lecturing	2 - 10
Small Group teaching	1 - 10
Teaching by telephone	2 - 10
Video-tape lectures (TVI)	3 - 10*
Audio-vision	10 - 20*
Teaching text	50 - 100**
Broadcast tv	100 or more**
Computer Aided Learning	200 or more*
Interactive video disc	300 or more**

*   requires support staff
** requires several support staff

Source: Sparkes, J. (1984) 'Pedagogic differences between media', in Bates, A.W. (1984) The role of technology in distance education, London, Croom Helm Ltd., p. 219.

Establishing equivalent workloads

It is possible to establish an equivalency between the overall workload involved in the development of various kinds of materials for the distance programme, a conventional teaching load, and the load involved in teaching distance students, by the simple expedient of equating the full-time loads for various activities (eg. a full-time load is equivalent to either producing seven 60 page books or 40 audio-cassettes or a teaching load of 15 hours per week in the conventional programme). This allows one to determine a full-time load for an individual member of staff working on two programmes: for example, the development of two books would account for $2 \div 7 = 0.29$ of the staff member's time, while a teaching load of 9 hours would account for $9 \div 15 = 0.6$ of his or her time (Rumble, 1986:42). Birch and Cuthbert's approach, discussed above, establishes an equivalency between the workload involved in teaching conventional and distance students.

The utility and dangers of staffing formula

The formula approaches discussed above can help to determine in broad terms (at the planning level) the number of staff that may be required to staff a distance education system, but there are pitfalls in this approach. The number of staff actually required will depend on a range of factors including, for example, the following (in respect of writing materials):

- the way in which individual staff members work and how they are motivated. For example, the rate of production of teaching texts appears to be much higher where there are incentive payments or where contracts are issued which effectively provide payment for results.
- the extent to which staff are working in an area in which they are already expert, or in one where they first of all need to undertake basic research before they can start writing.
- the complexity of the subject matter, and what is expected in terms of 'learner outcomes'.
- the precise role of the staff member. Some staff may only write texts, others may fulfil a variety of non-writing roles.
- the individual's capabilities. Some staff find it easier to write than others.

Experience shows that individual staff differ widely in the rate at which they produce materials, from those who produce none to those who produce an exceptional amount. The way staff are led and motivated is in the end much more important than 'management by production rates', although the monitoring of production rates can be an important indicator of performance (with the implication that management's task is to increase the rate of production without diminishing the quality of the output). Certainly, whatever their utility as abstract planning tools and measures of performance, production rates should not be used to allocate staff. There is, after all, something essentially illogical in a situation in which additional staff are allocated to areas with lower production rates, in order to increase their absolute output. Low productivity is an issue requiring managerial intervention rather than an injection of additional manpower.

Conclusions

This chapter has concentrated on two issues: firstly, on the staffing categories typically found in distance education systems, and secondly, and more specifically, on the determination of academic staffing levels in distance education systems and the means of equating the workload of those who develop distance materials and teach distance students with that of conventional teaching staff. On neither of these issues is there a single 'right' approach to the problem. The kind of staff appointed to distance education institutions and the way in which their jobs are determined can vary significantly, while the numbers of staff required to carry out particular duties is also subject to wide variation. For example, distance education institutions which rely heavily on short-term contract staff to develop their materials may have a relatively small pool of full-time permanent academic staff; low productivity (and hence an apparent need to increase staffing levels to boost output) may reflect poor academic leadership rather than an absolute need for more staff. What is clear is that the factors which consistently come through as the significant determinants of the shape of an institution are its underlying educational philosophy (institution-, individual- or society-centred), the nature of the institution (purpose-built, mixed-mode, or consortium), its size, its choice of media, and the level of service which it provides to its students.

Chapter Eight

PLANNING AND BUDGETING

The political process underpinning the establishment of a distance education system will normally lead to a statement of fundamental institutional aims or objects ('mission' statement) which expresses in the broadest terms the kind of instituion being set up. This statement alone will be insufficient to guide those planning the institution. Goals and specific objectives will need to be set.

It is normally the case that as an institution develops and new staff are appointed, so goals and objectives proliferate and become less rather than more clear. Perry (1976:222) commented that as the British Open University developed so the 'family' atmosphere (in which everyone knew each other and all policy papers were written by himself or one of his close colleagues) broke down, to be replaced by a government and decision-making structure which began to proliferate committees. By 1971 Perry felt that the contact he was able to maintain with the affairs of each of the University's faculties was becoming more tenuous and that 'the University [had] changed from a very tightly controlled and centrally organised institution, to a much more diffuse one with a much wider spread of authority and a consequential lack of tightness of policy control' (ibid.:225).

So long as resources are plentiful, institutions can expand and the untrammelled proliferation of programmes and activities can proceed broadly unchecked. Typically, this kind of growth is relatively unplanned. Although it can be controlled through the allocation of additional resources to budgets, the tendency is to try to ensure that the available resources are spent rather than consider whether the object of expenditure is desirable in itself. As a result goals and objectives may change and may distort the institution's original 'mission'.

Where funds are constrained or reduced, educational institutions have to make more effective and efficient use of their resources. For a while, it may be possible to continue to support the existing range of goals and objectives (formal or informal, overt or covert) by improving efficiency. Savings may be sought on the basis of expediency, with financial cuts falling on those budgets where there is immediate flexibility, and where savings can be made without cutting the essential staffing and infrastructure of the institution. In the long term, while this approach buys time, it is essentially unplanned and unrelated to the priorities of the institution. Ultimately continuing financial cutbacks and a general shortage of resources will force institutions to review their goals and objectives and make choices between these.

Externally, too, changes in the complex environment within which the institution is operating (demographic, economic, technological, political, etc) may require concomitant changes within the institution, including alteration of its mission, goals and objectives.

These tendencies require that the goals and objectives of the institution should be made more specific and that its activities should be examined critically. The problem is that this is by no means as easy as it might appear to be. Thus Hinman (1980), reporting on the first stage in the implementation of a planning and evaluation programme at the University of Michigan designed to develop, integrate and assign priorities to departmental objectives, observed that 'the quandary of goals statements for universities is that, to be stated in a form which elicits widespread agreement, they must be ambiguous and nonoperational; if concrete and measurable, they either provoke dissension or are too mundane to arouse enthusiasm'.

Yet the attempt needs to be made if institutions are to survive and continue to attract students in the face of changing patterns of demand and economic circumstances. It is the planner's task to channel this process.

The planning process

A fundamental distinction needs to be drawn between:

• strategic planning, concerned with the long-term prospects of an institution or system (broadly up to ten to twenty years),
• operational planning (broadly working within the short- to medium-term timescales of from two to five years within which institutional managers are required to plan), and
• the budget (the detailed financial and volumes-based plan for the institution for the immediately forthcoming period - normally one year).

Figure 8.1 reflects these different levels and their timescales.

'Mission' statements

The statement of fundamental roles or 'mission' contained in legal instruments establishing distance education systems are couched in varying degrees of specificity. For example, the Bill establishing the Indira Gandhi National Open University laid down under Article 4 the following objects for the University:

> ... to advance and disseminate knowledge by a diversity of means, including the use of any communication technology, to provide opportunities for higher education to a larger segment of the population and to promote the educational well being of the community generally; to encourage the Open University and distance education systems in the educational pattern of the country and to co-ordinate and determine the standards in such systems, ...

Mission statements express underlying beliefs about the nature of the institution and its characteristics. A well-formulated statement helps make explicit the differences between the institution and others operating at the same educational level, and can be useful both externally, to identify the institution clearly in the minds of politicians, the public and other institutions, and internally as a means of initiating a more rigorous and definition of goals.

Planners have found it useful to link mission statements to planning goals through the use of the 'cascade' structures commonly found in American universities and colleges, in which the mission ('objects') of the institution are progressively

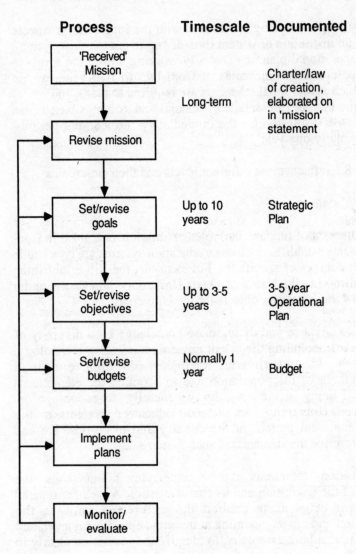

**Figure 8.1
Levels of planning**

Table 8.1
Cascade structure of mission statements and goals

Mission:

1. To provide education at university and professional levels
2. ... by distance means...
3. ... to meet the needs of non-traditional students and
4. to contribute to the educational well-being of the community in general

Goals:

Academic programmes	Student characteristics	Communic-ations and teaching strategy
1. To provide education in the liberal arts and sciences at degree level 2. To provide courses in the liberal arts and sciences of interest to the community 3. To provide professional and vocational education 4. To provide in-company courses on a contract basis	1. To provide courses for adults 2. To provide part-time education 3. To provide courses to students unable to attend conventional educational institutions 4. To provide learning materials suitable for use by independent learners and community-based groups	1. To teach by distance means 2. To exploit and develop new communications technologies for this purpose 3. To favour those technologies best able to support home-based learning and courses

refined and made more specific through the definition of goals. Table 8.1 shows how this process might be applied within the context of a distance education system.

Goals: the focus for strategic planning

The legal instruments establishing an institution may define the mission in more detail through the establishment of general goals. The Decree setting up the Universidad Estatal a Distancia in Costa Rica (Ministerio de Educación Pública, n.d.) laid down the following missions (objects) for the university under Article 2:

a) To encourage the values upon which the Costa Rican State is founded.

b) To provide university-level higher education through the use of new technical mediums of communication.

c) To incorporate into higher education, through suitable and flexible methods, those who have not been able to join the formal university system.

d) To contribute to research for the cultural, economic and social progress of the country.

e) To provide adequate means for the permanent improvement and education of all the people.

f) To serve as a vehicle for the diffusion of culture.

g) To reach agreements with the other universities for the realisation of educational and cultural activities proper to them or of common interest.

h) To contribute to the non-university level education of adults, establishing means of cooperation and coordination with the organisations and institutions specialising in this field.

and, under Article 3, specified as its goals:

a) To offer degrees in harmony with the country's needs, culminating in the securement of university-level titles and degrees.

b) To develop research programmes in areas fundamental for the development of the country.

c) To offer courses of training and improvement to the country's teachers and the rest of the civil service.

d) To bring to fruition cultural extension programmes.

e) To recognise studies, titles and degrees authorised by other universities.

f) Whatever other functions that are proper to its state as a university and accord with its mission [objects].

Irrespective of whether or not the legal instruments establishing a system define the general goals of the institution, the next stage in the planning process is to move from a general definition of role or mission to a more focused strategy which will guide decision-making over the longer-term future. To do this, the environment within which the institution is likely to operate needs to be delineated.

Table 8.2 indicates in broad terms some of the factors which may need to be taken into account in evaluating this environment. The strategic planning process should seek to explore the opportunities open to the institution having regard to both institutional mission, the aspirations of staff, and the strengths and weaknesses of the institution and its constituent parts (subject areas, media development and production facilities, teaching systems, and administrative support areas). A major requirement of any planning process must be to help in the articulation of aspirations both to develop new areas and to strengthen or withdraw from existing ones. This can best be done through the establishment of informal groups outside the main government structure of the institution which can be charged with the task of identifying both the future environment within which the system will operate and the academic aspirations of its staff.

The existing strengths and weaknesses of an institution can be analysed using Doyle and Lynch's (1979) modification of the 'product portfolio' concept developed by the Boston Consulting Group. This aims to analyse the institution's share of the market against its potential size. Doyle and Lynch suggest that an institution's academic programmes and courses may be characterised as 'stars' - courses with an acknowledged reputation in areas of high national demand; 'props' - courses with an acknowledged reputation attracting applicants but in an area of small national demand; 'problem areas' - courses lacking an established reputation and relatively unattractive to potential applicants, but in areas of high national demand; and 'dogs' - unattractive courses in areas of low national demand. They suggest that 'star' areas should be given the highest level of support; 'props' should be maintained because they enhance the institution's reputation, but they are not areas for potential expansion; 'problem areas' may need to be rationalised, with the institution seeking to move a number of these into the 'star' category through a programme of expansion, while closing others; 'dogs' should be considered as candidates for closure.

Sizer (1982a:21) has argued that Doyle and Lynch's model, while valuable in itself, needs to identify between high growth, low growth and declining market areas. He has therefore adopted

Table 8.2
Environmental factors

Demographic	Size and characteristics (age, geographical distribution, occupational structure, etc.) of the population based on long-term projections
Provision/demand	Educational provision by level (primary, secondary, tertiary) and sector (formal and non-formal); provision of training and opportunities for continuing education; and provision of education and training by mode (full- or part-time, conventional, distance or open studies)
	Likely growth in market (demand for education and training) by level, sector, and mode, including growth in developing subject areas
Environment	Political, socio-economic, technological:

- government priorities
- public expenditure trends/living standards affecting disposable income
- technological trends affecting communications strategies

---

the directional policy matrix approach used by a number of companies (Shell Group, General Electric Company) to identify future trends and possibilities. Figure 8.2, which is based on Sizer's directional policy matrix, indicates potential policy options (growth, selective growth, consolidation, and planned withdrawal and redeployment from subject areas depending on the strengths of the institution and the attractiveness of the market).

In parallel with the analysis of threats and opportunities, and

• Demographic trends • Market size (potential and frustrated) • Market growth rate (socio-economic & technological factors) • Market diversity • Competitive structure - range & costs of other providers • Political trends - government and opposition attitudes • Technological and scientific trends • Media and communications developments • Industrial importance • Attitude of business • Employment prospects of students • Environmental factors • Cultural importance • Optimal size of institution • Cost • Relationship to institutional strengths

PROGRAMME OR SUBJECT AREA
ATTRACTIVENESS

• Size and range of institution's programmes • Market share • Accessibility of programme to potential market • Demand • Reputation • Quality of staff • Recognition of awards • Employment prospects of graduates • Media • Resource mobility (age structure of staff) • Costs

INSTITUTIONAL STRENGTHS IN PROGRAMME OR SUBJECT AREA

	High	Medium	Low
High	Growth	Selective growth or consolidation	Consolidate
Medium	Selective growth or consolidation	Consolidate	Planned withdrawal/ redeployment
Low	Consolidate / planned withdrawal/re- deployment	Planned withdrawal/ redeployment	Planned withdrawal/ redeployment

Figure 8.2
Directional policy matrix

Based on Sizer, J. (1982) 'Institutional performance assessment under conditions of changing needs', Journal of Institutional Management in Higher Education, 6 (1), 17-28: Figure 2 on page 22.

strengths and weaknesses, a statement of the key elements of the institution's strategy needs to be drawn up. These key strategic factors are the tests against which opportunities are measured. They may be fundamental and they may well be based on the mission statement: for example, an institution offering secondary level courses at a distance would need to satisfy nationally approved standards of accreditation and meet any nationally approved curriculum objectives. The various key strategic factors should be rated as essential, highly desirable, or desirable. Once this process has been completed, the opportunities available to the institution (including the opportunities to withdraw from existing areas of activity) need to be tested against the key strategic factors. As a result of this process some opportunities may be discarded ('its an opportunity but not supported by a key strategic factor, so we will not pursue it') and some weak areas may be closed down.

The institution is now in a position to draw up a strategic plan which selects from among the opportunities available those which will be pursued. The strategic plan should rank these in order of preference. Figure 8.3 shows the planning process from refinement of mission through to the emergence of a strategic plan.

The statement of goals that emerges should reflect realisable aspirations and not be so remote from reality as to be unachievable. The goals need to support the institution's mission and should express clear intentions. Examples might be:

- To develop a distance taught degree in French
- To increase the level of support accorded to persons with disabilities (particularly the blind) with a view to enabling them to study the institution's courses at home
- To gain access to a satellite with a European 'footprint'

What is notable about such statements is that they are still unspecific as to (1) the timescale for implementation (although it is implicit that they will be implemented within the planning horizon covered by the strategic plan) and (2) the precise volume of activity represented by the activity.

Operational Plans and Budgets

Once the strategic plan has been agreed (and it needs to be remem-

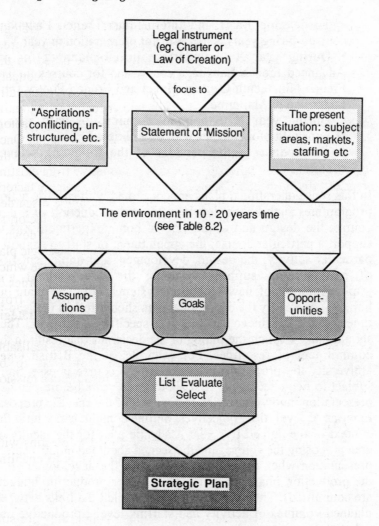

Figure 8.3
The Planning Process: From Mission to Strategic Plan

bered that it is not a fixed plan but is subject to continuing review), the institution can move on to make specific choices at the operational planning level. What distinguishes operational plans are that the objectives specified in them are specific in terms of both quantity and time. Examples might be:

151

- To develop Basic and Intermediate French Language courses during years X and X+1 for presentation in year X+2
- During year X to undertake initial planning for the Advanced French Language course and for courses on The French Nineteenth Century Novel and French Poetry from Lamartine to Mallermé.
- During year X to appoint a counsellor with special responsibility for students with disabilities.
- To produce braille versions of the following science courses: ....

In this sense operational plans are concerned with specific action programmes such as the development and production of a new course; the design and acquisition of home experiment kits to support a particular course; the appointment of staff to support a particular activity; the design, development and implementation of new student support systems; the development and implementation of new computer systems, etc. The planning horizon covered by the operational plan should reflect the lead-in times needed to achieve the objectives specified in the plan. They should make explicit the timing of the decisions that result in the commitment of resources. For example, at the British Open University the proposal to develop a new course is essentially subject to two checks, the first about three years before planned presentation involving academic approval of the specific proposal in terms of level, title, objectives, outline content, etc. within the context of the agreed five year academic plan for the faculty or area proposing the course; and the second about ten months before presentation when the course moves from the development into the production phase (at which point major production budgets are committed). The plan should make explicit the links between planned volumes of activity and staffing levels, productive and delivery capacities, and space and accommodation constraints.

The operational plan should be set within the context of the short- to medium-term financial situation. The first year of the operational plan will normally correspond to the immediate budget year. However, it is desirable that a longer term perspective should be obtained as to the cost of activities, not least because the time-scales for initiating action in distance education systems (and hence for committing elements of the budget) are frequently in advance of the formal budget setting exercise.

Again, at the British Open University the budget for the next operating year is not finalised until after the university receives notification of its grant from government - normally just before or just after the budget year begins. However, by the time the budget is formally settled the University has committed the vast majority of its expenditure in supporting among other things (1) staff on permanent or fixed term contracts, (2) commitments to statutory and contractual obligations (insurance, rents for regional offices, etc.), (3) the production of new courses (confirmed ten months before their first presentation), (4) the presentation of existing and new courses (confirmed about nine months before the new financial and academic year begins in January), and (5) the admission of new students to the undergraduate programme, provisionally agreed eleven months before the start of the new year and confirmed six months before it begins. Thus approval of the budget, except in cases where the it is being cut and activities are being stopped in mid-term, is more a question of fine-tuning rather than an event of major strategic importance.

The really significant budgetary decisions are thus those that are taken well before the budget for a particular year is formally agreed. Given this, planners need to provide an indication of the financial implications of major decisions at the time those decisions are taken. Such financial forecasts should not only indicate the costs of the decision itself (for example, the cost of developing, producing and presenting the courses built into the plans of academic units) but should place this within the context of the likely budget and other demands on it (eg. major capital replacement projects). To this extent financial forecasting will reflect the gradual closing of options and reduction of flexibility as the budget year approaches and decisions affecting it are taken.

The operational plan will also need to be supported by various models, notable student number forecasting models, an assessment of the course presentation load (eg number of broadcast transmissions, number of tutors, etc.), staffing models, space models, etc. Such models should facilitate the planning process, making it possible to evaluate the costs of alternative courses of action, and provide timely and relevant information to managers and decision-makers.

Finally, the operational plan may well include data on performance (in the form of performance measures) which can be used to monitor the developing situation and indicate where corrective action may be needed. The indicators may be fairly mundane in themselves (for example, average space per member of staff by department in square feet or meters) or reflective of more fundamental processes within the oganisation (eg. the average number of student study hours registered per student as a measure of rate of throughput, the ratio of enquiries to registered new students as a measure of the attractiveness of a programme, information on the age of courses, and the production rate of media per member of materials development staff). Such indicators should be chosen for their utility in pinpointing issues which may require more serious investigation. In addition the results of other evaluative exercises should be fed into the planning process as a matter of course. The whole issue of evaluation is dealt with in greater detail in chapter 11.

Some concluding comments on planning

The planning process outlined above may appear all-embracing and rational at the theoretical level. In practice it is likely to be 'messy' and anything but all-embracing. The external environment within which educational systems operate is both volatile and unpredictable. Keeping track of the external influences likely to affect the future of a distance education system operating in a number of sectors (formal academic programmes, vocational and professional in-service training, in-company contract training, community education, etc.) is a major task. It is inevitable that some aspects will be overlooked.

Secondly, education is both a service industry with people as its clients and, notwithstanding the substitution of capital for labour in distance education systems, a significant employer. Planning should be concerned as much with human relations as with the technical issues of managing and directing a distance education system. This includes the provision of incentives designed to motivate staff, and measures for the retraining and redeployment of staff from areas of low priority and declining demand to areas of expansion.

Thirdly, institutions may not be autonomous. Where this is the case, their goals and objectives may be determined by a supra-institutional body such as a regional or sectoral planning authority, or government ministry. The Botswana Department of

Non-Formal Education (formerly the Botswana Extension College) is a ministerial department. Its objectives are restricted and it lacks freedom to experiment. Similarly, the Mauritius College of the Air is a parastatal body which is a part of the Mauritius Educational Broadcasting Authority. It too is subject to direct government involvement and control. Such conditions may inhibit the search for new goals and objectives, and the abandonment of old ones (Dodds, 1983:116-7).

Those distance education units that operate as departments of conventional institutions may not be able develop distance studies in new subject areas not covered by the existing university staff, even though there is a perceived market for them, because they are not empowered to appoint staff on their own initiative. More significantly, they may not even be able to offer the full range of courses on offer to the conventional students because some departments refuse to participate in distance studies at all. Bynner (1985:521) reports that 'even in the [Australian] universities with the largest commitment and strongest reputation for external teaching, some departments have steadfastly refused to participate'. He lists the Schools of Science and Architecture at Deakin University, the Faculties of Science and Rural Science at the University of New England, nine of the thirteen faculties at the University of Queensland where there is a long standing commitment to external studies, and five out of the twelve faculties at Macquarie University (ibid.:520). The restricted mission of the parent body may also restrict the mission of the distance teaching unit. Thus for example the distance teaching 'wing' of the Universidad Pedagógica Nacional in Mexico is effectively restricted to the in-service training of un- and under-qualified teachers by the fact that its parent body is a teacher training university.

Budgeting

The efficient management of finance is one of the crucial tasks facing any educational institution. The approach taken is however heavily dependent on the prevailing economic climate and may range from incrementalism through revenue budgeting and zero-based budgeting to supplemental budgeting. Incremental budgeting occurs where resources are plentiful, existing budgetary baselines go virtually unchallenged, and the budget is steadily increased to pay for expansion and developments. Revenue budgeting occurs where resources are tight but unlikely to fall significantly below current levels, so that there is reasonable predictability as to the financial future of the organisation. Zero-based budgeting occurs when resources are scarce and the entire budget is subject to review. In supplemental budgeting there is not even an agreed annual budget which budget holders can control. Instead the budget is in effect built up throughout the year as individual items of expenditure are agreed by a central authority. Supplemental budgeting is fairly common in third world countries and is the complete negation of planning. Indeed under such conditions a long-term view becomes increasingly hard to sustain.

Yet distance education systems are frequently required as a matter of course to take decisions which will commit resources in advance of the budget settlement. As well as the kind the decisions mentioned in the previous section on planning, they are required to make financial provision for the purchase of stocks of materials (print, home experiment kits, etc.) which will then be consumed over several years (in the case of print and consumable materials in kits) or used for a number of years during the presentation of a particular course. The cost of providing sufficient stocks of materials for large population science courses with a home- or local centre-based experimental component can be considerable. The institution may have to pay for the stocks over several years if it cannot afford to meet this cost in a single year and if it is not allowed to hold money over from one budget year to another to pay for stocks. Certainly where publicly funded institutions are concerned it is unusual for them to be allowed to carry unspent budget balances forward against future commitments.

To ease the process of budgeting and identify the growing commitments to expenditure as they occur and in advance of the formal settlement of the budget, the institution needs to develop a financial model that will identify in broad terms the costs of its activities and project these forward against planned volumes. Where resources are plentiful relatively crude forecasting models can be used (such as, for example, the one used by the British Open University during the mid-1970s [described in chapter 4] and the approach adopted by Snowden and Daniel [1980:76-82] at Athabasca University). Where resources are less plentiful such simple approaches break down and prove inadequate (Rumble,

Neil and Tout, 1981:235). To deal with this problem the institution needs to develop means of costing its activities and programmes. As Rumble (1986:5) points out, this requires the prior identification of activities and programmes, which in itself may prove to be a difficult exercise, particularly where activities and outputs contribute to more than one programme, thus raising the problem of 'joint supply' (ibid.:23-7). Rumble (ibid.:11-17) discusses the practical problems of coding budgets and expenditure to allow costs to be analysed on a nominal basis by type of expenditure (salaries; premises, grounds and fixed plant; supplies and services; transport and movable plant; agency services, etc.); on a functional basis using Kaye and Rumble's systems-based model of distance education (materials development, production and delivery, teaching, administration, etc.); and on a programme basis related to outputs (teaching, by programme [undergraduate, postgraduate, community education, secondary, etc.] and course). Table 8.3 lists some of the typical costs incurred in the development, production and presentation of distance taught courses. The aim should be to assign the various costs to individual projects and courses within programmes (using spread sheet analysis) to provide 'activity costs' (ie. information on the total direct fixed and variable costs of each course or programme).

The activity costing model can be extended to cover overheads if this is felt to be desirable. Full absorption costing (in which all overheads are assigned to programmes or courses) is possible although not always very meaningful. There is certainly no absolutely right way of apportioning overheads. The best way is to assign indirect costs or overheads to cost centres, functional activities and programmes (as required) on the basis of the proportion of services that they consume. Common methods include the apportionment of overheads relative to the number of students, full-time equivalent students, staff, space, etc. which the primary unit has or utilises. Where this is not possible, the overheads may be assigned to cost centres, functional activities or programmes on the basis of that unit's share of the institution's total direct expenditure. Rumble (1986:58-60) discusses this problem in greater detail.

While full absorption costing may give an idea of the full costs of an activity, it should not be assumed that the closure of a programme or the development of a new one will automatically

Table 8.3

Typical costs incurred in the development, production and presentation of distance taught courses

Development phase#

Staff costs
  Academic, Secretarial, Editorial,
  Design, Course managers,
  Educational technologist
Academic consultants
External editing
External design
Development costs:
- Computer Assisted Instruction

- home experiment kits
- ancillary materials
Academic assessors
Discretionary and sundries
Developmental testing
- cost of materials
- payment to testers
- running expenses

Production phase

Print fixed costs*
- Keyboarding, film assembly,
  pre-press, machine make-ready,
  cover preparation, etc
- Copyright clearance
Television and video production*
Stocks of video-cassettes**

Radio and audio production*
Stocks of audio-cassettes**
Home experiment kit production*
Stocks of kits**
Ancillary materials production*
Ancillary materials stocks**

Presentation phase

Academic and other staff costs -
  course maintenance
Variable print costs (including stocks)
- Machine working, binding, paper,
  cover working, cover artboard, etc.
Cost of other materials provided each
year of presentation:
- Audio-cassettes
- video-cassettes
- filmstrips
- slides
- records
- scientific equipment and consumables
- textbooks
- maps
- other bought-in materials
Storage costs
Distribution and transmission

- packing costs
- postal costs
- carriage
- radio transmission
- television transmission
- broadcast repeat fees
Teaching costs:
- Tutor marked assignments
- Computer marked assignments
- Face-to-face tuition
- Telephone tuition
- Tutor training
- Examination centre hire
- Local centre hire
- Examinations invigilation
- Examinations script marking
- Laboratory hire
- Computer line charges

These costs may also be incurred during re-development
* including appropriate staffing costs
** where materials are returnable. Additional stocks costs may arise.

Based on Rumble, G. (1986) *Costing distance education*, London, Commonwealth Secretariat. Reproduced with permission.

lead to a reduction in all the overhead costs assigned to it, or to an across-the-board increase in its overheads. The development of new activities generally results in marginal changes in cost including the direct additional costs of the activity being expanded together with a possible increase in some overheads, the cost of the latter depending on the size of the increase in activity. Where activities are closed, direct variable costs will be saved with immediate effect, but fixed costs whether they are direct or indirect may not be so easy to reduce. Thus, for example, a reduction in the number of new courses under development and production will result in immediate savings in the direct variable costs of the activity (eg. cost of print, consultants, etc.), but, short of declaring permanent staff redundant, it will not immediately affect the 'fixed' costs of the staff employed to develop these courses. In the long run, though, all costs are variable and can be reduced. From a managerial point of view, and in general, it is the marginal change of cost arising from increases or reductions in the volume of activities that is important.

Conclusions

Planning is an essential part of the management of any distance education system. As this chapter has made clear, it needs to be conducted at a variety of levels - definition of mission, strategic and operational planning and budgeting - the higher levels defining the parameters for the lower one, while the lower levels should be consistent with the choices that have been made at the higher ones.

The plans should also be consistent with the broad financial situation facing the institution: at the strategic level they may reflect aspirations while not being wholly unrealisable; at the operational level they should be consistent with the funds available. This places a premium on financial forecasting. In certain situations this is extremely difficult if not impossible, either because the agency funding the distance education project is unable to give any assurances about its medium- and long-term financial prospects, or in situations where inflation is high. With so much of the budget effectively committed well in advance of the normal budget setting timetable (in order to meet production and delivery schedules), distance education systems can be peculiarly vulnerable to sudden cut-backs in expenditure. Given this, planners need to make explicit, through the use of financial models based on activity costing, the likely levels of costs tied up in particular programmes of activity and the timescales involved in the commitment of resources. They should also pay particular attention to the political climate within which the institution has to operate, ensuring that those responsible for allocating resources to support the institution have a good understanding of its needs.

Chapter Nine

ACADEMIC MANAGEMENT

Although the management of educational institutions has been the subject of many studies in recent years, the concept of management is by no means clear cut. Management can be defined as the judicious use of means to accomplish an end. It has also been defined as an activity involving responsibility for getting things done through people. In this book there is no attempt to define it more closely.

Various models of educational management have been advanced. These include, for example:

- The analytical-rational model. This model is premised on the assumption that management as a process involves the rational and systematic analysis of situations leading to the identification of possible courses of action, a subsequent exercise of choice between these, followed by implementation, monitoring and evaluation. It lays stress on planning, the identification of objectives, and the achievement of efficiency and effectiveness. The model is generally supported by and consistent with a systems approach.
- The pragmatic-rational model. This lays stress on management as a practical activity. It accepts that complete agreement on objectives is not always possible (although a broad consensus is presumed) and that decisions are not always taken on rational grounds. However, the process of policy-making itself is held to be more or less rational in that it moves through defined phases of formulation, determination and implementation. While policy has to be developed within the context of constraints (of which the

161

existing structure is one), the model presumes that change may be engineered through negotiation and gradual shifts in the allocation of resources.

• The hierarchical model. This model is characterised by a well-defined framework in which authority is conferred from above and there are recognisable chains of command, pre-determined regulations and procedures, and clearly-specified roles. It is common in the administration but may be found in academic departments under an autocratic head.

• The collegiate model. In collegiates, authority is subject to ratification from below, members enjoy equal rights in policy-making, decisions have to be exposed to possible dissent, and individuals are subject to minimal constraints. This model tends to be found in academic departments where there is reasonable uniformity of view and respect for consensus and democratic values. Academic staff are regarded as members of an association which 'cannot instruct [them] to undertake any particular activities other than obey the rules' (Jacques, 1976:92), and in which the necessary direction and control is achieved not through managerial accountability and controls but through group decisions taken by governing bodies made up of elected representatives (ibid.:345).

• The political model. This model assumes that conflict is endemic in organisations. It holds that there is no consensus within organisations as to goals and purposes. The institution is a collection of loosely-structured interest groups, authority is derived from personal power, and decisions are arrived at through a process of conflict which leads to the emergence of policies based on both democratically arrived at decisions and on compromise. Management is seen as a process of engaging in and regulating conflict through bargaining, negotiation and the exercise of power. At an initial stage emphasis is given to the formation of groups of individuals anxious to promote a commonly held policy. At a later stage the focus is on the management of decision-making organs, and particularly committees. The model may be found both at the departmental level and institutionally.

• The 'organised anarchy' model. This model stresses ambiguity of goals, fluid participation by individuals in the decision-making process, and lack of clarity as to means. In anarchical models, authority is eroded by external loyalties, individual autonomy is emphasised, there is a plurality of values which makes it difficult for managers to identify unambiguous goals or find ways of achieving such shared purposes as may exist, and influence is based on expertise. Management concentrates on securing certain minimal conditions for organisational survival and flexibility. Departments subject to ideological splits may exhibit these features, as may the institution as a whole where there is no strong central set of goals or authority.

The various models presented above provide perspectives from which the management of distance education systems can be analysed and then compared and contrasted with that of conventional educational systems. This is not to say that conventional educational institutions conform to a particular model. They do not. Indeed, elements of each model may be present in the same institution, at the same time, depending on circumstances. Nor is it just a question of identifying the different tasks undertaken by managers in distance education - an aspect discussed in the next chapter where the management of distance education systems is related to production and operations management. It is far more a question of trying to identify whether particular management and leadership models or styles are more or less suitable in distance education systems than others, and whether distance education systems on balance exhibit different features to those found in conventional educational institutions.

Management and leadership in distance education systems

The question arises whether traditional forms of academic management can be transferred from their conventional to a distance education setting. Clearly, distance education systems exhibit a range of features not found in conventional ones which make their management qualitatively different (Kaye and Rumble, 1981:177). These include their use of instructional media with a concomitant requirement for specialist staff, the quasi-industrial processes of production and distribution, and the distance between themselves and their students which requires access to reliable and rapid means of communication for administrative and teaching purposes. The sections which follow discuss a number of aspects related to the management of distance education systems.

The management of materials development

While teachers in conventional educational systems do rely on professional administrative and support areas to provide a range of services (for example, audio-visual materials, photocopies, access to rooms, purchasing, etc.), they exercise almost complete control over the process of teaching. Most decisions are localised and have very little impact outside the department in which they are taken. Departments (or schools or faculties) retain complete control over the teaching/learning process.

In a few cases - notably in very small departmentally-based distance teaching systems (for example, the kind of system that was initially developed within the School of Education at the University of the South Pacific and in the Department of Physics at the University of Waterloo, Ontario) the department also retains overall control over the whole process of teaching students at a distance. Generally, however, academic departments do not control the whole development - production - distribution - teaching process in distance education systems. Instead a 'collective' of functionally distinct departments, both academic and non-academic, together have responsibility for the realisation of the teaching programme.

Individual subject areas may still be organised on departmental and faculty/school lines similar to those found in conventional systems, with full-time permanent academic staff and with academic leadership of the subject area (both of teaching and where appropriate of research) vested in a head of department. In some distance teaching institutions, for example, the Fernuniversität in the Federal Republic of Germany, control over the development of distance teaching materials is vested in traditional academic departments led by a Professor (although much of the material is actually written by outside consultants). In others, the British Open University is perhaps the best known example, responsibility for the development of courses has been vested in 'course teams' made up of academic and other staff drawn from a number of faculties and non-academic departments.

In yet others there may be no academic departments in the generally accepted meaning of the term. For example, the Universidad Estatal a Distancia in Costa Rica uses contract staff to prepare course materials, and hence differs from other (conventional) Costa Rican universities in that it is not organised in schools or departments.

The organisation and management of the development and production of instructional materials is a difficult area. Stone (1975) suggests that there are four different approaches:

• In the specialised approach the various tasks involved in the development and production of instructional materials are allocated to professional staff. In the first stage the educators do the curriculum planning and define the contents. The communicators then write the scripts. Finally the studio staff record the programmes. Each specialist works on his or her own tasks, the analogy being with an assembly line.

• In the chain approach the discontinuities and lack of integration of the specialist approach is overcome to some extent by ensuring that each specialist participates in both the stage immediately prior to and that immediately after his or her own.

• In the interdisciplinary team approach, persons from different specialisms are brought together and given join responsibility for the overall development and production o the materials or course.

• In the matrix approach 'projects' are staffed by borrowing appropriate specialists from functional departments to perform specific tasks on the project. The head of each functional area retains responsibility for the quality of the work done by the specialist staff assigned to the project, while the project manager has responsibility for ensuring that the project is completed on time and that overall coordination is achieved.

The main problems with the specialist approach are those of discontinuity of work, poor communication between the specialists, and the fact that there is no integrated overview of the project. Its apparent efficiencies may be negated by the fact that the quality of the product can be impaired. The chain approach attempts to ameliorate the compartmentalism of the specialist

165

approach.

Initially the Universidad Nacional Abierta (Venezuela) adopted a specialist type approach towards course development. Curriculum designers, instructional designers, media experts and evaluation experts were involved in turn in the design of aspects of each course leading up to the preparation of a brief for the academic content specialists. The latter wrote materials to a design which they had not been instrumental in agreeing. The draft texts were then given to the instructional design team for vetting and transformation into self-instructional distance-teaching format. It seems that there were two extreme responses to this situation: academic content specialists either ignored the instructions and wrote what they considered to be better texts, handing these over for production at a stage when there was nothing which the instructional designers could do about it short of cancelling the course, or they accepted the instructions and wrote texts which they personally felt to be inappropriate and to which they had lost any sense of commitment (Rumble, 1981c:188). Similarly, at the Universidad Estatal a Distancia in Costa Rica, a specialist Office of Curriculum Design within the Planning Vice-rectorate prepares a curriculum plan for each professional degree programme and its constituent courses. The Academic Vice-rectorate working through Academic Producers in the various subject areas identifies and contracts external specialists to write the course books. Their draft texts are vetted at various stages by the Academic Producers, who serve as both editors and educational technologists, transforming the materials into distance teaching texts. Assessment and examination papers are then prepared by Tutor Coordinators within the Academic Vice-rectorate. A particular weakness of this system arose from the fact that neither the authors (contracted by the Academic Vice-rectorate but working to a specification laid down by an Office within the Planning Vice-rectorate) nor the Tutor Coordinators (working in the Academic Vice-rectorate on assessment and examinations questions designed to test the objectives laid down by the Curriculum Planners), actually met the Curriculum Designers. As a result neither the Curriculum Planners nor the authors had an appreciation of the teaching processes (Rumble, 1981c:188-9).

Both the Universidad Estatal a Distancia and the Universidad Nacional Abierta exhibited a tendency to structure their organisations in terms of the linear flow-charts with which they portrayed on paper the processes of course development, production and distribution. In practice those involved in the work cannot operate in compartmentalised boxes, but the organisation was constructed as if this was the case. In both universities the problem was recognised at an early stage and resolved through the establishment of informal lines of communication at the Universidad Estatal a Distancia and the introduction of the concept of Integrated Design Units (Unidadés Integradas de Diseño) - in effect small course teams - at the Universidad Nacional Abierta.

In any system relying on academic editors to 'rework' material prepared by an external contract author, the role of the editor is crucial. At both the Fernuniversität (Smith, 1980:65) and the Universidad Estatal a Distancia the materials seem to be more subject-orientated than student-orientated. In other words, 'matters of course design seem to play a smaller part and the influence of instructional designers is less apparent' (Smith, 1980:65). One possible way of solving this kind of problem is the 'transformer model' which has been advocated by Macdonald-Ross and Waller (1969) and Waller (1977/8). They envisaged a team of subject experts supported by an educational technologist who would decide on the subject matter of the course and then produce course outlines and, possibly, draft texts. The products of their work would then be handed over to a second team of transformers who would consist of subject matter specialists, educational technologists, broadcast producers, editors, graphic designers, and course managers, some of whom must have been members of the first team. The subject matter experts drawn into the second team would be teaching-orientated, whereas some of those in the first team would be research-orientated and would not wish to join the second team. The second team would convert the outline materials and drafts into a complex multi-media course that teaches effectively. Whether the system would work satisfactorily or not is an open question, as it has not to date been adopted by any distance education system.

The course team approach might be seen as an answer to many of these problems. It was pioneered by the British Open University and has since been adopted in modified form in institutions such as Athabasca University, Deakin University, and the Universidad Nacional Abierta.

The origin of the course team approach sprang from the conviction that the content and teaching of each Open University course could not be left to the whim of the individual department or academic member of staff (Perry, 1976:83). It was also clear that no single individual could produce interdisciplinary courses of the length envisaged by the British Open University (equivalent to either 225 or 450 hours of student work). The result was the course team concept. Essentially each Open University team consists of a number of subject matter experts (from 3 to 20, but typically of 5 to 10 members), one of whom is appointed course team chairman, an educational technologist, and a BBC producer, an editor, a staff tutor (responsible for tutorial services in one of the University's regions), and a course administrator. Some of the material may be written by outside consultants. Secretaries, designers, technicians, librarians, project control staff (concerned with the scheduling of the materials' development, production, distribution and use by students) and accountants provide support in specialist fields but are not members of the team. The BBC (British Broadcasting Corporation) producers, while full-members of the team, remain ultimately responsible to their line manager within the BBC's Open University Production Centre, and the BBC formally clears their work before it is presented to the course team for approval.

The course team approach adopted by the British Open University mixes the interdisciplinary team and matrix approaches identified by Stone, in the sense that the academic members are given joint responsibility for the development of the course while many of the non-academic members are 'lent' to the project but remain ultimately responsible to their professional management.

Perry (1976:91) has claimed that 'the concept of the course team is the single most important contribution of the Open University to teaching practice' and that 'a course produced by this method will inevitably tend to be superior in quality to any course produced by an individual' (ibid.:91), but he has also admitted that it is an expensive way of developing materials and can only be justified if the materials are going to be used by large number of students.

Analysing the factors which favour the course team approach, Northcott (1978:20, 22) mentioned (1) the project based nature of course development, (2) the need to bring in educational technologists to help academics write good materials, (3) the inter-disciplinary nature of many of the early Open University courses, (4) the need to integrate the broadcasts and printed materials, (5) the size of the task - many people were needed to develop an Open University course in the timescales available, and (6) the fact that innovation and creativity is encouraged by group interaction within course teams.

The way course teams work varies enormously. Perry (1976:85-6) commented that in some subject areas at the British Open University (particularly the arts and social sciences) academic course team members write texts, circulate them for comment, receive and consider comments, and then revise their work - retaining their personal responsibility for the finished product and deciding which critical comments to take account of in their revisions. In other subjects (notably science and mathematics) the draft texts, although prepared by an individual, are considered to be the product of the whole team, and each one is approved by the team before it is passed on to production. Here the finished product can be the work of many hands.

Working in a course team can be very stressful. Perry (1976:86) noted the occurrence at times of bitter and acrimonious argument, particularly at the stage when the course syllabus and content are being defined. Studying course teams at the British Open University, the Tavistock Institute spoke of them as having a harrowing, destructive and punitive environment which engendered great psychological stress. Nicodemus (1984) provides further evidence of conflict within an Open University course team, while Linder and Lonsdale (1975) noted that at the Rocky Mountain Satellite Demonstration (STD):

> time constraints made it impossible to achieve consensus among team members across team lines. The democratic organisation implicit in the theoretical structure of the courseware team concept requires time; time, however, became an unaffordable luxury at the STD ... The people who did not adapt had several reactions. Some reacted defensively; they attempted to form cliques and garner support among other team members. Others reacted aggressively; they tried to attack the other team members' integrity, knowledge and products. Still others reacted indifferently; they tried to

ignore the requisite process by acting unilaterally.

Drake (1979:50) has claimed that course teams are 'a menace to the academic output and reputation of the Open University - where good courses have been produced and maintained, this has been in spite of rather than because of it'. Mason (1976:32) noted that 'a feeling of hopelessness is quite frequent in my experience of course teams'. On the other hand, others have found it to be a valuable experience and the method has its defenders (Blowers, 1979; Costello, 1979).

In a number of institutions course teams transcend traditional patterns of seniority and departmental affiliation. In the Open University senior academics may work as members on a course team chaired by a relatively junior member of staff. This can cause problems (Gough, 1978:32-3). For instance, 'if the chairman of the team is a junior member of staff, it can cause severe dissonance if a senior team member insists on being senior' (Crick, 1980:133). Perry (1976:90) was convinced that course team chairmen should be appointed for their managerial skills. The role of the course team chairman is crucial to the operation of the course team. However, course team chairmen rarely get much training in managing groups. Northcott (1978:24), warning of the danger of course teams degenerating into committees, mentions evidence supporting the use of nominal group technique (NGT) and Delphi technique to keep the team process vigorous.

Since course team chairmen may have no authority outside the team, and indeed outside it may be subordinate to some of their team members, leadership depends on the moral authority which the chairman can exercise. The personal qualities of the chairman are also important. A disorganised chairman can lead to a team that is disorganised. This raises questions about who should be a course team chair. Some institutions believe that the team should elect its own chairman, thus conferring legitimacy and moral authority on its choice, but such elections could themselves be divisive. Others (eg. the University of Mid-America) believed that the chairman should be a non-academic, an idea that finds favour with some (eg. Mitchell, 1978:2).

The academic members of course teams should be experts in their field since it is on the quality of their work that the institution will be judged. Dodds (1983:105) stresses three main qualities that are required of academics in distance education systems: subject expertise, teaching ability, and writing skills. There may however be other qualities that are needed. Academics often find it hard to work in a quasi-industrial environment where it may be necessary to cooperate with non-academic colleagues and defer to their expertise; accept the judgements and criticisms of academic colleagues in respect of their own work; adhere to production timetables; and be cost conscious and remain within budget. A tactless remark can lead non-academics to withdraw their good will, to the detriment of the course. The strain of working to deadlines can be considerable. Newey (1975:49), writing from the basis of his experience in Open University course teams, says that 'as deadlines approach, each member of the team has his own problems to worry about, and even though the will may be there, he becomes less and less inclined to read and comment on his colleagues' draft [texts] - and even to attend course team meetings'. Mason (1976:33) remarks on the fact that academics are so dominated by deadlines 'that any sense of the whole [course] is dissipated by the time the course is half finished', while towards the end, with the project winding down, it is the case that 'sometimes only the editor and chairman even know that [the course] is finished'. Fear of criticism can lead people to submit their drafts late - so that the choice is between having an unvetted text or no text at all (Crick, 1980:134). The feeling that someone on the team is not pulling their weight can cause friction. Equally, individuals may withdraw from the team if they feel that other members lack confidence in them or that their work is being unduly criticised. Psychologically, course team life can seem like a production treadmill, engendering tiredness and a consequential fall in standards. Personal qualities are important. A course team can seem a liberating experience, or a prison in which the 'academic-prisoner' suffers intolerable inroads into personal freedom of intellectual activity (Crick, 1980:133-4).

This suggests that course teams do not always achieve their objective of integration. Certainly they may facilitate the integration of staff by providing a structure in which the various specialists can work as a group, thus transcending the discontinuities that normally exist between the work of one specialist or group of specialists and another. They will not, however, necessarily transcend the boundaries between roles which can occur where there are major discontinuities in technology. Miller (1959) equates discontinuities of technology with differences in the material means of the production process, the skills required of individuals for the perfomance of given tasks, and techniques. The greater the discontinuity of technologies, the stronger are the forces towards differentiation. This is particularly true if the skills of some members of the group are so specialised that others cannot aspire to them, so that some interchange of roles (or even any real understanding of roles) between members of the total group becomes impossible or impractical.

The notion of distinctive competencies is present in any organisation using a number of technologies, where the organisational structure is built up around clusters of specialised skills and equipment. These differences can often be exaggerated by the people most directly involved, so that the preservation of 'role-distinctiveness' becomes a primary aim of specialist staff (Rumble, 1981c:190). Stone (1975) noted that even where teams were established, 'usually the team ends up dividing the tasks according to the background and interests of the members, which is just a reversion to the specialist approach'. The task of the team leader must be to ensure that these tendencies do not develop, as they can sometimes do, to the point at which they become destructive.

Rumble (1981c:189) argued that the best course team approach allows for a flexible response to the varying tasks involved in the development of materials, while Stone and Oliveira (1980), studying professional conflict in the production organisations at seven Brazilian educational television systems, concluded that the fewer the tasks the average staff member performed in a given project (ie. the more specialised the division of labour), the greater the conflict in that project. They also found that ambiguity about final responsibilities and about the criteria for performance evaluation also increased conflict. These findings led McAnany, Oliviera, Orivel and Stone (1982:345-6) to suggest that there are strong arguments against organisational structures where roles are highly defined. They felt that Rumble's observations presented compelling arguments against a high level of role definition. Ambiguity is clearly a problem, but it can be solved by taking a flexible attitude towards the professional roles of staff working on the project in the assignment of duties, while making it clear, once agreement on roles has been reached, who individually is responsible for carrying out specific tasks.

Generally, the notion of distinctive competencies can be more or less encouraged or inhibited through the conscious structuring of the organisation and of the tasks which individuals undertake. If jobs are closely designed and if staff work along 'assembly line' models, then the inherent divisions in their roles will be accentuated and the essential co-dependence of tasks will be obscured. Anyone concerned with the management of distance education must consider means by which cross-functional integration can be achieved. There are a number of ways of achieving this - project teams, working groups, the appointment of persons with specific responsibilities for coordination. At least in respect of the development of materials and their integration into the teaching process, the course team approach, notwithstanding its drawbacks, does seem to be a good way of achieving cross-functional integration.

The management of student services

Not all distance education systems provide their students with support services. Some may only register and examine them. However, the vast majority do provide some form of backup in the form of tutorial, counselling and advisory services. This support may be provided in a number of different ways - through face-to-face contact, by telephone, and by correspondence.

From a managerial point of view the problem is that many of these services are likely to be provided at a distance from the student. The capacity of distance teaching systems to provide a great deal of face-to-face tuition and support is limited, not least by cost considerations. However, some systems do provide face-to-face tutorial support to students through local centres. In other systems there are no local centres. Quite often the tutor is only a script marker (as in pure correspondence systems). In more sophisticated systems, tutors fulfil other roles (advisory, counselling) but again these services are often provided at a distance.

All contact at a distance raises questions about the effectiveness of the communications systems which have to be solved. It also raises questions about the capability of the institution to check on the quality of the service being provided - a factor of particular importance where tutors are grading students' work. Furthermore, if an element of face-to-face tuition is provided, it makes sense for the tutors to be recruited locally. This means that the institution not only has problems of communicating with its distance students, but also with its equally distant tutors; and it has the added problem of ensuring that these 'remote' tutors are serving the needs of the students adequately.

A further problem is that there may be a divide between those who develop the teaching materials and those who are responsible for helping students to study. True, in some small distance teaching systems academic staff are responsible for both developing the material and teaching the students. Even in the British Open University there are some small guided-study courses which are developed by an individual academic (who produces reading lists and some limited course notes) who then tutors the course. The number of students on such courses is necessarily small (from 20 to 30) and the fact that the students can be distributed throughout the country effectively rules out any face-to-face tuition. Generally, however, distance education courses are developed with large numbers of students in mind, and those who develop them simply cannot also tutor all the students on 'their' course.

Some institutions encourage the central materials developers to do some tutoring. At the Universidad Nacional Abierta the full-time staff travel out to local centres to undertake some tutoring, but the majority of the work is done by part-time tutors. In other institutions (the Open University is an example) nearly all tutoring is done by part-time staff who have not been involved in the development of a course. Given the scale of the programme this is inevitable, and it is then incumbent on the institution to train and induct its part-time tutorial staff. What is less understandable is the failure of some institutions to *require* their full-time staff to be involved in the teaching process, either through tutoring a group of students (both face-to-face and by correspondence) or to be involved in examination boards. The reason why this is surprising is that the division of responsibilities leads to the creation of a functional barrier which need not exist (at least to the extent that it does) and which severely limits the experience of the materials development staff.

Some of the problems of 'quality control' over the work of 'remote' tutors can be solved through the appointment of full-time senior tutors who may both (as in the British Open University) represent the 'teaching' view to course teams developing a new course and also supervise the work of the part-time tutors in the field. Supervision may involve visiting tutors when they are conducting face-to-face sessions and also operating a system whereby scripts marked by the tutors are intercepted on a random sampling basis (and if necessary by exception) to check on the quality of the feedback given by the tutors. Where necessary the senior tutors should intervene to correct faults, solve problems, and provide training in areas of weakness.

In institution-centred models, the purposes of group learning are laid down by the institution. The tutor's role is to support learners' efforts to master objectives that have been determined by the institution through the study of materials that it has provided. The objective of management is both to facilitate this process and to ensure that it happens.

This approach contrasts strongly with the organisation and role of groups in society-centred models. Here groups come together in response to pressing problems in the community (community action) or to effect change in the community (community development). The groups determine the problems which will be tackled, the adult educator acting as a facilitator. The educator may in fact support the work of many groups. Lovett (1982:128) found when working on the Liverpool Educational Priority Area Project that the crucial issue was the organisation of learning in the community. His experience suggested that the adult educator should be at the centre of a network of existing organisations involved in community development and education, acting as a 'network agent'. This is very different to the hierarchical organisational structure found in the management of institution-centred group learning, where tutors are responsible to an institution for what they do and are expected to work within defined limits. Lovett would regard such hierarchical structures as inappropriate in the kind of community development programmes with which he has been involved.

Managing the interface between academic and operational areas

The process of education at a distance cannot be divorced from the operational and logistical services that support it. Rather it is heavily dependent on and constrained by them. As Daniel and Snowden (1979:218) said, 'the management of [distance] learning requires the creation of a complex and interdependent system that needs constant administrative attention and teamwork'. This has a profound effect on decision making because, even where policy making is formally vested in representative committees whose membership is largely academic, the administrative and operational areas of the system define the technical boundaries and constraints within which decisions can be made. Informal decision-making processes in which administrative staff play a crucial role, may well identify the parameters within which decisions can be made before issues are put to formal academic committees. Inevitably this leads to situations in which instructional staff may see their autonomy threatened (Snowden and Daniel, 1980:88).

Certainly the functional divisions found in distance education systems affect the pattern of decision-making and the distribution of effective power between teaching and administrative staff. The organisational structures established to support materials development, production and distribution, the administration of students and the organisation of the teaching-learning process, are markedly different to those found in conventional educational institutions, and bring into the decision-making forum a range of managers drawn from non-academic areas of the institution.

Where tasks and technologies are well defined and jobs are specialised, coordination can be achieved through established plans, procedures and line management. The consensual and democratic models of policy formulation commonly found in areas formulating academic policy are quite inappropriate to the management of materials production and distribution processes.

The experience of the British Open University is germane to the point. Initially there was an elaborate committee structure coordinated by an 'Operations Board' to oversee the whole area of production and distribution, the purpose of which was to ensure that these areas were subject to academic control. Quite early on, however, the concept of academic control over these areas came to be seen as inappropriate and most of the committees including the Board were swept away. The detailed day-to-day management of operational units was then left to departmental managers (publishing, design, audio-visual, mailing services, warehouse) who reported to the Vice-Chancellor on a regular basis through a newly established post of Director of Operations. The whole 'flavour' of the area is one of production and operations management.

The assumption that distance education systems are in some ways 'more managerial' than conventional ones can nevertheless be overstressed. While hierarchic values may dominate the decision-making process in materials production and distribution areas, those charged with managing the staff developing course materials or organising local groups, particularly in systems providing social-action orientated community education programmes, are as likely to rely on consensual and democratic methods of leadership. It is precisely here that the problem lies since these styles of leadership tend to result in continual shifts in policy as each new group developing or teaching a course seeks to adapt or develop solutions that will satisfy their members.

This essentially localised, departmentally-based process of formulating policy is consistent with practice in conventional educational establishments, where decisions which affect the whole institution tend to be avoided or couched in ways that permit a variety of interpretations. In universities in the United States and Britain, for example, there is frequently no common supra-departmental policy on admissions or study requirements, nor is this felt to be a problem. The role of the professional administration is to keep a watching brief over the activities of largely autonomous departments and, where necessary, to initiate requests that departments meet minimal central requirements. Even within the department there may be little attempt to manage the teaching process. What happens within the classroom, in terms of the definition of learning goals, content, pacing and the assessment of students, is left to the discretion of the individual academic. Similarly, in schools individual teachers may have considerable local autonomy in respect of how they teach.

In distance education systems, however, departments cannot normally determine unilaterally how the teaching process is to work. At the British Open University Perry saw the problem in terms of differentiation between policy formulation (the preserve of the academic sitting in committee) and policy implementation (1976:221): 'Academics, jealous of their rights as the supreme academic authority, tend to want to retain control of the implementation as well as of the formulation of policy ... and to be hesitant about delegating decision-making about implementation, save in routine and trivial matters, to administrators over whom they feel they have no control' (ibid.:212-13).

While there is an element of what might be referred to as the academic desire to keep their fingers in every pie, the problem is more fundamental than this. Institutionally either administrative and operational areas have to be strengthened to match proliferating academic goals and objectives, or else those goals have to be constrained. The first raises questions about resources for non-academic areas while the second raises questions about the managerial and leadership capabilities of the institutional head. Unless they are checked, academic goals will tend to proliferate, creating a diversity of teaching/learning models each requiring different systems to develop, produce and distribute them, and each reliant on different transactional patterns in terms of the interaction between students, intermediaries, and student administration and services.

Within the decentralised departmental structures common to conventional education, where student numbers on any course are often small and there is a direct correlation between the number of academic staff (the 'managers' of the teaching/learning process) and students, a proliferation of models can usually be accommodated.

In distance eduction where students are dealt with *en masse* (ie. excluding small scale individual-centred systems), this is not possible. The head of a distance education institution must ensure that the policy proposals put forward by academic areas are capable of implementation by administrative and operational areas with which academics may have little sympathy or understanding. It is the management of this interface between the academic and the administrative and operational areas that is crucial. Styles of leadership which work in the management of academic departments may be quite inappropriate for the management of this interface. Generally speaking distance education systems require tighter management than is commonly found in conventional educational institutions (Snowden and Daniel, 1980:86) and have an unusually strong need for good leadership (ibid.:88). Again, the management of the operations and administrative areas will need to be hierarchic, rather than collegial, and analytical-rational/pragmatic-rational rather than overtly political or anarchic. The overall conclusion must be that certain styles of management found in conventional educational institutions are not conducive to the good management of distance education systems.

Institutional Leadership

The success of innovative projects depends on strong leadership during their early development, not only to move from vision to reality, but also to ensure political backing. Strong leadership has been noted as a factor in the El Salvador ETV project, the SACI/EXERN project in Brazil, and the Fundação Maranhense de Televisão Educativa project, also in Brazil (McAnany, Oliveira, Orivel and Stone, 1982:347). Strong leadership was also in evidence at institutions such as the British Open University, the Universidad Nacional Abierta in Venezuela, the Universidad Estatal a Distance in Costa Rica, the Sukhothaithammathirat Open University in Thailand, and at Athabasca University.

McAnany et al. (1982:347) suggest that there is a contradiction between innovation and institutionalisation, and that 'charismatic leadership must become institutionalised if the cause it espouses is to survive'. It is certainly the case that as organisations increase in size so the top job-holders cease to be able to control policy formulation and execution at any level of detail, and instead need to rely more on formal documentation and standard procedures, rather than personal supervision, to coordinate activities and maintain control.

At the Universidad Estatal a Distancia, the first Rector, Dr. F. Pacheco, initially retained a tight control over decision-making. Corporate management of the University was exercised through the weekly meetings of the Rector's Council, which consisted of the Rector and his three Vice-Rectors (Academic, Planning and Administrative). Below this level, each Vice-rector had a weekly meeting with their office heads. Only in very rare cases did specialist subordinate staff attend the Rector's Council to provide direct advice, and it was also rare for staff from one vice-rectorate to attend the meetings of another vice-rectorate. The management of the institution was strongly hierarchical, with very few committees. While this made for speedy decision-making, there was little cross-functional integration, and the work of those committees that existed was undermined because they were wholly advisory, and since neither the Rector nor the Vice-rectors attended them, their status was low. Committee members also lacked any sense of collective responsibility, with the result that it was not uncommon for disaffected members to try to overturn recommendations through the exercise of their influence within the hierarchical structure (Rumble, 1981d:34-6). Some of the problems arising from the lack of cross-functional integration at the Universidad Estatal a Distancia have already been noted.

Perry (1976:225) comments on the way in which the British Open University as it grew in size changed from 'a very tightly controlled and centrally organised institution, to a much more diffuse one with a much wider spread of authority and a consequent lack of tightness', with the consequential loss of personal control that this entailed. Whereas coordination had been achieved largely through weekly meetings of a Vice-Chancellor's Committee and monthly meetings of the Senate, with policy very largely being developed in short-lived working groups, by 1971 a more formal committee structure was being established, enabling greater representation and participation to occur, but also slowing down the rate at which business could be agreed.

Such developments are altogether healthy: problems arise where they do not occur, as at the El Salvador ETV project where the Minister of Education, Walter Beneke, retained close day-to-day control over decisions, so that 'most division leaders were, in fact, dependent on the Minister's judgement and reluctant to act on matters without his approval. This tendency impeded problem solving at lower administrative levels and retarded communication and cooperation between divisions' (Mayo et al., 1976). On the other hand, there is a balance to be struck between the proper representation of all views and the need for clear sighted direction of policy towards agreed goals and objectives. Too great a reliance on government by committee can be equally bad.

Conclusions

This chapter began by considering the management of educational institutions. No attempt was made closely to define management as an activity, nor the work of managers. Also, in spite of the title given to this chapter, there are a whole range of managerial functions which are dealt with in other parts of the book, including those of deciding on the structure of the organisation (chapter 6), defining work roles (chapter 7), planning and particularly the identification of goals and objectives (chapter 8), production and operations management (chapter 10), budgetary control (chapter 8), and the evaluation and monitoring of performance (chapter 11).

This chapter has been concerned more with issues related to leadership and the management of staff involved in key areas - particularly the development of materials and the support of student learning - and the management of the interface between the academic and operational and administrative areas of distance education systems. Management, it is suggested, needs to ensure integrated decision making across a range of functionally distinct areas. This can best be achieved through joint decision making processes which involve both academics and operational and administrative staff. It is also most likely to be achieved by rational and possibly hierarchical approaches to management, rather than by approaches which tolerate collegiality, politicization and organised anarchy. This does not mean that these latter models are not found in distance education systems. They may well be present, but the overall management of the institution must be both stronger and more rationally orientated than is necessarily the case in conventional educational institutions.

Chapter Ten

PRODUCTION/OPERATIONS MANAGEMENT

A major function of management in any education system is to ensure that students are taught in accordance with agreed plans. These plans include the basic scheduling of classes, tutorials, lectures and examinations. In distance education systems management also has to ensure that the materials required by the students reach them on time. This involves planning, scheduling and managing the materials development, production and distribution subsystems.

In business these tasks are covered by the terms 'production management' and 'operations management', the two terms being synonymous in that they describe the management of the resources required to produce the goods (production management in a manufacturing company) or provide the services (operations management in a non-manufacturing company) to be sold. Distance education systems are normally involved in both the manufacturing of materials and the provision of services.

Goods are tangible items which can be purchased and used. Services are intangible, consumed at the time of being provided, with the customer taking away or retaining the benefit of that service. The students of a distance education system will both take away goods (eg. teaching texts, audio-cassettes) and make use of the services that are provided (tutorials, assignment correction, etc.). Some of the goods that are produced by the institution will be used internally to provide a service to the students. For example, the tape of a television programme may be used by the institution to provide a service (a transmitted television programme). Similarly some of the services provided by the institution's departments may be used internally to support the

182

manufacturing process. Thus the editorial and graphic design departments are providing services to the materials producers which enhance the quality of the eventual goods that are produced.

The task of production and operations management is complex involving design and development, the planning of capacity against forecast requirements (orders), the layout of production facilities, the method of working, the acquisition of materials, the process of manufacturing and/or providing the service, the delivery of the product or service, and the control of quality.

Production management

The previous chapter discussed inter alia the management of the academic process of materials development and of the interface between academic areas and production and distribution departments. This section of the chapter is concerned with the process of production management in distance education systems: that is, with the production and subsequent distribution of the learning materials which students make use of during their studies. This includes (1) in respect of print, copy editing, design, page layout, print preparation, printing, collation, and binding, (2) the production of audio-visual materials including production of master tapes etc. and subsequent production and distribution of copies, (3) the production and assembly of items of equipment, (4) packing and (5) despatch. Where items are lent to students, it includes their receipt at the end of the term or year (when the students have finished with them), and their checking, refurbishment and repacking prior to use by the next batch of students.

Design specification

The design of the various items of material will need to be agreed and specified. The design of printed materials will need to take account of size, the number of pages per binding, the method of binding, page layout, the use of illustrations, typography, and so on. The design of home experiment kit materials will need to take account of safety aspects in respect of carriage and use, labelling and packaging requirements, etc. Design will also need to take account of questions of house style, the ease with which the material can be used by students (either in the home, office or local centre), and (at least in respect of electrical components and chemical apparatus), safety. Those developing and producing the materials will need to ensure that the design specification is being followed.

Specialisation of products

Distance education systems share many of the characteristics of manufacturing and service industries, but in one respect the task of production and operations management is made infinitely harder, and this is in respect of the question of standardisation. Industrial manufacturing is based on product standardisation. The principle of standardisation is to reduce the number of components or materials required to provide the range of products or services which are being sold. This allows costs to be reduced by lowering holdings of components and materials, longer production runs, and bulk purchasing.

Generally speaking, while distance education systems may manage to purchase materials in bulk (eg. paper, blank audio-cassettes), a large number of 'products' (in the form of items of course material) are needed to support a range of courses. In spite of superficial similarities in respect of, for example, the format of printed materials, the number of 'titles' of course texts, audio-cassettes, video-cassettes, items of ancillary materials, etc. is likely to be considerable. More significantly, their number is likely to grow rapidly as an institution develops and begins to present more and more specialised courses.

The more specialised the courses, the fewer students they are likely to attract, with the result that production runs tend to reduce in length. It may be possible to produce materials to meet the needs of a specific course over a number of years, thus increasing the production run by, for example, printing to meet likely student demand for a number of years. The benefits of doing this, however, have to be weighed against the fact that this makes it virtually impossible to change the materials in, say, the second year of presenting a course, without either dumping unused stock or adding to the material going to students in the form of errata slips and so on. Also, materials stockpiled for future years have to be stored properly and the costs of this taken into account.

Production/operations management

Product identification

The number of items developed and produced for a course can be significant, including major texts, supplementary items of printed material, audio-cassettes, items of equipment, substances for inclusion in home experiment kits, and so on. The production, distribution and refurbishment of all of these items will need to be monitored. As a result each item will need to have a distinct code assigned to it which provides a basis for production scheduling, stock control and distribution.

Demand

Some estimate of demand is required so that the requisite number of copies of each item of course material can be ordered and provision made for storage. It is difficult to forecast student demand for particular courses accurately, although previous experience may give some guidance where the institution has offered courses of a similar level in a similar subject area before (eg. final year literature courses). Estimates of demand can nevertheless be seriously wrong. Obviously, overproduction is something which needs to be avoided, but equally no one likes turning students away because stocks of materials are insufficient to meet demand. Sometimes, however, this is unavoidable - for example, where a course is in its final year of presentation and it would be very costly to run off a few additional copies, or where particular items of equipment that are loaned to students are very expensive or capacity is limited (eg. places at residential schools). In such cases a quota may need to be imposed on the number of students taking a course.

Capacity planning

Medium- to long-term requirements in respect of production, storage and distribution need to be established to enable staffing and space requirements to be properly planned. Institutional capacity may relate to the number of people employed (eg. editors, designers), the capacity of the equipment carrying out the process (eg. audio-cassette copying capacity), the facilities available (eg. number of studio-days available), and the size of the building (eg. pallet spaces in the warehouse). The production manager's task is to ensure that the volume of materials arising from a given range of courses is accurately predicted and scheduled to ensure that the production capacity is not exceeded. If the capacity of the internal production units is likely to be exceeded, arrangements need to be made to send material out to external producers.

Production planning and control

Once a course has been approved, the number of items of materials which it will require needs to be specified and its production planned. Materials production is a complex task. A major function of production management is to schedule the production, ensuring that the materials are delivered to the students in time for their use. Various forms of network have been developed to control production. It is likely that relatively sophisticated methods such as network analysis will need to be used. A detailed example of an early attempt to develop a production network for the preparation of materials for one British Open University course appears in Lewis (1971a:115-23). Lewis also comments on the problems that occur when, because of pressures of time, certain elements in a course have to be agreed in respect of their contents or form before other elements have been devised and written (Lewis, 1971b:192-3). For example, moulded polystyrene packaging may need to be designed before all the contents of a home experiment kit have been agreed. Obviously such instances should be minimised.

Where a task is completed by a single individual, or uses an integrated facility such as a studio, the loading, sequencing and scheduling tasks are simplified. In such cases a typical scheduling solution is to use a bar chart which provides an overall picture of the assignments loaded, the estimated completion of tasks, and the availability of staff or facilities to take on more work. Gantt charts may also be used.

Adequate time must be allowed for each activity to take place, culminating in a situation in which all the materials required for a particular package are ready and available for packing prior to distribution to the students. Lewis (1971b: 194-6), while recognising the utility of critical path analysis and associated techniques such as bar charts and Gantt Charts as a means of scheduling production, concludes that it is 'most unfortunate that these methods are almost totally inapplicable to the Open University's course production problems' (ibid.:194-5). The reasons which he gave for this conclusion were as follows (ibid.:195-6):

- there is no unique way of breaking down the overall course production task into distinct and clear-cut sequences. The way the work is approached can vary significantly. (This is generally the case during the design phase, but less true at the production phase, where critical path methods may be more useful.)
- for any breakdown that might be proposed, it is often impossible to assign meaningful time estimates to many of the subtasks. A conceptual model of a course, for example, may be prepared in a matter of minutes or hours, or take many weeks of discussion. (However, at the production stage, it is more likely that it will be possible to assign times to activities, thus making the application of critical path methods more likely.)
- it is not always certain that all the initially proposed subtasks will occur. Some texts may require heavy clearance of copyright material, others may not.
- the development of a course may run into problems, requiring those developing it to go 'back to the drawing board'.
- there may be valid differences of opinion as to the order in which certain activities should be scheduled. For example, should the audio-visual materials support the text, or vice-versa? Both approaches may be theoretically right, the one chosen reflecting differences of opinion in respect of the planning of a course.

Ideally, scheduling should take account of the earliest and latest dates at which particular work should be started or finished (ibid.:198). Lewis, however, sounds a note of caution. The air of precision implied by such techniques as critical path analysis and Gantt Charts is 'largely spurious' (ibid.:200) because activities can be sequenced in various ways, and because it is difficult, at least in respect of some tasks, to know to what extent progress has been made. For example, how does an author know that he has made one week's progress on a task scheduled to take four weeks?

Lewis's conclusions, as he himself admitted (1971b:197),

were not meant to imply that production planning should not be undertaken. Indeed, it is vitally important that it should be. What is important is that the work of each development and production team should be assessed and scheduled in a way that meets their needs. As Lewis says, the more detail that is put into the network, the more controversial the exercise becomes (ibid.:200). As he concludes (ibid.:200-01):

> The fact is that even the simplest networks do not stand up to close examination. What, then, is the point of constructing them? Well, there is the telling argument that even a controversial network and scheduling scheme is better than nothing at all. .... even the weakest attempt to construct a network and scheduling scheme can be salutary and rewarding. At the very least, it disciplines one's thinking and enables the major problems to be confronted in a systematic way. Secondly, it is necessary to remember that some planning and scheduling *must* go on - otherwise the course materials would stand very little chance of being produced on time, and to the required standards.

Provided that their limitations are recognised, networks provide a means of making explicit the tasks which need to be undertaken, and provide an indication of the timetable needed to complete a course on time.

Operations management

Operations management is concerned with the delivery of services to students. This includes the registration of students on courses and their allocation to local centres, tutors, tutorial or learning groups, counsellors, examinations, etc., tuition, the provision of advisory services, general counselling, and the maintenance of the students record. It also covers the recruitment, training, and supervision of tutors and counsellors.

Specialisation of services

So far as services are concerned, there may be pressures to increase the range of services and the form in which they are made available through the proliferation of study models. This is because each course or project is regarded as special by those creating it, with distinct educational aims and objectives needing special features that affect its presentation. This may include special requirements in respect of prerequisites for entry to a course, or particular forms of student support (such as the requirement at the Universidad Nacional Abierta [Venezuela] that students on certain courses should be required to gain work experience related to their professional degree course). These can usually be justified on academic grounds, but each new requirement for a special group of students leads to an increase in complexity as the range of study models is increased. The tendency to proliferate study models was noted in the last chapter, where it was argued that in distance education systems the administrative and operational effects of this are frequently unacceptable in as much as they lead to increasingly complex administrative systems.

Capacity planning

Some student services (such as general advice and correspondence tuition) can be provided fairly easily through postal, telephone and electronic mail services, the capacity of individual counsellors and tutors to provide the service being a function of the load on staff (see chapter 7). The provision of face-to-face contact is more difficult. Those systems which provide for face-to-face contact between students and tutors need to plan the frequency and location of such contact. The approach taken may well vary depending on the absolute numbers of students and their population density. In urban areas where there are considerable numbers of students, face-to-face contact may be provided in the form of fairly frequent but relatively short sessions at a local centre. Where there are fewer students, it may not be possible to provide regular tutorials in easy reach of every student, simply because there are too few students to warrant the expense of running classes. In such circumstances, a smaller number of longer sessions (day schools or weekend schools) may be provided in major centres, with students having to travel to the centres. Alternatively, tutors may be peripatetic, as at North Island College in British Colombia where 'campers' are fitted out as mobile tutor homes and/or study centres which move from community to community to serve the needs of remote students

(Salter, 1982).

Planning face-to-face sessions can be helped by the use of 'mapping techniques' which identify on a map where students are living and how their distribution relates to existing local centres - and in particular how far from existing centres they are in terms of their travelling time.

Operations planners also need to take account of demand for particular services. For example, the facilities available at study centres (such as television monitors for viewing video-cassettes of programmes, computer terminals, etc.) need to be planned having regard to the likely demand for these services from students.

The administration of the learning process

Öster (1965:71), speaking from his experience in commercial correspondence schools (Hermods), argued that the administration of correspondence systems (the giving of advice to students, the handling and despatching of students' assignments, the direction of studies through the means of timetables, etc.) is an integral part of the total organisation which needs to be planned and efficiently organised for two reasons: 'a good organisation has a stimulating effect on studies: both when choosing courses and during the studying period', and 'for commercial reasons: as an effective means of competition, by creating confidence in the particular school as compared with rival correspondence schools'. His comments are, however, appropriate to other kinds of distance education systems.

Öster (ibid.:74) argues that the administrative function operates efficiently when

> ... it directs the flow of data and other activities:
> a. in the shortest possible circuit time
> b. with correct delivery of instructional material
> c. with accurate registration of information data
> d. and manages all this at a reasonable cost.

The 'circuit time' is measured in terms of the average turn-round time for the handling of students assignments; the correct delivery of instructional material and accurate registration data can be measured by the number of complaints per assignment and registration; and the reasonableness of cost can be assessed by measures such as the salary cost per registration (ibid.:74).

The features which Öster identifies as contributing to the efficient administration of the process are standardisation of procedures, standard documentation and forms, accessible record systems which are not burdened with unnecessary information, clear divisions of labour in respect of tasks which are in themselves simple, with appropriate coordination between groups of workers, management evaluation of the processes to ensure their continued efficiency, and careful attention to administrative costs.

Öster's detailed discussion of the development of administrative procedures at Hermods, while retaining interest, is specific to the conditions there during the period he was writing about. They need not concern us here, but his general principles remain true today. In particular, efficiency demands that the number of study models is limited. The point was made in chapter 9 that there are tendencies inherent in academic decision-making processes which result in a proliferation of study models, with a consequential loss in administrative efficiency. To minimise this problem, it is important that academic decisions should not be taken in isolation from the productive, distributive and administrative systems that support them, nor should it be assumed that these systems can always support every academic goal or objective. This requires joint decision-making in which both academic, operational, administrative and financial considerations are all taken into account.

Holmberg (1985:109), noting that 'the organisation and administrative aspects of distance education naturally vary with the cultural and sociological contexts', identifies the particular task of the administrative section as being:

- Correct, competent and courteous treatment of all letters, correct delivery of instructional material, information circulars, etc. and proper reception of students calling in person or on the telephone.
- Short turn-around time for assignments submitted in writing, on audio-tape and other media and for letters applying for information.
- Practical provision for the educational use of the telephone, the computer and other aids included in working methods.
- Accurate, easily available registration of data.

- Checking on students' progress and procedures, contacting those who fall behind or seem to be in danger of dropping out.
- Facilities (when needed) for supplementary teaching (telephone tuition, oral refresher courses, laboratory instruction, etc.).
- General efficiency in all the above activities at reasonable cost.

Student administration

Many distance education systems, in common with other administrative systems, are computerised, although there is no absolute reason why they should be. Where records are kept on a 'local centre basis', it may well be sufficient to keep manual records in conventional files. For example, records of individuals who have contacted the Instituto Centroaméricano de Extensión de la Cultura are kept on index cards. As recently as 1969 experience in the use of data processing in the administration of distance education systems was limited (Sorensen, 1969:107).

At about the same time as Sorensen was writing, the British Open University's planners were deciding to set the computer at the centre of the University's administrative processes (Perry, 1972:95). This enabled the University to establish a highly centralised model of administration and to design systems of great complexity. The latter has created problems for the institution: when, for example, the University moved from a batch processing computer using magnetic tape to a more advanced model using direct access disks, with a database and terminal network, it took 30 years-worth of work to convert the University's existing stock of systems to the new computer. Not until this was completed was it possible to begin the work of redesigning systems to take advantage of the new facilities. This work began in 1975. It was 1980 before the first of the second-generation student computer systems came on stream. As Friedman (1982:294) comments, this gives some idea of the gestation period of large-scale computer systems. Since the systems reflect academic policy in respect of admissions, student progress, examinations and assessment, etc., this has major implications for the University's ability to introduce changes in academic policy. Friedman (ibid.:295) comments that given these long gestation periods, 'the problems of asking policy makers and strategy implementors what sort of systems they would like in four or five years time remains'.

The use of computers nevertheless enables distance education systems to process large amounts of data about many thousands of students. Friedman (1984:156) has commented on the need to process changes in information about students quickly and with minimum loss of information. At the British Open University the two most common changes in information about students are changes of address and changes of current course. The speedy processing of these is vital. The batch processing procedures used by the University in its early days engendered some delay - on top of the time it took students to notify the University of such changes through the post. The introduction of online and demand processing, by putting the University's administrators and clerks online, 'greatly reduced the delay caused by transactions [ie. changes in information] waiting in batches for their turn to update the main file' (Friedman, 1984:157).

Friedman believes, however, that the University has still not got to the heart of the problem. Advances in computing and communications mean that students will eventually be able to be online themselves, thus allowing them to maintain some fields on their own files (eg. address) and input their preferences for courses, residential school places, etc. This could have a significant impact on the number of clerical staff employed by the University (ibid.:158) and the pattern of transactions (in the sense introduced in chapter 1) that take place between the institution and its students.

New technology

New technologies are having a major impact on the development, production and distribution of materials and particularly print.

Development and production

At present most distance education systems develop their printed materials through a series of drafts which are typewritten. The typewritten manuscripts are then edited. The material is then produced either by reprographic techniques (roneo, photocopying), or by traditional print technologies involving galley and page proofs followed by printing.

The advent of word processors has already begun to transform the writing and editing of texts. The work of individual authors is changing radically. Experience at EIES (Electronic Information and Exchange System) at the New Jersey Institute of Technology suggests that groups working through computer conferencing systems find this a very effective means of achieving consensus and preparing joint group reports. Kaye (1985:11) has suggested that such systems might usefully be employed for the discussion of course aims and content, and the development of printed course materials.

Timmers (1986) has described how, at the Open Learning Institute (British Columbia, Canada), a computer network was established to help facilitate the development of the second half of a chemistry course. Each member of the course team was provided with a Rainbow microcomputer, a printer, a modem, communications software and self-paced training materials on how to set up and use the computer. The course writer keyed the draft into the microcomputer using word processing software and, when ready, transmitted it electronically to an assessor who commented on it. These comments were transmitted back to the author who then revised the draft and transmitted it to a full-time course developer at the Open Learning Institute (OLI). The latter edited it, transmitted the edited version to the author, and then at a prearranged time discussed all the proposed changes with the author over the telephone, the two of them simultaneously scrolling through the work as they discussed it. Once agreement was reached, the work could be re-edited into its final production-ready form and transmitted to the production unit (Timmers, 1986:17-18).

At OLI the author, assessor and course developer need not meet. Thus, for example, OLI is developing a mathematics course in conjunction with the British Open University in which the author is in England, the assessor at the University of British Columbia, and the course developer at OLI (Timmers, 1986:23).

OLI compared the development and production procedures for the chemistry course where the first half was produced by conventional means and the second using computer-based technologies. Timmers (ibid.:18) comments that:

- the nature of authoring changed. Drafts prepared on word processors look better than the 'scissors and paste' amended

manuscripts revised after typing.
- the assessor knew that the author could easily revise the text, so the comments provided were more extensive.
- it was easier and less time-consuming for the author to incorporate the assessor's comments.
- electronic communication made it easier to transmit drafts between the three people involved. There was no lost time waiting for the manuscript to come through the post.
- editing was easier. The text was 'cleaner' and queries and alternative expressions could be inserted into the text.
- the writer was more involved in discussing and agreeing editorial changes.
- the time required to prepare production-ready copy decreased. Timmers suggests that the development time per page dropped from 120 hours to 50.
- the production unit required less time to produce word-processed manuscripts.

Wordprocessing packages can be set up to accord to house style, thus reducing the work of both author and editor. Proof-reading tools can scan texts for spelling mistakes, vague or anomalous usages, article usage, etc. Wordprocessing and graphics packages can be merged and an infinite number of page layouts tried out before printing occurs. Experience at OLI shows that the use of programs incorporating pre-determined layouts and house styles ('course authoring templates') speeds up the course development process (Timmers. 1986:23). Such templates are in use at Universitas Terbuka, the new distance teaching university in Indonesia, where they are entered into Apple microcomputers (Timmers, 1986:23). Computerised typesetting can be used in conjunction with wordprocessing systems (using direct electronic communication or optical scanners for both text and graphics). Laser printers allow authors to produce camera ready copy from discs on which text and graphics have been merged (the method used to prepare this book). These developments in 'desk-top publishing' are likely to have a profound affect on distance education systems and on publishing in general.

Courses may now be delivered on disc rather than on paper. A San Francisco based company, TeleLearning, now offers via the 'Electronic University' a wide range of courses (both preparatory to the College Level Examination Program examinations and on professional/career development topics) through a computer network. The majority of the course materials are provided to students on floppy discs which can be created quickly to meet demand (although they could equally be provided in printed form, the printed copies being created rapidly from a master disc that can be continually updated as the need arises). Students who require a 'hard copy' of the material can print one using their own microcomputers and printers.

TeleLearning's approach minimises the costs to students that would arise if they were required to access materials from a central computer via their own terminals. However, it is also possible to store course texts on a computer and require students to access them by calling the central computer from their own home terminals. Telecommunications software can then be used to 'download' the centrally produced materials for further or later reading. This in effect constitutes on-demand printing which is student controlled.

Presentation

New technology is also having a significant impact on the teaching and learning processes. The development of computer-mediated communication systems (CMCS) 'allows individuals and groups of people to carry out discussions and conversations over a computer network regardless of time and place constraints via messages keyed in to microcomputers connected by telephone to a central computer' (Kaye, 1985:5). Kaye mentions four features which make CMCS attractive:

- once the equipment is in being and the necessary software and network facilities are in place, communications costs are very low.
- communications are asynchronous, messages being entered and retrieved when convenient to users of the system.
- all communications can be stored until deliberately deleted from the file - a feature not found with face-to-face communication and telephone comunication.
- the processing power of the mainframe computer and its CMCS software can be used to organise and structure inputs, outputs and communication patterns in a variety of ways,

including:

- electronic mail, both one to one and one to group, with automatic signalling of unread mail.
- computer conferencing with the ability to assign specialist roles to different participants (full membership with read and write facilities, read-only membership, moderator, secretary, etc.) and with different categories of conference (open, closed, private)
- private notepads for personal notes and documents
- signalling of on-line participants giving the possibility of synchronous communication
- membership directories
- on-line text editing
- free text search and retrieval
- voting and polling on forced-choice questions, with instantaneous display of the results
- file transfer, both to and from other systems and to and from the user's microcomputer (Kaye, 1985:5-6).

Kaye reports on a number of CMCS-based systems, including: COSY (COnferencing SYstem) at the University of Guelph, Ontario, where a course on 'Adult education: principles and practice' was first offered in 1984 to a group of graduate students in the School of Extension Education; EIES (Electronic Information and Exchange System) developed at the New Jersey Institute of Technology, which is used by, for example, the New School for Social Research in Manhattan to provide on-line courses for credit through its 'Connected Education' project; and PARTICIPATE at the New York Institute of Technology, where a range of distance study versions of on-campus courses in the Independent Study Program are now being offered to students. As Kaye (1985:10) points out, the way in which CMCS is being used varies, being an adjunct to on-campus classes in some of the courses offered at the University of Guelph, an adjunct to essentially print-based distance education versions of on-campus courses at New York Institute of Technology, and the principal teaching medium in the Connect-Ed courses at the New School of Social Research EIES-based system. Most of the courses have small numbers of students, but distance education systems are beginning to consider the use of CMCS on larger courses.

It seems likely that the introduction of CMCS will have a major impact on the organisation of distance education systems. The hierarchical structure commonly found in institution-centred distance education systems is likely to be replaced by a 'networked organisation' in which a large number of linked subgroups and individuals (particularly at the 'middle management' level) will begin to interact with each other using fluid and overlapping channels of communication. Thus for example, tutors on a course will communicate directly with each other (rather than through 'their' senior tutor or the central academic staff), and students too will be able to communicate more freely not only with other students (both within and outside 'their' group) but also possibly with other tutors. Such changes will have a profound effect on existing 'transactional' patterns.

Internal organisation

Computer conferencing and electronic mail facilities are also likely to affect the way in which those working for a distance education system interact with each other. Hierarchical relationships are likely to be less important as people 'network' with each other on problems of mutual interest. At the same time the span of control of top management is likely to increase because management can scan the electronic mail and computer conference messages. People's understanding of the organisation is likely to increase. Jobs and positions may become less clear-cut. As a result, the identification of objectives and the assignment of personal responsibility for achieving these may become more important. As Johansen (1984:7) points out, 'basic changes in organisations are almost always slow, and it is organisational change that is the main event in a teleconferencing implementation, whether or not this is recognised by the implementors'.

Conclusion

The need to integrate academic and educational processes such as curriculum planning, course design and teaching with the production and operations management approaches to materials development, production and distibution, and the delivery of services, is a distinguishing feature of distance education. More than any other feature, it reflects the 'industrialisation' of education which Peters (1973) regards as one of the defining characteristic of distance education. It is certainly true that production and operations management techniques have to be brought to bear on the materials production and distribution and service delivery aspects of distance education, but, as Lewis indicated, there are limitations to their 'pure' application.

One other theme has been developed in this chapter, and that is the implications of the new technologies currently being developed for the development, production, distribution and delivery of distance education. All the indications are that these changes are likely to be profound, ushering in a new era that will be characterised by the development of 'information technology-based distance education' systems. These developments are likely to affect the pedagogy of distance education, transactional relationships in individual distance education systems (see chapter 1), the cost structure of distance education (chapter 4), and the jobs of those working in distance education. Given the pace of technological development, these changes are likely to be extremely rapid.

Chapter Eleven

EVALUATION

Evaluation is the activity of examining and judging value, quality, significance, quantity or condition. The purpose of evaluation may be to provide a general assessment or appraisal of the value of an activity or it may be to produce information which can be used in educational decision-making. In industrial settings, most of what is described as *evaluation* in an academic setting is usually called *management information* or *market research*.

Evaluation can be defined as 'a systematic search for, and analysis of information' (McIntosh, 1974:54). Since collecting information has a cost, some consideration must be given to the *value* of the information collected. The high investment in the development and production of distance teaching materials leads McIntosh (ibid.:55) to place considerable emphasis on formative evaluation (defined as evaluation that is conducted in conjunction with the development of a new educational programme with the aim of influencing that development). She suggests that summative evaluation (ie. evaluation used to assess the effectiveness of an existing programme) may on occasions be less appropriate (eg. in cases where a course is not going to be remade).

Not all evaluation costs a great deal of money. Kemmis and Hughes, who define evaluation as 'the process of marshalling information and arguments which enables interested individuals or groups to participate more fully and more effectively in the critical debate about a program' (1979:10), argue that there is always a low but significant level of informal evaluative activity of a self-critical kind going on, and that this does constitute a defensible form of essentially practical evaluation of courses and administration.

Evaluation presupposes the notion of satisfactory performance, about which Soumelis (1977:26) commented:

> The notion of a system operating satisfactorily relates to both its 'output' and its specific operations. A direct relationship may be postulated between output and the operation of a system. In other words, if a system operates as it ought, its output is expected to correspond and vice versa. However, this relationship may not always hold. In most cases we may be more interested in the nature of the output rather than in the system's operation per se. In the case of the educational system, for example, we are usually interested in the pupil as the system's output rather than in the operation of, say, teaching. We are interested in teaching in so far as it contributes to the amelioration of the output.

> The above suggests that the evaluation could start from the output and move to evaluating specific operations only when the output is found to be defective in some respect, in order to locate the cause of the output's defectiveness.

Evaluation can take place at a number of levels. Soumelis' comment suggests that there are two levels: evaluation of the output, and evaluation of internal processes. The latter, he suggests, need only be done where the former indicates that there are problems. Such a strategy, while expedient, can nevertheless hide inefficiencies. Kemmis (1980:23) suggests that evaluation might be considered at four levels: (1) programme evaluation, concerning general institutional relationships, (2) curriculum evaluation, concerning the educational arrangements of whole curricula and particular courses, (3) the evaluation of student learning, concerning the opportunities for learning created by a particular teaching/learning encounter, and (4) student assessment, concerning the outcomes of student learning. McIntosh (1974:46) distinguishes sets of people interested in evaluation, each of which may have differing objectives. These are (1) society as a whole, (2) the institution or group making a course, (3) the designers of a course, (4) the institution that runs the course, (5) the student who is the 'user' of the course, (6) the employer of the student, if any, and (7) other people who may be affected by the student's participation in the course. To this list

Evaluation

might be added (8) politicians and funding bodies with responsibility for the use of public resources. Finally, evaluation may be formative, conducted in conjunction with the development of new programmes, or summative, used to assess the effectiveness of existing programmes.

Approaches to evaluation.

The major problem faced by those evaluating distance education programmes is that the student is separated from the teacher. In conventional education, teachers have direct contact with their students. This allows immediate feedback from the students to the teachers, allowing the latter to adapt their approach to teaching where necessary. Evaluation is often instinctive. In distance education, in contrast, this contact with the students is lost, and course designers and teachers therefore have to rely on 'evaluation techniques' which are in many cases undertaken by professional evaluators who are intermediaries between the teacher as course developer and the students.

There are a number of different approaches to evaluation, all of which have their advantages and drawbacks.

Evaluation as 'test and measurement'

Until the early 1970s educational evaluation was identified with curriculum evaluation, a field within which the 'test and measurement' model of evaluation was dominant. This model attempted to apply scientific approaches to the measurement of educational outcomes, and in particular to measure results under controlled experimental conditions. It assumed that there were agreed curriculum and/or course aims which could be expressed as objectives, that experiences could be provided which would enable the learners to behave in ways that would help them achieve the objectives, and that attainment of these by students could be measured. The model was criticised by Scriven (1973) who argued that evaluators should not just look for the intended effects of the programme but for other effects as well ('goal-free' evaluation), and by those who feel that teachers and students may choose to pursue objectives that are different to those laid down by a programme's developers. There are also considerable problems in devising valid and reliable tests to measure discrepancies between desired and actual achievements. A number of people (eg. Parlett and Hamilton, 1976; Stake, 1967) have argued that the test and measurement model does not adequately explain why a programme fails.

Evaluation as 'illumination'

There are alternative approaches. Parlett and Hamilton (1972, 1976) introduced an alternative model which they referred to as 'illuminative evaluation'. Their approach used research techniques derived from social anthropology and in particular participative observation. Stake (1975) elaborated a 'responsive' approach which attempted to focus on programme activities rather than programme intents. His approach is to respond to issues of particular concern to participants, and take account of the various value-perspectives present in reporting on the success or failure of a programme. Hamilton et al. (1977) complained of (1) 'an under-attention to educational processes including those of the learning milieu', (2) 'an over-attention to psychometrically measureable changes in student behaviour', and (3) 'the existence of an educational research climate that rewards accuracy of measurement and generality of theory but overlooks both mismatch between school problems and research issues and tolerates ineffective communication between researchers and those outside the research community'. They argued that inter alia research should be (1) 'responsive to the needs and perspectives of differing audiences', (2) 'illuminative of the complex organisational, teaching and learning processes at issue', and (3) 'relevant to public and professional decisions forthcoming'. Needless to say the approach was not without its critics who held that it was 'subjective', 'impressionistic' and 'qualitative' as against the more rigorous 'quantitative' and 'objective' approaches of the test and measurement school.

McIntosh (1974:43), considering some of the problems of evaluating multi-media educational systems, commented that:

> increasingly the traditional approach to evaluation ... is found to be inadequate as evaluators are confronted by innovatory educational programmes of a wide variety. It is quite clear, in particular, that the evaluation of multi-media educational systems cannot even confine itself to curriculum evaluation,

and certainly cannot confine itself to the 'test and measurement' model.

She criticised the test and measurement approach on the grounds that it requires controlled conditions which can rarely be produced in an educational setting, and certainly not in systems catering for heterogeneous adult home-based populations who are learning from a variety of media, all of which may not be equally accessible to all learners (McIntosh, 1974:51). On the other hand she felt that 'participant observation as a research form can find little place in a mass home-based learning system', although the 'learning milieu' concept could perhaps be applied to face-to-face sessions at local centres (McIntosh, 1974:44). This is certainly the case in respect of institution-centred programmes, although the learning milieu approach would be highly relevant in the evaluation of community-based educational models such as those discussed in chapter 2.

Evaluation as part of 'rational management'

Another approach - the organisational model to evaluation - seeks to meet the needs of managers and decision makers, providing them with a range of information which will enable them to decide whether or not the institution is on the right track. Kemmis (1980:28) characterises this approach as 'one of rational management'. Among the various factors taken into account are the determination of institutional goals and educational objectives, the measurement of educational and other outcomes, and the evaluation of learning experiences in terms of desired outcomes, use of resources to achieve desired outcomes, and planning and decision-making processes (Dressel, 1976:419-22). Clarke and Birt (1982:8-12) have drawn attention to various check lists of items which universities, for example, may use to help plan intra-institutional evaluations, including lists drawn up by the Australian Williams Committee of Inquiry into Education and Training (Williams, 1979, R 18.23:809-810), Miller (1979) in the United States, and Fielden and Lockwood (1973) in the United Kingdom.

The task set by those adopting an organisational review approach to evaluation is not only daunting: there is, as Kemmel comments (1980:28), 'a tremendous spuriousness and misplaced earnestness about such lists of relevant factors.... the notion that any evaluation can achieve all of the data-gathering, analytic and reporting tasks set out is absurd'.

The model starts with organisational goals (and can therefore be criticised on the grounds that as an evaluation system it is not goal-free), goes to absurd lengths to control institutional complexity, attempts to be comprehensive and hence defies genuine application, swamps managers and decision makers with reports, and may actually obscure those issues which they can do something about (Kemmis, 1980:28). McIntosh (1979:82) commented that the 'very richness and profusion' of the data collected by institutional researchers at the British Open University 'has become a barrier to its use. The problem is a serious one of organising and storing it in such a way that it is accessible'. On the other hand, she accepts that the existence of a broad data bank which can be scanned to give a swift reaction to a variety of general questions is useful.

Obviously exactly what data are collected should be determined by the purpose which they will serve. Some data can be collected as a matter of course as a by-product of routine administrative procedures. Other data will need to be collected specifically. Sizer (1979:61) argues the need to define the specific information needs of each managerial position and policy making committee, design control reports and agree these, and establish an information system to generate the reports.

One way of approaching the problem is to set out to identify the 'Critical Success Factors' that apply - that is, those things that are done by managers that are crucial to achieving the institution's agreed objectives. There is often considerable disagreement among managers as to what the Critical Success Factors (CSFs) are. They can be established by canvassing individual manager's views, and the CSFs that best represent the consensus view of management can then be identified and agreed. Once this has been done, managers need to review the information they receive and decide to what extent it supports the CSFs. Irrelevant data is then discarded as a waste of time. Meanwhile gaps in the current information system are identified and the information system is overhauled, the new system being designed to monitor the CSFs.

However, while in some cases it will be possible to predefine information needs, in others it will not, so that evaluators and administrators will have to respond as best they can in the time available. It is quite usual for information which decision makers feel they would like to have not to be available at all or in the right format at the time it is needed. All too often assumptions made about what information is needed serve rigidly to predetermine the sort of information that can be provided. Equally, as Marris (1985:242) shows, the information which one chooses to collect has a powerful circular relationship with the agenda of what is regarded as important.

Conclusion

It is now generally agreed that no one technique or paradigm is likely to be adequate to meet all the needs of institutional research. The choice of research strategy needs to take account of and hence follow on from the identification of the problem requiring solution, and not be dictated by the latest intellectual fashion. However, the strategy adopted may also depend on the time available to undertake a study. One of the problems of illuminative evaluation is that it requires time to undertake it. Unfortunately this is not always available. Ideally, the planning function should indicate well in advance when a particular review will be undertaken or decision made, so that research can be commissioned, carried out and analysed in time to inform decision makers. Equally, Critical Success Factors should be identified and the information system developed to support these as a matter of course.

Criteria for evaluating distance education programmes

There are many criteria by which distance education programmes could be evaluated. Many of them are common to distance and conventional programmes. Gooler (1979:46-50) listed seven criteria which seemed to him to be particularly relevant to distance education programmes; Rumble (1981b:71-8) identified four basic criteria; and Keegan and Rumble (1982b:225-43) provided a framework for assessing the effectiveness of distance teaching universities. The analysis which follows is based on Gooler's criteria but takes into account various criteria listed by other researchers.

Access

A number of distance education programmes have been set up specifically to extend educational access to new groups of people, while others offer a second route to an existing clientele. Among the measures used here are the absolute numbers served, and the numbers belonging to specific target groups. However, it may not always be clear how many students are being served by a distance education programme. Many programmes do require their students to enrol formally, but some, for example, those using open network broadcasting, are 'open', and it may be difficult to identify the persons following the programme and therefore how many 'students' there are, and what kind of 'students' they are. Another crucial factor is the extent to which the programmes of study are actually available to the target populations for which they have been developed. A whole range of factors may be important here including geographical coverage, ease of access to the media used to deliver the programmes, the cost of the programmes to the student, etc. A further factor which needs consideration is the level of awareness of the programme among potential students and also among employers who might sponsor students to take appropriate courses. It is no good increasing opportunities for access if potential students do not know of the existence of the programme.

Relevancy to needs and expectations

Individual distance education institutions may serve a variety of needs. Everyman's University in Israel and the Allama Iqbal Open University in Pakistan have a variety of programmes of study - academic, technical, vocational and functional courses - each serving distinct needs. Other institutions have more limited aims (eg. the Correspondence Course Unit, Kenya which is concerned solely with teacher training). Clearly the wider the spread of programmes available, the more likely it is that something will appeal to a given individual.

Some institutions are established specifically to serve perceived national needs. For example, the Universidad Nacional Abierta had as one of its objectives that it should help meet the national needs for trained professionals identified in the fifth national development plan (1976-80). Other institutions, particularly those engaged in community-based education, set out to meet local needs. Some institutions serve company needs for in-house training. Employers may support students on appropriate courses. Students may also have individual needs. It is by no means easy to identify needs and evaluate whether or not they are being satisfied. Buoyant application rates will indicate that some kind of need is being satisfied, while the level of frustrated demand (those who apply but cannot be offered a place) will indicate a pool of unsatisfied demand. Neither the level of satisfied demand nor the level of frustrated demand provides a clear indication of the level of potential demand (ie. those who might apply one day).

The fact that there is a demand does not mean that the products of the institution will meet the needs of the labour market. Where this is judged to be an important criterion, information will need to be collected about the employment of graduates including, in the case of part-time adult students many of whom will already have a job, details of post-study-related promotion, change of job or career, and improved pay.

Given the level of investment required to develop a distance education programme, there is a considerable need for adequate market research to identify potential levels of demand. It is not always easy to do this prior to the launch of a programme. In any case, the existence of a need does not necessarily mean that distance education is the best means of satisfying it. For example, distance education is not a good vehicle for teaching manipulative skills (Holmberg, 1981:14).

Quality of programme offered

There are a number of ways in which the quality of a distance education programme can be judged. One way is to look at the quality of the materials. This may be intuitive - a question of whether or not they 'feel right' - or it may be based on their acceptance by external assessors (where these exist), their adoption for use by other educational institutions, and the quality of any reviews in journals. A more formalised way is to obtain feedback from those using the materials, both students and tutors, on the utility of the materials and the difficulties which they encountered in using them. Routine feedback can obtain a great deal of information on, for example, the amount of time that students spent on elements of the course, on whether or not they are on schedule or behind schedule on paced courses, and on what they felt about the material. Tutors may report on any difficulties which students have in understanding the material.

McIntosh (1978:13) argues that theoretically it is both necessary and desirable to evaluate at the microlevel of individual components, but admits that this is very costly. There is another problem too, and that is that unless the evaluation is specifically being undertaken with a view to improving a component, and the resources are made available to enable this to happen, there is the danger that the results will sit on the shelf unheeded while course writers and producers go on to work on other projects. All too often 'evaluation is retrospective, and can only be used negatively to point out what has gone wrong or what has not worked' (McIntosh, 1979:83). However, where the evaluators work closely with the academics from the very beginning of a project, the research is generally both better planned and more likely to be used (ibid.:83).

Attention also needs to be directed to the quality of the educational experience. There are those who find it difficult to accept that distance education provides an *educational* experience at all. Escotet (1980a:11-12, 15-17), for example, argues that distance education provides *instruction*, not *education* : he bases this contention on a belief that education presupposes a social and cultural context. Similar views are expressed by Carnoy and Levin (1975:396) who argue that much of the value of a university education is captured in its 'socialization content', and that this cannot be provided by a distance teaching university. Yet in fact many distance teaching systems do provide opportunities for face-to-face contact between teachers and students, and students and students.

Another issue which needs to be addressed is the ease or likelihood of the materials being used successfully by the students. There is little point in developing materials which the learner finds difficult or hard to use. A large number of studies have concentrated on the practical problems of using multi-media distance education materials. The evaluation practices adopted by the British Open University are discussed by Bates, Hawkridge and Henderson (1982), while McIntosh (1978) provides an account of the evaluation of one Open University course.

Bates, Hawkridge and Henderson (1982) suggest that even

before a course is presented, the materials can be evaluated in a number of ways - through expert appraisal by content specialists, educational technologists, and so on, and through developmental testing. Subsequently the course can be evaluated using informal feedback from tutors and students (likely to be 'impressionistic and ... of dubious value' [ibid.:44]), routinely through information on students' performance on assignments and examinations, and through formal tailor-made evaluation surveys using questionnaires. Both Bates et al. and McIntosh argue that the real problem is implementing the findings of such evaluation. As the former point out, 'much of the feedback collected on the old course may be irrelevant' to the design of a new course (Bates, Hawkridge and Henderson, 1982:46).

The quality of the programme may also be reflected in the quality of the learning achieved by the students and the recognition that this is accorded. Among the measures here may be the extent to which other educational institutions recognise the distance studies for credit transfer purposes, the acceptance of the degrees, diplomas and certificates awarded as qualifying the student to go on to higher level studies, the recognition of awards by employers and professional associations, and the general esteem in which the programmes and awards are held by the community at large.

Learner outcomes

The evaluation of learner outcomes can be summarised as the issue of 'who learns what'. Many distance education programmes have as an objective the education of their students to a sufficiently high standard to obtain a degree, diploma or certificate. It is clearly important to evaluate success or failure in this endeavour, particularly as the evaluation of learner outcomes has been the historical focus of much evaluation effort and remains a major indicator of success or failure in the eyes of funding bodies. Among the measures which are important here are the output: input ratio, which measures the number of graduates as a proportion of the number of students entering a course or programme of study, and the response time test, which measures the amount of time it takes to produce a graduate (ie. the elapsed time between a student embarking on a programme of study and graduating). The latter takes account of course failure and repetition rates. The evaluation also needs to take account of the student's objectives. It is quite common for students to follow a course and undertake formative assessments but not sit the final examination upon which credit is awarded, simply because their objective is to learn, not to gain credit. Drop-out or desertion is an acknowledged problem in many distance education programmes.

The evaluation should also take account of qualitative factors, including the quality of the output (discussed above) and the difference between the quality of the input and the output. Some distance education institutions only accept students with regular qualifications for entry to the educational level they are serving; others have adopted an open admissions policy and will accept both qualified and unqualified students; yet others waive normal entry standards for certain groups of students. Any evaluation should take account of variations in entry qualifications and also of the elapsed time between the end of formal full-time schooling and the start of distance studies.

Effectiveness and efficiency

Effectiveness is concerned with outputs: an organisation is effective to the extent that it produces outputs that are relevant to the needs and demands of its clients. Efficiency is concerned with the cost of achieving these outputs: an organisation becomes more efficient to the extent that it maintains outputs with fewer resources or increases outputs with a less than proportionate increase in inputs. Effectiveness is an overriding concern for many people who seek to evaluate distance education programmes. However, where the distance programme is reaching new target populations it may be very wrong to judge its overall effectiveness on whether or not it is as effective as a conventional system.

On the other hand, there are distance education institutions which have been established with the aim of educating similar target population to those served by conventional institutions at a lower cost per student. Failure to achieve this objective may well be a significant factor in any decision to continue the programme. The significant measures here are the average cost per student and the average cost per graduate, but, taken at face value, even these measures may be flawed. Generally speaking there is an assumption that the students and graduates whose costs are being measured are similar entities in terms of quality and so on, but this may not be the case. The achievement of a lower cost per student or graduate may be negated by the fact that their quality and hence their value is less.

A further problem arises in respect of the analysis of costs. All too often the total system costs are understated. Governments may be interested only in the average cost of a student or graduate supported by government funds, ignoring the contributions of other agencies. Such contributions may not necessarily be provided in cash (commonly what is given is access to facilities at marginal or no cost). Researchers may concentrate on the average institutional cost of a student or graduate, forgetting that many costs are born by students. Such factors may make it extremely difficult to compare the costs of different institutions. However, various 'cost finding' procedures have been developed to ensure that costs are not overlooked or underestimated. A recent review of the application of cost analysis procedures to higher education is provided by Adams et al. (1978), while Lindsay (1982:183) cites recent literature in the field and Rumble (1986) has discussed some of the problems arising in the costing of distance education.

Efficiency should always be a matter for concern. Both efficiency and effectiveness were discussed in chapter 5.

Impact

A distance education programme may have an impact on individuals, other programmes and other institutions. As Gooler comments (1979:49) 'people who are interested in utilizing an impact criterion regard the ripple effects of distance education programs to be a significant factor in judging the success of a program'. A conspicuous success may lead other institutions to implement distance education programmes of their own. Observation of distance education practices may lead other institutions to modify their own instructional approaches. Conventional teachers who tutor for distance education systems may moderate their behaviour in some ways. Successful systems may lead to a re-examination of educational needs, of assumptions about the way in which people learn, and of educational policies including those governing the financing of education. Sizer (1979:62) notes that concentration on short term output indicators of performance (such as the cost per student) may obscure the need to evaluate the long-term impacts and benefits of an institutions's programmes.

Generation of knowledge

Finally, distance education programmes will almost certainly generate greater understanding of 'the problems, issues and practices in the field of delivery of educational opportunities', about the nature of the adult learning population, and about the use of technologies in the service of education (Gooler, 1979:50).

The measurement of institutional performance

There has recently been, at least in the United Kingdom, considerable interest in the development of performance indicators both as an aid to educational management and as a means of monitoring the overall performance of an institution and permitting comparisons with other educational institutions.

Just as in industry there are a number of key measures which can be applied (eg. profit to sales, profit to assets employed, sales to assets, working capital to sales, stock to sales, current liabilities to current assets, earnings per share, etc.) so it is felt by many that there should be a series of performance indicators that can be used in non-profit making organisations to measure the effective and efficient accomplishment of the expectations of the institution's constituencies (Romney, Bogen and Micek, 1978). Non-profit making institutions exist to provide a service rather than earn a profit. Sorenson and Grove (1977) have summarised the objectives and properties of service indicators: availability, awareness, accessibility, extensiveness, appropriateness, efficiency, effectiveness, outcome benefits/impacts, and acceptability (see Table 11.1). It is generally agreed that 'services provided' are harder to measure than profits (Sizer, 1982:35), but that nevertheless the goals and objectives of the organisation can, albeit with difficulty, be identified, quantified and agreed. In this process there is a tendency to concentrate on those aspects of an institution that can be measured with some precision, and also to concentrate on process indicators rather than outcome measures or ones that substantiate progress towards achieving objectives.

This is not to deny that many of the process measures used by those managing non-profit making institutions (such as staff:

Table 11.1
Service perfomance indicators applied to distance education

Focus of measure	Use	Content
Availability	What can be obtained? User satisfaction	Number and type of course, materials for sale or use, service available (eg to students with special dis-advantages), range of media available.
Awareness	Who knows about what is available?	Knowledge of DE system among user population (courses offered, services available, entry require-ments); knowledge of media available among those developing courses.
Accessibility	Ease of access	Hours of opening of local study centres, broadcast transmission hours, access media in the home.
Extensiveness	'How much?' but not 'How well?'	Student enrolments against target numbers/quotas, number of users of special services, percentage use of media
Appropriateness	Is quantity/ quality of what is offered what is required?	Demand for course/service; mismatch between demand and availability (computing facilities for students)
Efficiency	How much resource was used?	Cost per service (disabled student, broadcast trans-mission), per student per course, etc.
Effectiveness	Characteristics, duration, content, effect, proportions served, variance from budget, standards	Comparison of planned to actual; percentage utilising facility or service; graduate success in employment etc.; budgeted to actual cost; planned to actual cost per student course; planned to actual wastage rates

Outcomes/ Benefits/ Impacts	Monetary and non-monetary effects	Increased earning power of ex-students/graduates, benefits to society, local community, other educational institutions, etc.
Acceptability	User satisfaction	Demand for courses, number of complaints about course content or services, complaints about speed of service (eg assignment turn-round time)

student ratios and cost per full-time equivalent student) are not valuable for internal planning, control and resource allocation processes. Hijmans (1980) has suggested that 'process-directed evaluation is probably less obnoxious to academe than the evaluation of teaching or research itself, as it does not threaten academic freedom in a direct way'. Still, there are considerable dangers in relying on simple quantitative approaches to the measurement of educational performance. There are 'the difficulties of capturing in a set of measurements the intangibility of the multiple objectives and outputs in education and the different values placed on them by people with differing perspectives' (Lindsay, 1982:179). All too often these difficulties are not recognised. On the other hand, as Toombs (1973:13-14) commented, 'input-output ratios offer an analytical and descriptive device of great simplicity that can be applied to many levels in a complex organisation. ... input-output analysis is a good place to start, but we should not expect it to yield sophisticated results'. Sizer (1979:71), concluding his review of institutional performance indicators, has indicated that simple ratios 'provide a starting point for managerial judgements'.

A study by Romney (1978) of measures of institutional goal achievement indicated some resistance to traditional process measures among respondents at the 45 American colleges and universities which he surveyed. Measures attempting to show the impact of higher education (eg. satisfaction, ability to apply knowledge, publications, value added) were preferred. Romney argues that institutions should concentrate on developing measures that substantiate progress towards the achievement of institutionally important goals. Sizer (1982), while agreeing that there is a strong case for developing progress measures (p.42), warns that such measures need to assess long-term impacts and also the quality of the outcomes (p.39).

An approach to the appraisal of course and programme effectiveness and efficiency has been proposed by Birch and Latcham (1985:115-20). They identified a number of effectiveness and efficiency measures for individual courses which provide for the routine monitoring of performance at the individual course level. They identify the attainment of a satisfactory level of student intake against planned intake numbers, completion rates (ie. students who have enrolled and have not dropped out but have participated throughout the course), pass rates or successes (ie. students who have satisfied the assessment system and been allowed to proceed to the next level or graduated), and post-graduation employment or enrolment in higher level courses. So far as efficiency is concerned they suggest that this is best done by way of average costs, although such measures as the student:staff ratio, average class size, student taught hours and lecturer class contact hours can also be used since a knowledge of such factors is important for an understanding of the deployment of academic staff. Efficiency can be examined at any level of output - eg. places, enrolments, successful end-of-course students, successful end-of-programme graduates, etc. Their approach requires that critical outcomes are identified, satifactory levels of performance are set, and data definitions and measurement rules agreed. It also requires that management agrees to consider taking appropriate action in cases where the appraisal indicates that courses, subject areas or programmes are not performing adequately. It is this final element that constitutes the vital element of control which leads to adaptation, change and improvement.

The appraisal model outlined in figure 11.1 is based on Birch and Latcham's model but has been extended and adapted to take account of the development and production of distance taught courses and to incorporate Sizer's institutional directional policy matrix (discussed in chapter 8 - see figure 8.2).

Conclusions

Evaluation is important for a number of reasons. Broadly, it helps one:

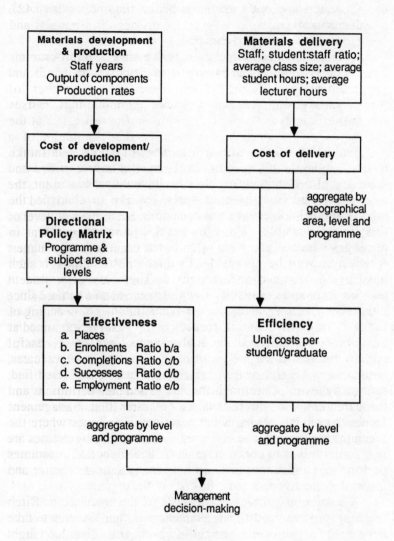

Figure 11.1
Course and programme appraisal model

Based on Birch, D. and Latcham, J. (1985) 'Measuring college
performance', in Further Education Staff College (1985) Assessing
educational effectiveness and efficiency, Coombe Lodge Report 18
(3), Blagdon, The Further Education Staff College.

- understand one's operation better, thus improving one's decision-making.
- monitor one's performance.
- learn about one's operation, with a view to improving it.
- satisfy oneself and external agencies that one is effective in achieving one's aims and objectives.
- satisfy oneself and external agencies that one is cost-efficient.

Evaluation takes place at a number of levels - informal, formal, global, highly specific. In the normal course of events a great deal of evaluation takes place in conventional education on a day-to-day and hour-by-hour basis, leading to changes and modifications in objectives and behaviour. In distance education, this is not possible. While informal evaluation occurs, the messages which it gives are often based on anecdotal evidence which may well be unreliable. Evaluation strategies therefore have to be designed and structured. There are a number of possible techniques available. Illuminative evaluation may help in internal evaluation and also in the evaluation of group activities, but it is of limited use in respect of the evaluation of mass home-based learning systems. It also seems clear that evaluation cannot be restricted to traditional 'test and measurement' approaches. A great deal of information can be collected on a routine basis, either through the analysis of student records or through the use of questionnaires designed to provide regular feedback or to answer particular questions. The danger is that too much information will be collected, thus reducing its utility. One way round this is to concentrate on Critical Success Factors and performance indicators that can help management monitor and assess the effectiveness and efficiency of the organisation.

A particular problem in respect of the evaluation of the teaching process in distance education is that the courses are developed for use over a number of years. Once they have been produced, it can be very costly to change them. Pre-production evaluation may help in this respect (for example, the use of external and other assessors, and strategies such as developmental testing), but on the whole it is much harder to change a distance-taught course once it has been produced than is the case in conventional education. It is also much harder to evaluate how students study and make use of the materials, simply because there is little contact with them. Where courses have been evaluated during their presentation phase, it is difficult to apply the lessons that have been learnt to the next course, which may be very different in form and content. All these factors make the evaluation of distance education more difficult than that of conventional education. In spite of this, it is important that distance education systems should be evaluated, for the reasons given above. Indeed it is arguable that it is more important to evaluate non-traditional educational programmes than is the case in respect of conventional ones, in order to show external agencies that the maintenance and improvement of their effectiveness and efficiency is a matter of concern to management. Certainly, distance education can be both effective and efficient, and hopefully the results will show this to be the case.

Chapter Twelve

CONCLUSION

This book is concerned with the planning and management of distance education. One conclusion that might be drawn from it is that, ultimately, there is no single right way of planning and managing a distance education system. There are, however, a number of themes running through the book. The purpose of this chapter is to make these explicit.

Educational models and distance education

Chapter 1 provided a definition of distance education based on Keegan (1986:49-50), who identified seven principal characteristics of distance education:

- the separation of teacher and student
- the influence of an educational organisation
- the use of technical media
- the provision of two-way communication
- the absence of group learning, with students taught largely as individuals (while retaining the possibility of occasional seminars)
- the industrialisation of the educational process, which is not a necessary defining feature of distance education, but which is evident in distance education systems (Keegan, 1986:48)
- the 'privatisation' of learning (ie. learning takes place in private rather than in groups)

Chapter 2 discussed three educational models, based on

Bertrand (1979):

- institution-centred models
- person-centred models
- society-centred (or community-centred) models

Each of these models is found in distance education, but the dominant model is the institution-centred model. The three models were related to Keegan's seven defining characteristics of distance education (in table 2.1). This suggested that institution-centred models and those society-centred models which are based on campaign-type approaches exhibit more of the features identified by Keegan than do, for example, society-centred models based on social-action principals, or individual-centred models based on contract learning or project work.

Society-based community education projects raise the biggest problem in relation to Keegan's defining characteristics, since they must involve group-based learning and social-action. To this extent they clearly contradict Keegan's principal that 'the separation of the learner from the learning group throughout the length of the learning period is a characteristic feature of [distance] education which distinguishes it from conventional, oral, group-based education' (Keegan, 1986:46). Indeed, it is doubtful whether Keegan would accept as a form of distance education society-centred social-action type projects of the kind found in the radio clubs of francophone Africa or the many radiophonic schools of Latin America, where centrally produced radio and printed materials are used to support local social-action orientated groups under the direction of an animateur.

Examples of such systems abound - Acción Cultural Popular in Colombia, Acción Cultural Popular Hondureña in Honduras, the Radio Associación La Voz de Atitlán in Guatemala, Escuelas Radiofónicas Populares in Ecuador, Radio Educativa de Veraguas in Panama, Escuelas Radiofónicas de la Tarahumara in Mexico, L'heure rurale Radio Club in Togo, and Radio Clubs du Niger. More are listed in the 'Directory of Distance Teaching Projects' in Young et al. (1980:162-233).

Keegan (1986:51) also excludes from the concept of distance education:

- 'the use of printed, audio-based, video-based, computer-based learning materials in classrooms, lecture theatres, seminars, tutorials and laboratory sessions for on-campus programmes'. This leads him to exclude projects such as Radio Mathematics in Nicaragua, Radio Santa Maria in the Dominican Republic, the Mauritius College of the Air, Telesecundaria in Mexico, etc. where educational technology and media are used to support learning in the classroom. He also excludes (ibid.:52) flexi-mode, multi-mode or mixed-mode programmes which use distance education materials for conventional students, with a reduced attendance rate at classes.
- 'the use of printed, audio-based, video-based learning material and computer in private study'.

The 'theory in use' in this book has been to exclude private study and the use of structured learning materials within the school or college from any definition of distance learning, but to take a more relaxed approach towards the definition of distance education, and to include as forms of distance education those systems where local groups within the community, under the guidance of an animateur, extension worker or adult educator, make use materials that have been specially prepared by a materials development and production agency for this purpose.

While in practice this book has tended to concentrate on institution-centred distance education systems, one theme explored in it (not always explicitly) has been the differences between those distance education systems that are institution-centred, person-centred, and society-centred. Table 12.1 attempts to summarise some of these differences.

Models of distance education: systems and transactions

Chapter 1 also introduced three models of distance education: a systems model, a holistic ('political') model, and the idea of transactional models.

Two of these models, the systems one and the transactional one, have been used extensively although not always explicitly in the analysis presented in this book. The systems approach was used by members of the British Open University's Centre for

Conclusion

Table 12.1
Educational models: influence on the planning and management of distance education

	Institution-centred	Society-centred	Person-centred
Audience focus			
	Mass	Local community	Individual
Educational model			
	Information-processing (arguably training and instruction, not education)	Social-action	Humanistic/open
Political purpose			
	Egalitarian; Provide places for disadvantaged; Modernisation; Adult education; Continuing education; Control education (curriculum and students); Lower cost of education	Social-action; Rural development; Community education	Open education
Economics and costs in: **(a) purpose-built systems and consortia:**			
• materials subsystem			
	Fixed; high level of investment in materials	Fixed; low, medium or high level of investment in materials	Fixed; low investment in materials
• student subsystem			
	Variable; significant cost but needs to be kept lower than in conventional systems	Variable; institutional cost likely to be low	Variable; high cost relative to materials though low in absolute terms

Conclusion

• infrastructure

Significant investment in management systems to support materials and student sub-systems	Significant investment in systems to support materials subsystem	Low

(b) in mixed-mode systems

• general

Materials development costs and some admin. costs 'shared' between distance and conventional systems; student system requires funding	Materials development costs and some admin. costs shared between conventional and distance system	Costs differ little from conventional costs

Planning

Focus tends to be on media and course development and production	Focus needs to be on the community, group, and group leader and his/her interaction with members	Focus on the individual learner and his/her mentor/supervisor

Evaluation

Need to evaluate at a distance. Focus on formal evaluative techniques. Use of questionnaires. Illuminative approach of limited use.	Need for multiple approach to evaluation; illuminative approach useful for evaluation at group level	Evaluate at a distance but scope for informal evaluation by mentor/supervisor

---

International Cooperation and Services both in the planning and evaluation of distance education systems (Rumble, 1978; Pengelly, Rumble and Wilson, 1978; Rumble, 1979:60-2) and as the organising framework for a course on the planning of distance learning systems which subsequently became the basis of a book written by members of the Centre and edited by Kaye and Rumble (1981). It is a powerful analytical tool for the planning and management of distance education systems, and is used in this book as a means of organising much of the material presented in chapters 5 to 10.

The transactional approach was developed by Henri and Kaye (1985:122-35) and provides an alternative and equally powerful analytical framework which can be used to understand the way in which distance education systems function. As is made clear in this book, transactional patterns vary considerably depending in part on the underlying educational model and the mix of media, and in part on the communications systems in use. An argument made in this book in a number of places is that the new Computer-mediated Communications Systems (CMCS) will radically change the transactional patterns found in distance education systems, leading to a networked rather than a hierarchical organisational structure.

The business-orientated nature of distance education

Distance education is different from conventional education:

- a wide range of media is used, some of which are uni-directional but some of which allow for two-way communication
- long lead-in times are required to develop and produce materials and courses
- the long lead-in times mean that the operational planning horizon is extended over several years, during which time the institution has relatively little scope for implementing radical changes. This places a premium on strategic planning
- developing a distance taught course using media requires considerable investment in staff time, with the result that individual teachers often have to work together to realise the course. Various solutions to this problem have been sought (eg. the course team approach, the academic-editor/ consultant approach)
- the teachers who develop the courses are unable to realise their programmes alone, but instead have to rely on a range of non-teaching staff - editors, designers, audio-visual

producers, warehouse operatives, etc. - if their programmes are to be produced and delivered to the students. The development process in particular brings a range of specialist academic and non-academic staff together in project teams or as a 'production-line'

• individual academic staff experience a loss of control over the products of their labour which is not found in conventional educational systems

• the development and production of distance teaching materials requires a production management approach

• the teachers developing the course materials, at least in large-scale systems, cannot hope also to tutor all the students, thus leading to a division of labour between those who develop courses and those who tutor students. The teacher qua course developer is thus separated from the learner, and any face-to-face contact has in general to be provided through intermediaries (tutors etc.) who are also remote from the central materials developers

• the development of new computer-mediated communication systems may reduce the transactional distance that currently exists between teacher and student, teacher and tutor, and student and student, without changing the fundamental physical separation of teacher and student, teacher and tutor, tutor and student, and student and student

• extensive administrative systems are required to keep track of students and administer their progress through the institution

• online student access to their records and to the administrative process in respect of course choice etc. will affect existing transactional patterns and may lead to further capital intensification as work which is currently done by clerical staff is undertaken by students using online computing

• an operations management approach to the delivery of services is required

• the cost structure of distance education is different, involving significant investment in course materials and administrative systems before a single student is enrolled in the system

• traditional approaches to budgeting and to the

determination of staffing levels are not readily transferable to distance education systems

• the introduction of new technologies increasingly requires students to have access to them before they can take part in the learning process. The cost structure of distance education may therefore change againas capital costs increase. This raises the issue of who pays, for what. If students have to pay, this may affect access

• the use of media has led to increased specialisation of jobs revolving around the distinctive technologies used in distance education

• the organisational structure is dominated by functional divisions

• currently, the management of distance education requires a greater degree of hierarchical control than is found in conventional educational systems. New communications technologies may change this, resulting in a networked as opposed to a hierarchical form of organisation

• more learning takes place out of sight of and beyond the direct control of the teacher

• evaluation has to be formalised to overcome the problem of the distance between the teacher and the learner

• proposals for improving the learning materials may be difficult to implement given the nature of the materials and the fact that changes can not be readily made to them

• non-traditional educational systems generally need to show that they are effective and efficient. This places an increased premium on evaluation

While by no means implying that the planning and management of conventional education is necessarily easy, these features add to the complexity of the management process in distance education systems. Greater emphasis is put on hierarchical management, and there is lower tolerance of collegial, politicised and anarchic models of academic management. This is not the same thing as saying that distance education is an industrialised form of education. The production-line analogy does not bear too great a scrutiny. Distance education is, however, a more business-orientated form of education - a factor that is reflected in its origins in commercial correspondence schools, the mail-order analogy descriptive of some of its processes, and its heavy involvement in publishing, audio-visual production and communications. It is this theme, more than any other, that underpins this book.

REFERENCES

Adams, C.R., Harkins, R.L., Kingston, L.W. and Schroeder, R.G. (1978) *A study of cost analysis in higher education*, Washington, D.C., American Council on Education, 4 volumes.

Advisory Committee (1966) *A University of the Air*, London, HMSO, Cmnd.2922.

Bååth, J. (1981) 'On the nature of distance education', *Distance Education*, 2 (2), 212-3.

Bakken, A. (1984) 'The Norwegian State Institution for Distance Education - experience with a model based on co-operation', in Universidad Nacional de Educación a Distancia (1984) *Evaluación del rendimiento de la enseñanza superior a distancia*, Madrid, Universidad Nacional de Educación a Distancia.

Bates, A.W. (ed.) (1984) *The role of technology in distance education*, London, Croom Helm.

Bates, T, ['A.W.'], Hawkridge, D. and Henderson, E. (1982), 'Evaluating the British Open University's teaching', in Brown, J.W., and Brown, S.N. (eds.) (1982) *Educational media yearbook 1982*, Littleton, Colorado, Libraries Unlimited Inc.

Beeby, C.E. (1966) *The quality of education in developing countries*, Cambridge, Mass., Harvard University Press.

Bertrand, Y. (1979) *Les modèles éducationnels*, Montréal, Université de Montréal, Service Pédagogique.

Bewley, D. (1979) 'Community resources in distance education', in Neil, M. (1981) *Education of adults at a distance*, London, Kogan Page.

Birch, D.W. and Cuthbert, R.E. (1981) *Costing open learning in*

229

References

further education, London, Council for Educational Technology.

Birch, D.W. and Cuthbert, R.E. (1982) 'Academic staff costs in open and distance learning', in Scottish Education Department (1982) *Distance no object. Examples of open learning in Scotland*, Edinburgh, HMSO.

Birch, D.W. and Latcham, J. (1985) 'Measuring college performance', in Further Education Staff College (1985) *Assessing educational effectiveness and efficiency*, Coombe Lodge Report, 18 (3), Blandon, The Further Education Staff College.

Blowers, A. (1979) 'Carry on course teams', *Teaching at a Distance*, 16, 54-7.

Bynner, J. (1985) 'Collaborative schemes and the ethos of distance education: a study of Australian and New Zealand universities', *Higher Education*, 14, 513-33.

Carnoy, M. (1975) 'The political consequences of manpower formation', *Comparative Education*, 19 (1), 115-28.

Carnoy, M. and Levin, H.M. (1975) 'Evaluation of educational media: some issues', *Instructional Science*, 4, 385-406.

Carter, C.F. (1973) 'The economics of the Open University: a comment', *Higher Education*, 2, 69-70.

Casas Armengol, M. (1981) 'La Universidad Nacional Abierta de Venezuela', in Peñalver, L.M. and Escotet, M.A. (n.d.) *Teoría y praxis de la universidad a distancia*, Caracas, Fondo Editorial para el Desarrollo de la Educación Superior [FEDES].

Cirigliano, G. (1983) *La educación abierta*, Buenos Aires, Librería 'El Ateneo' Editorial.

Clarke, A.M. and Birt, L.M. (1982) 'Evaluation reviews in universities: the influence of public policies', *Higher Education*, 11, 1-26.

References

Committee on the Establishment of an Open University (1982) *Towards an open learning system,* Hyderabad, Andhra Pradesh, Osmania University Department of Publications and Press.

CONARE [Consejo Nacional de Rectores] (1975) *Plan nacional de educación superior 1976-1979,* San José, Costa Rica, Oficina de Planificación de la Educación Superior, Consejo Nacional de Rectores.

Costello, N. (1979) 'The curse of the course team: a comment' *Teaching at a Distance,* 16, 53-4.

COUNA [Comisión Organizadora de la Universidad Nacional Abierta] (1977) *Universidad Nacional Abierta: Proyecto,* Caracas, Universidad Nacional Abierta.

Crick, M. (1980) 'Course teams: myth and actuality', *Distance Education,* 1 (2), 127-41.

Daniel, J.S. and Smith, W.A.S. (1979) 'Opening open universities: the Canadian experience', *Canadian Journal of Higher Education,* 9 (2), 63-74.

Daniel, J.S. and Snowden, B.L. (1979) 'The management of small open universities', in Neil, M. (ed.) (1981) *Education of adults at a distance,* London, Kogan Page.

de Moor, R. (1982) 'Plan to reality: the Netherlands Open University', in Daniel, J.S., Stroud, M.A. and Thompson, J.R. (eds.) (1982) *Learning at a distance. A world perspective,* Edmonton, Athabasca University/International Council for Correspondence Education.

de Moor, R. (1983) 'The planning of an Open University. The case of the Netherlands', CRE-Information, New Series No. 64 (1983 [4]), 57-69.

Department of Education and Science (1980) 'Continuing education: post-experience vocational provision for those in employment', London, Department of Education and Science: cited in Advisory Council for Adult and Continuing Education

References

(1982) *Continuing education: from policies to practice*, Leicester, Advisory Council for Adult and Continuing Education.

Diaz Bordenare, J.E. (1980) 'Latin America initiates a new approach to rural communication', *Educational Broadcasting International*, December 1980, 163-7.

Dieuzeide, H. (1985) 'Les enjeux politiques', in Henri, F. and Kaye, A. (eds.) (1985) *Le savoir à domicile: pédagogie et problématique de la formation à distance*, Québec, Presses de l'Université du Québec/Télé-université.

Dodd, J. (1985) 'Progettare un sistema di instruzione a distanza in Italia', in Keegan, D. and Lata, F. (eds.) (1985) *L'Universita' a Distanza. Riflessioni e proposte per un nuovo modello di universita'*, Milano, Franco Angeli.

Dodd, J. and Rumble, G. (1984) 'Planning new distance teaching universities', *Higher Education*, 13, 231-54.

Dodds, T. (1983) *Administration of distance-teaching institutions. A manual*, Cambridge, International Extension College.

Dolce, P.C. (1981) 'The consortium approach: preserving college decision making', in Information Dynamics, Inc. (ed.) (1981) *National conference on technology and education - 1981*, Washington, D.C., Institute for Educational Leadership.

Doyle, P. and Lynch, J.E. (1979) 'A strategic model for university planning', *Journal of the Operational Research Society*, 30 (7), 603-9.

Drake, M. (1979) 'The curse of the course team', *Teaching at a Distance*, 16, 50-3.

Dressel, P. (1976) *Handbook of academic evaluation*, San Francisco, Jossey-Bass.

Duchastel, P.C. (1979) 'On being an educational technologist', *British Journal of Educational Technology*, 9 (3), 164-6.

Eicher, J-C., Hawkridge, D., McAnany, E., Mariot, F. and Orivel, F. (1982) *The economics of new educational media, Vol. 3. Cost and effectiveness overview and synthesis,* Paris, The Unesco Press.

El-Bushra, J. (1973) *Correspondence teaching at university,* Cambridge, International Extension College.

Emery, F.E. and Trist, E.L. (1965) 'Socio-technical systems', Paper presented to the Sixth Annual International Meeting of the Institute of Management Sciences, reprinted in Frank, H.E. (ed.) (1971) *Organisational structuring,* London, McGraw-Hill.

Erdos, R.E. (1975) *Establishing an institution teaching by correspondence,* Paris, The Unesco Press.

Escotet, M.A. (1978) 'Factores adversos para el desarrollo de una universidad abierta en América Latina', *Revista de Tecnología Educativa,* 4 (1), 66-83.

Escotet, M.A. (1980a) *Tendencias de la educación superior a distancia,* San José, Editorial Universidad Estatal a Distancia.

Escotet, M.A. (1980b) 'La educación superior a distancia en latinoamérica', *Revista de Tecnología Educativa,* 6 (3/4), 239-51.

Escotet, M.A. (1981) 'La educación superior a distancia frente al paradigma de instrucción y formación', in Peñalver, L.M. and Escotet, M.A. (n.d.) *Teoría y praxis de la universidad a distancia,* Caracas, Fondo Editorial para el Desarrollo de la Educación Superior [FEDES].

Fanon, F. (1967) *The wretched of the earth,* Harmondsworth, Penguin.

Feasley, C.E. (1983) *Serving learners at a distance. A guide to program practices,* (ASHE-ERIC Higher Education Research Report No. 5), Washington, D.C., Association for the Study of Higher Education.

Fielden, J. and Lockwood, G. (1973) *Planning and management in universities. A study of British universities,* London, Chatto and Windus/University of Sussex Press.

Freire, P. (1969) *La educación como práctica de la libertad,* México, D.F., Siglo Veintiuno Editores, sa.

Freire, P. (1970) *Pedagogy of the oppressed,* Harmondsworth, Penguin.

Freire, P. (1970) *Pedagogy of the oppressed,* London, Sheed and Ward.

Friedman, H.Z. (1982) 'The contribution of data processing to student administration at the Open University', in Daniel, J.S., Stroud, M.A. and Thompson, J.R. (eds.) (1982) *Learning at a distance. A world perspective,* Edmonton, Athabasca University/International Council for Correspondence Education.

Friedman, H.Z. (1984) 'Computers in academic administration', in Bates, A.W. (ed.) (1984) *The role of technology in distance education,* London, Croom Helm.

Gale, J. (1980) 'Proteus in a kaleidoscope: the educational technologist in Open University course production', *Journal of Educational Television and Other Media,* 6 (1), 4-7.

Glover, I (1985) 'Management of organisations', in Elliott, K. and Lawrence, P. (1985) *Introducing management,* Harmondsworth, Penguin.

Gooler, D.D. (1979) 'Evaluating distance education programmes', Canadian Journal of University Continuing Education, 6 (1), 43-55.

Gough, J.E. (1978) 'Course teams - some comments on the Deakin experience', in Northcott, P., Gough, J.E. and Kerns, L. (1980, 2nd. ed.) *Course teams,* South Australian College of External Studies, Distance Education Series No. 8, Adelaide, College of Technical and Further Education.

Government of India (1985) The Indira Gandhi National Open

References

University Bill (1985), as introduced to the Rajya Sabha on 21 May 1985. Bill no. XVII of 1985.

Great Soviet Encyclopedia (1975) "Correspondence education', New York, Macmillan.

Gueulette, D. and Hortin, J. (1981) 'Instructional media for the 80s: home telecommunication centres, home computers and the super school', in Harvey. B. et al. (1981) *Policy and research in adult education*, Nottingham, University of Nottingham Department of Adult Education.

Guiton, P. (1982) 'Resource allocation in the Australian two-mode universities', in Daniel, J.S., Stroud, M.A. and Thompson, J.R. (eds.) (1982) *Learning at a distance. A world perspective*, Edmonton, Athabasca University/International Council for Correspondence Education.

Hall, J.W. and Palola, E.G. (1979) 'Curricula for adult learning', Paper presented to the Open University Conference on the Education of Adults at a Distance, Birmingham, UK, 18-23 November 1979.

Hall, P., Lund, H., Parker, R. and Webb, A. (1975) *Change, choice and conflict in social policy*, London, Heinemann.

Halperin, S. (1984) *Any home a campus: Everyman's University of Israel*, Washington, D.C., The Institute for Educational Leadership, Inc.

Hamilton, D., et al. (1977) *Beyond the numbers game: a reader in educational evaluation*, London, Macmillan Education.

Harbison, F.H. and Myers, C.A. (1964) *Education, manpower and economic growth*, New York, McGraw-Hill.

Harris, D. (1976) 'Educational technology at the Open University: a short history of achievement and cancellation', *British Journal of Educational Technology*, 71, 43-53.

Hawkridge, D. (1981) 'The telesis of educational technology',

British Journal of Educational Technology, 12 (1), 4-18.

Henderson, E. (1979) Intenal memorandum, Open University, 22 October 1979, cited in Gale, J. (1980) 'Proteus in a kaleidoscope: the educational technologist in Open University course production', *Journal of Educational Television and Other Media,* 6 (1), 4-7.

Henri, F. and Kaye, A. (1985) 'Enseignement à distance - apprentissage autonome?', in Henri, F. and Kaye, A. (eds.) (1985) *Le savoir à domicile: pédagogie et problématique de la formation à distance,* Québec, Presses de l'Université du Québec/ Télé-université.

Hijmans, R. (1980) 'The role of government in institution performance evaluation', paper presented to the Ninth Special Topic Workshop of the Institutional Management in Higher Education (IMHE) Programme, OECD/CERI, Paris, 10-12 December 1980.

Hinman, M.M. (1980) 'Planning and evaluation at the University of Michigan', paper presented to the Ninth Special Topic Workshop of the Institutional Management in Higher Education (IMHE) Programme, OECD/CERI, Paris, 10-12 December 1980.

Holmberg, B. (1977) *Distance education: a survey and bibliography,* London, Kogan Page.

Holmberg, B. (1981) *Trends and status of distance education,* London, Kogan Page.

Holmberg, B. (1985) *Status and trends of distance education,* Lund, Lektor Publishing.

Houle, C.O. (1974) *The external degree,* San Francisco, Jossey-Bass.

Hughes, L.J. (1980) *The first Athabasca University,* Edmonton, Athabasca University.

Jacques, E. (1976) *A general theory of bureaucracy,* London,

References

Heinemann.

James, A. and Arboleda, J. (1979) 'El Proyecto Universidad Desescolarizada: a feasibility study of teaching at a distance in Colombia, S.A.', *Higher Education,* 8, 269-77.

Jevons, F. (1984) 'Distance education in a mixed institution: working towards parity', *Distance Education,* 5 (1), 24-37.

Johansen, R. (1984) *Teleconferencing and beyond,* New York, McGraw-Hill.

Joyce, B. and Weil, M. (1972) *Models of teaching,* Englewood Heights, Prentice-Hall.

Karmel Committee (1975) *Open tertiary education in Australia. Final report of the Committee on Open University to the Universities Commission,* Canberra, Australian Government Publishing Service.

Kaye, A. and Rumble, G. (1981) *Distance teaching for higher and adult education,* London, Croom Helm.

Kaye, T. [A.] (1985) 'Computer-mediated communication systems for distance education. Report of a study visit to North America, September/October 1985', Milton Keynes, Open University Institute of Educational Technology, Project Report CCET/2, November 1985. Mimeo.

Kaye, T. (1981) 'Some possible limitations of distance education', paper presented to the Australian and South Pacific External Studies Association Fifth Biennial Forum, Suva, 1981.

Keegan, D. (1980) 'On defining distance education', *Distance Education,* 1 (1), 13-35.

Keegan, D. (1986) *The foundations of distance education,* London, Croom Helm.

Keegan, D. and Rumble, G. (1982a) 'Distance teaching at university level', in Rumble, G. and Harry, K. (1982) *The distance teaching universities,* London, Croom Helm.

Keegan, D. and Rumble, G. (1982b) 'The DTUs [Distance Teaching Universities]: an appraisal', in Rumble, G. and Harry, K. (eds.) (1982) *The distance teaching universities,* London, Croom Helm.

Kemmis, S. (1980) 'Program evaluation in distance education: against the technologisation of reason', *Open Campus,* 1980 (2), 19-48, Geelong, Deakin University, Centre for Educational Services.

Kemmis, S. and Hughes, C. (1979) 'Curriculum evaluation in higher education: self reflection in a critical community', *Open Campus,* 1970 (3), 7-23, Geelong, Deakin University, Centre for Educational Services.

Laidlaw, B. and Layard, R. (1974) 'Traditional versus Open University teaching methods: a cost comparison', *Higher Education,* 3, 439-68.

Lawless, C. and Kirkwood, A. (1976) 'Individualising induction for educational technologists at the Open University', in Clarke, J. and Leedham, J. (eds.) (1976) *Aspects of educational technology,* Volume X, London, Kogan Page.

Leonard, J. (1985) 'Yomping across the airways', *The Guardian,* 13 August 1985, page 11.

Leslie, J.D. (1979) 'The University of Waterloo model for distance education', *Canadian Journal of University Continuing Education,* 6, 33-41.

Lewis, B. (1971a) 'Course production at the Open University II: activities and activity networks', *British Journal of Educational Technology,* 2 (2), 111-23.

Lewis, B. (1971b) 'Course production at the Open University III: planning and scheduling', *British Journal of Educational Technology,* 2 (3), 189-204.

References

Linder, G. and Lonsdale, H. (1975) *The use of courseware teams for achieving content objectives in television production*, Denver, Federation of Rocky Mountain Styates, Inc.

Lindsay, A.W. (1979) 'Institutional performance in higher education: the efficiency dimension', *Review of Educational Research*, 52 (2), 175-99.

Lovett, T. (1982) *Adult education, community development and the working class*, Nottingham, University of Nottingham Department of Adult Education.

Lovett, T., Clarke, C. and Kilmurray, A. (1983) *Adult education and community education*, London, Croom Helm.

Lowe, J. (1983) 'The future of adult education worldwide', in Tight, M. (ed.) (1983) *Opportunities for adult education*, London, Croom Helm.

Lumsden, K. and Scott, A. (1982) 'An output comparison of Open University and conventional university students', *Higher Education*, 11, 573-91.

McAnany, E.G., Oliviera, J-B., Orivel, F. and Stone, J. (1982) 'Distance education: evaluating new approaches in education for developing countries', *Evaluation in Education: an International Review Series*, 6 (3), 289-376.

Macdonald-Ross, M. 'Janus the consultant. Educational technology at the Open University', *British Journal of Educational Technology*, 7 (1), 65-75.

Macdonald-Ross, M. and Waller, R. (1969) 'The transformer', in *Penrose Graphic Arts International Annual*, London, Northwood Publications.

Mace, J. (1978) 'Mythology in the making: Is the Open University really cost-effective?', *Higher Education*, 7, 295-309.

Mace, J. (1984) 'The economics of education: a revisionist's view', *Higher Education Review*, 16 (3), 39-56.

References

McIntosh, N.E. (1974) 'Evaluation of multi-media educational systems - some problems', *British Journal of Educational Technology*, 5 (3), 43-59.

McIntosh, N.E. (1978) 'Evaluation and institutional research: the problems involved in evaluating one course or educational program', *International Journal of Institutional Management in Higher Education*, 2 (1), 5-19.

McIntosh, N.E. (1979) 'Barriers to implementing research in higher education', *Studies in Higher Education*, 4 (1), 77-86.

McIntosh, N.E. (1981) 'Demand and supply in the education of adults', *Educational Analysis*, 3 (3), 21-36.

Mackenzie, N., Postgate, R. and Scupham, J. (1975) *Open learning: systems and problems in post-secondary education*, Paris, The Unesco Press.

Malassis, L. (1975) *Ruralidad, educación y desarrollo*, Buenos Aires, Editorial Huemul SA/ Paris, Editorial de la UNESCO.

Malavassi, G. (1978) *Comprender lo comprensible*, San José, Costa Rica, Instituto Centroaméricano de Extensión de la Cultura, 2 volumes.

Marriott, S. (1981) *A backstairs to a degree. Demands for an open university in late Victorian England*, Leeds, University of Leeds Department of Adult Education and Extramural Studies.

Mason, J. (1976) 'Life inside the course team', *Teaching at a Distance*, 5, 27-33.

Mayo, J. Hornik, R. and McAnany, E. (1976) *Educational reform with television: the El Salvador experience*, Stanford, Calif., Stanford University Press.

Miller, E.J. (1959) 'Technology, territory and time: the internal differentiation of complex production systems', *Human Relations*, 12, 243-72.

References

Miller, E.J. and Rice, A.K. (1967) *Systems of organisation: the control of task and sentient boundaries,* London, Tavistock Publications.

Miller, R.I. (1979) *The assessment of college performance,* San Francisco, Jossey-Bass.

Ministerio de Educación Pública (n.d.) *Proyecto de ley: Universidad Estatal a Distancia,* Costa Rica, Ministerio de Educación Pública.

Ministry of Education, Science and Culture (1975) *Report on the survey for estimating educational needs for the University of the Air,* n.p., Ministry of Education, Science and Culture, Japan.

Mitchell, I. (1978) 'The concept of course teams', Adelaide, College of the Arts and Education. Mimeo.

Moore, M. (1973) 'Towards a theory of independent learning and teaching', *Journal of Higher Education,* 44, 661-79.

Moore, M. (1983) 'The individual adult learner', in Tight, M. (ed.) (1983) *Adult learning and education,* London, Croom Helm.

Muta, H. (1985) 'The economics of the University of the Air of Japan', *Higher Education,* 14, 269-96.

Neil, M. (1981) *The education of adults at a distance,* London, Kogan Page.

Newey, C. (1975) 'On being a course team chairman', *Teaching at a Distance,* 4, 47-51.

Nichodemus, R. (1984) 'Lessons from a course team', *Teaching at a Distance,* 25, 33-9.

Northcott, P. (1978) 'Course teams - some theoretical considerations, with particular reference to the Open University experience', in Northcott, P., Gough, J.E. and Kerns, L. (1980, 2nd. ed.) *Course teams,* South Australian College of External Studies, Distance Education Series No. 8, Adelaide, College of

References

Technical and Further Education.

OECD [Organisation for Economic Co-operation and Development] (1976) *Framework for comprehensive policies for adult education,* Paris, OECD.

Ortmeier, A. (1982) *External studies in Australia,* Armidale, Institute for Higher Education.

Öster, L. (1965) 'Problems concerning the office organisation of a large correspondence school', in European Council for Education by Correspondence [CEC] (1965) *CEC Yearbook 1965,* Leiden, CEC.

Otsuka, H. (1984) 'On the radio and television universities of the People's Republic of China', MME Research Note of the National Centre for Development of Broadcast Education No. 7, 65-118, cited in Muta, H. (1985) 'The economics of the University of the Air of Japan', *Higher Education,* 14, 269-96.

Pacheco, F.A. (1978) 'La Universidad Estatal a Distancia de Costa Rica y la transferencia de technología', paper presented to the Seminario Interaméricano sobre la Transferencia de Tecnología en Educación, Viña del Mar, Chile, May 1978; reprinted in Peñalver, L.M. and Escotet, M.A. (eds.) (n.d.) *Teoría y praxis de la universidad a distancia,* Caracas, Fondo Editorial para el Desarrollo de la Educación Superior.

Pagney, B. (1982) 'The role of learning at a distance in national educational systems', *Distance Education,* 3 (1), 107-15.

Parlett, M. and Hamilton, D. (1972) *Evaluation as illumination,* Edinburgh, Centre for Research in the Educational Sciences.

Parlett, M. and Hamilton, D. (1976) 'Evaluation as illumination: a new approach to the study of innovatory programmes', in Towney, D.A. (ed.) (1976) *Curriculum evaluation today: trends and implications,* London, Macmillan Education/Schools Council Research Studies.

Penberthy, J. (1982) 'Elementary education of children at a

References

distance', in Daniel, J.S., Stroud, M.A. and Thompson, J.R. (eds.) (1982) *Learning at a distance. A world perspective,* Edmonton, Athabasca University/International Council for Correspondence Education.

Pengelly, R.M., Rumble, G.W., and Wilson, K.P. (1978) *A report on the present and future development of the Universidad Estatal a Distancia, Costa Rica,* Milton Keynes, Open University Centre for International Co-operation and Services. Not publicly available.

Perraton, H. (1980) 'Overcoming the distance in community education', *Teaching at a Distance,* 18, 54-61.

Perraton, H. (1981) 'A theory for distance education', *Prospects,* 11 (1), 13-24.

Perraton, H. (1982) *The cost of distance education,* Cambridge, International Extension College.

Perry, W. (1972) *The early development of the Open University. Report of the Vice-Chancellor, January 1969 - December 1970,* Milton Keynes, The Open University Press.

Perry, W. (1976) *Open University. A personal account by the first Vice-Chancellor,* Milton Keynes, The Open University Press.

Perry, W. (1981) 'The growth of distance education', in Neil, M. (ed.) (1981) *Education of adults at a distance,* London, Kogan Page.

Perry, W. (1984) *The state of distance-learning worldwide. The first report on the index of institutions involved in distance-learning,* Milton Keynes, International Centre for Distance Learning of the United Nations University.

Peters, O. (1973) *Die didaktische Struktur des Fernunterrichts Untersuchungen zu einer industrialisierten Form des Lehrens und Lernens,* Weinheim, Beltz.

243

References

Planning Committee (1969) *The Open University. Report of the Planning Committee to the Secretary of State for Education and Science,* London, HMSO.

Riley, J. (1986) 'The evolution of professional practice at the Open University', *Programmed Learning and Educational Technology,* 23 (1), 7-14.

Rogers, C. (1969) *Freedom to learn,* Columbus, Ohio, Charles E. Merrill Publishing Co.

Romney, L.C. (1978) *Measures for institutional goal achievement,* Denver, Colorado, National Center for Higher Education Management Systems.

Romney, L.C., Bogen, C. and Micek, S.S. (1978) 'Assessing institutional performance: the importance of being careful', paper presented to the Fourth General Conference of the Programme on Institutional Management in Higher Education, OECD/CERI, Paris, 11-13 September.

Rumble, G. (1976) 'The economics of the Open University', paper presented to the Anglian Regional Management College/Organisation for Economic Co-operation and Development 'International Management Development Programme for Senior Administrators in Institutions of Higher Education, Danbury, Essex, 1976-77', Milton Keynes, Open University, Academic Planning Office.

Rumble, G. (1978) *A Report on systems-based planning for the Universidad Nacional Abierta,* Milton Keynes, Open University Centre for International Co-operation and Services. Not publicly available.

Rumble, G. (1979) 'Planning for distance education', in Hakemulder, J.R. (ed.) (1981) *Distance education for development,* Bonn, German Foundation for International Development.

Rumble, G. (1981a) 'The cost analysis of distance teaching: Costa Rica's Universidad Estatal a Distancia', *Higher Education,* 10,

375-401.

Rumble, G. (1981b) 'Evaluating autonomous multi-media distance learning systems: a practical approach', *Distance Education,* 2 (1), 64-90.

Rumble, G. (1981c) 'Organisation and decision-making', in Kaye, A. and Rumble, G. (eds.) (1981) *Distance teaching for higher and adult education,* London, Croom Helm.

Rumble, G. (1981d) *Costa Rica's Universidad Estatal a Distancia: a case study,* Milton Keynes, Open University Distance Education Research Group, Monograph No. 4.

Rumble, G. (1982) 'The cost analysis of distance learning: Venezuela's Universidad Nacional Abierta', *Distance Education,* 3 (1), 116-40.

Rumble, G. (1986) *Costing distance education,* London, The Commonwealth Secretariat.

Rumble, G. and Harry, K. (1982) *The distance teaching universities,* London, Croom Helm/New York, St. Martin's Press.

Rumble, G., Neil, M. and Tout, A. (1981) 'Budgetary and resource forecasting', in Kaye, A. and Rumble, G. (eds.) (1981) *Distance teaching for higher and adult education,* London, Croom Helm.

Salter, D. (1982) 'Mobile learning centres in an open learning system', in Daniel, J.S., Stroud, M.A. and Thompson, J.R. (eds.) (1982) *Learning at a distance. A world perspective,* Edmonton, Athabasca University/International Council for Correspondence Education.

Schramm, W. (1977) *Big media, little media: tools and technologies for instruction,* Beverly Hills, Calif., Sage.

Schramm, W., Hawkridge, D., and Howe II, H. (1972) *An "Everyman's University" for Israel. Report to Hanadiv by Enquiry Commission,* Jerusalem, The Jerusalem Post.

References

Scriven, M. (1973) 'Goal-free evaluation', in House, E.R. (ed.) (1973) *School evaluation: politics and process,* Berkeley, Calif., McCutchan.

Sesame, (1979) *The first ten years. A special edition of 'Sesame' to mark the tenth anniversary of the Open University 1969-1979,* Milton Keynes, The Open University.

Siaciwena, R.M. (1983) 'Problems of managing an external degree programme at the University of Zambia', *Journal of Adult Education* [University of Zambia], 2 (1), 67-77.

Sine, B. (1975) *Education and mass media in Black Africa. Problems presented by the adaptation of educational technologies,* Paris, Unesco, Document ED-75/WS/55.

Singh, B. (1975) 'The role and organisation of an ideal distance education institute', in Ljosä, E. (1975) *The system of distance education. Papers to the Tenth ICCE International Conference, Brighton, Great Britiain, 12-16 May 1975,* Malmo, Hermods.

Singh, B. (1979) 'Distance education in developing countries - with special reference to India', in Hakemulder, J.R. (ed.) (1981) *Distance education for development,* Bonn, German Foundation for International Development.

Sizer, J. (1979) 'Assessing institutional performance: an overview', *International Journal of Institutional Management in Higher Education,* 3 (1), 49-77.

Sizer, J. (1982a) 'Institutional performance assessment under conditions of changing needs', *International Journal of Institutional Management in Higher Education,* 6 (1), 17-28.

Sizer, J. (1982b) 'Assessing institutional performance and progress', in Wagner, L. (ed.) (1982) *Agenda for institutional change in higher education,* Guildford, Society for Research into Higher Education.

Skinner, B.F. (1968) *The technology of teaching,* New York, Appleton-Century-Crofts.

References

Smith, K.C. (1979) 'External studies at New England - a silver jubilee review, 1955-79', Armidale, University of New England, reprinted in part in Sewart, D., Keegan, D. and Holmberg, B. (eds.) (1983) *Distance education. International perspectives,* London, Croom Helm.

Smith, K.C. (1980) 'Course development procedures', *Distance Education,* 1 (1), 61-7.

Snowden, B.L. and Daniel, J.S. (1980) 'The economics and management of small post-secondary distance education systems', *Distance Education,* 1 (1), 68-91.

Sorensen, L. (1969) 'Electronic data processing in the administration of correspondence education', in *Proceedings of the Eighth International Conference of the International Council for Correspondence Education,* Paris, ICCE.

Sorenson, J.R. and Grove, H.D. (1977) 'Cost-outcome and cost-effectiveness analysis: emerging nonprofit performance evaluation techniques', *The Accounting Review,* 52 (3), 658-75.

Sparkes, J. (1984) 'Pedagogic differences between media', in Bates, A.W. (ed.) (1984) *The role of technology in distance education,* London, Croom Helm.

Stake, R.E. (1967) 'The countenance of educational evaluation', *Teachers' College Record,* 68, 523-40.

Stake, R.E. (1975) *Evaluating the arts in education: a responsive approach,* Columbus, Ohio, Charles E. Merrill.

Stone, J. (1975) 'Alternative organisational structure for developing multimedia instructional materials', Educational Technology, 15 (10), cited in McAnany, E.G., Oliviera, J-B., Orivel, F. and Stone, J. (1982) 'Distance education: evaluating new approaches in education for developing countries', *Evaluation in Education: an International Review Series,* 6 (3), 289-376.

Stone J. and Oliveira, J-B. (1980) 'A dinâmica do conflicto em

References

organizações de producao de TV educativa', Estudos e Pesquisas, 17/18, cited in McAnany, E.G., Oliviera, J-B., Orivel, F. and Stone, J. (1982) 'Distance education: evaluating new approaches in education for developing countries', *Evaluation in Education: an International Review Series*, 6 (3), 289-376.

Swift, B. (1980) 'Outcomes of Open University studies: some statistics from a 1980 survey of graduates', Milton Keynes, The Open University, Survey Research Department. Mimeo.

Swinerton, E.N. and Hogan, T.P. (1981) 'A tested budget model for a nontraditional degree program', Madison, Wisconsin, University of Wisconsin. Mimeo.

Tiffin, J.W. (1978) 'Problems in instructional television in Latin America', *Revista de Tecnología Educativa*, 4 (2), 163-235.

Timmers, S. (1986) 'Microcomputers in course development', *Programmed Learning and Educational Technology*, 23 (1), 15-23.

Toombs, W. (1973) *Productivity: burden of success*, Washington, D.C., American Association for Higher Education.

TRU Commission (1975) *Distance education. An outline of the present situation and some organisational alternatives for post-secondary education. Summary of a TRU Commission report (SOU, 1975:72)*, Stockholm, TRU Commission.

Unesco (1983) *Distance education in higher education. Inter-country study-cum-mobile workshop, Sukhothai Thammathirat Open University, Thailand and Darling Downs Institute of Advanced Education, Australia, 6-16 September 1983*, Bangkok, Unesco Regional Office for Education in Asia and Pacific.

van der Drift, K.D.J.M. (1980) 'Cost-effectiveness of audiovisual media in higher education', *Instructional Science*, 9, 355-64.

van Enckevort, G. (1984) 'Problems of research for a new Open University', *Distance Education*, 5 (1), 72-83.

References

Vázquez-Abad, J. and Mitchell, P.D. (1983) 'A systems approach to planning a tele-education system', *Programmed Learning and Educational Technology*, 20 (3), 202-9.

Villarroel, A. (1980) 'The Venezuelan National Open University: an overview', paper presented to the Thirtieth International Conference of the International Communication Association, Acapulco, Mexico, May 1980.

Wagner, L. (1972) 'The economics of the Open University', *Higher Education*, 1, 159-83.

Wagner, L. (1975) 'Television video-tape systems for off-campus education. A cost analysis of SURGE', *Instructional Science*, 4, 315-32.

Wagner, L.. (1977) 'The economics of the Open University revisited', *Higher Education*, 6, 359-81.

Wagner, L. (1982) *The economics of educational media*, London, The Macmillan Press.

Waller, R. (1977/78) *Notes on transforming nos. 1-5*, Milton Keynes, Open University Institute for Educational Technology. Mimeo.

Weathersby, G.B. and Balderston, F.E. (1972) 'PPBS in higher education planning and management: Part 1, an overview', *Higher Education*, 1, 191-206.

White, M. (1982) 'Distance education in Australian higher education - a history', *Distance Education*, 3 (2), 255-78.

Willén, B. (1981) *Distance education at Swedish universities*, Stockholm, Almquist and Wiksell.

Willianson, O. (1975) *Markets and hierarchies: an analysis and antitrust implications*, New York, Free Press.

Woodley, A. (1981) *The Open University of the United Kingdom*, Amsterdam, European Cultural Foundation, Institute of

References

Education.

Young, M., Perraton, H., Jenkins, J. and Dodds, T. (1980) *Distance teaching for the Third World. The lion and the clockwork mouse,* London, Routledge and Kegan Paul.